IRON
FIST

THE
LIVING
WEAPON

COLLECTION EDITOR: **SARAH BRUNSTAD**
ASSOCIATE MANAGING EDITOR: **ALEX STARBUCK**
EDITORS, SPECIAL PROJECTS: **JENNIFER GRÜNWALD & MARK D. BEAZLEY**
SENIOR EDITOR, SPECIAL PROJECTS: **JEFF YOUNGQUIST**
BOOK DESIGN: **JEFF POWELL**
SVP PRINT, SALES & MARKETING: **DAVID GABRIEL**

EDITOR IN CHIEF: **AXEL ALONSO**
CHIEF CREATIVE OFFICER: **JOE QUESADA**
PUBLISHER: **DAN BUCKLEY**
EXECUTIVE PRODUCER: **ALAN FINE**

IRON FIST: THE LIVING WEAPON VOL. 1 — RAGE. Contains material originally published in magazine form as IRON FIST: THE LIVING WEAPON #1-6. First printing 2014. ISBN# 978-0-7851-5435-8. Published by MARVEL WORLDWIDE, INC., a subsidiary of MARVEL ENTERTAINMENT, LLC. OFFICE OF PUBLICATION: 135 West 50th Street, New York, NY 10020. **Printed in Canada.** ALAN FINE, EVP - Office of the President, Marvel Worldwide, Inc. and EVP & CMO Marvel Characters B.V.; DAN BUCKLEY, Publisher & President - Print, Animation & Digital Divisions; JOE QUESADA, Chief Creative Officer; TOM BREVOORT, SVP of Publishing; DAVID BOGART, SVP of Operations & Procurement, Publishing; C.B. CEBULSKI, SVP of Creator & Content Development; DAVID GABRIEL, SVP Print, Sales & Marketing; JIM O'KEEFE, VP of Operations & Logistics; DAN CARR, Executive Director of Publishing Technology; SUSAN CRESPI, Editorial Operations Manager; ALEX MORALES, Publishing Operations Manager; STAN LEE, Chairman Emeritus. For information regarding advertising in Marvel Comics or on Marvel.com, please contact Niza Disla, Director of Marvel Partnerships, at ndisla@marvel.com. For Marvel subscription inquiries, please call 800-217-9158. **Manufactured between 9/26/2014 and 11/3/2014 by SOLISCO PRINTERS, SCOTT, QC, CANADA.**

10 9 8 7 6 5 4 3 2 1

IRON FIST
THE LIVING WEAPON

RAGE

WRITER, ARTIST AND COVERS
KAARE KYLE ANDREWS

LETTERER
VC'S JOE CARAMAGNA

EDITOR
JAKE THOMAS

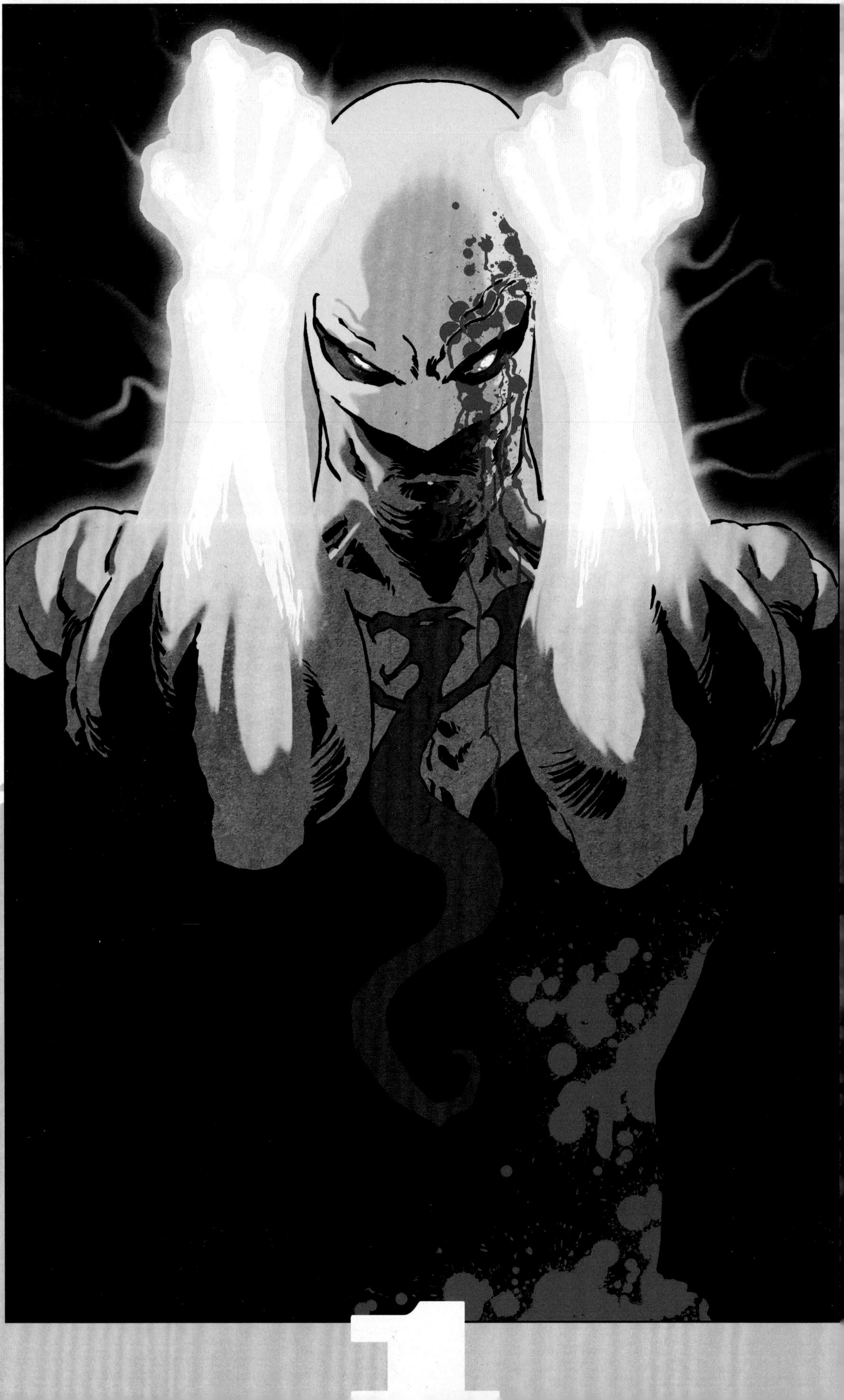

1

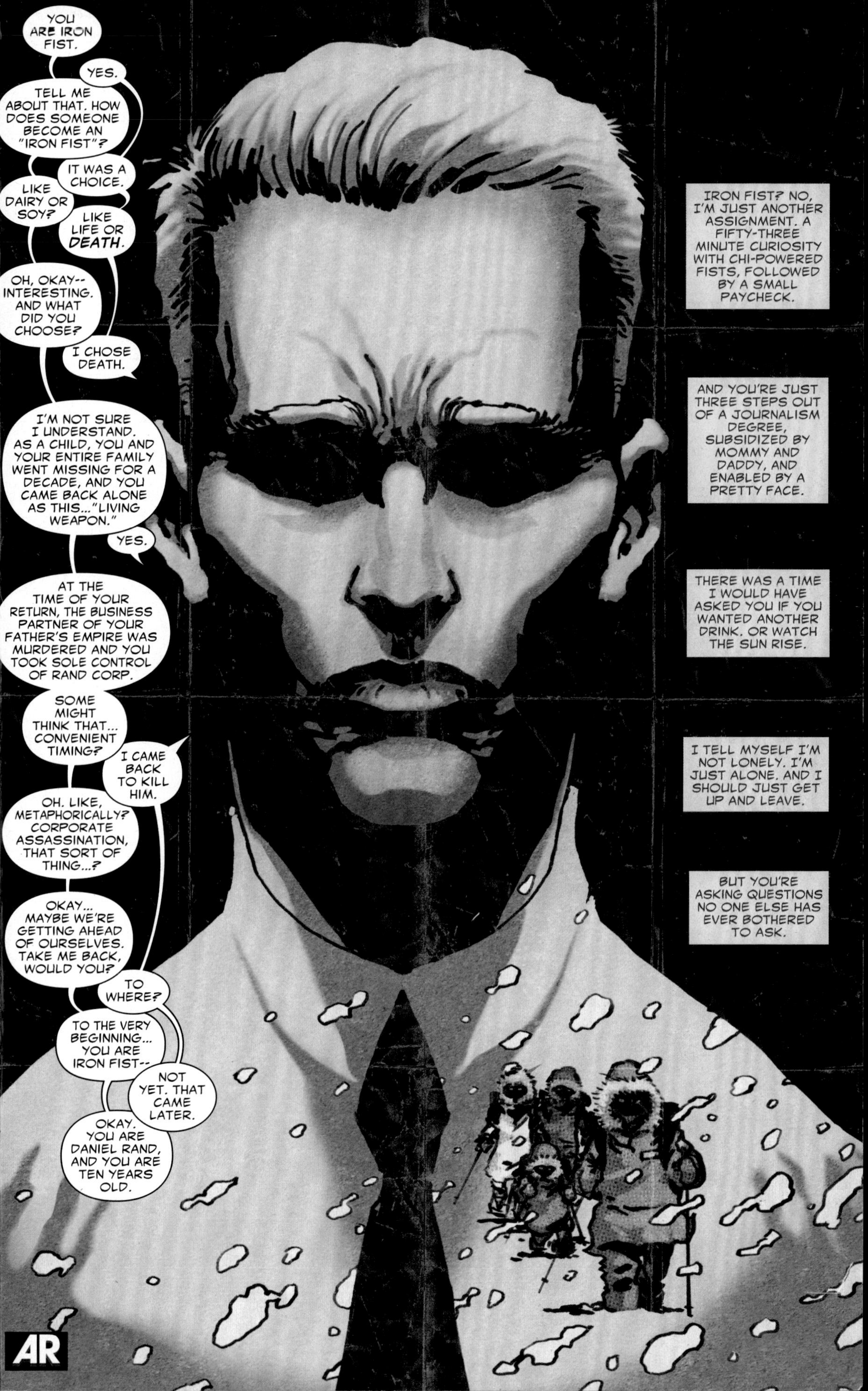
YOU ARE IRON FIST.
YES.
TELL ME ABOUT THAT. HOW DOES SOMEONE BECOME AN "IRON FIST"?
IT WAS A CHOICE.
LIKE DAIRY OR SOY?
LIKE LIFE OR DEATH.
OH, OKAY-- INTERESTING. AND WHAT DID YOU CHOOSE?
I CHOSE DEATH.
I'M NOT SURE I UNDERSTAND. AS A CHILD, YOU AND YOUR ENTIRE FAMILY WENT MISSING FOR A DECADE, AND YOU CAME BACK ALONE AS THIS..."LIVING WEAPON."
YES.
AT THE TIME OF YOUR RETURN, THE BUSINESS PARTNER OF YOUR FATHER'S EMPIRE WAS MURDERED AND YOU TOOK SOLE CONTROL OF RAND CORP.
SOME MIGHT THINK THAT... CONVENIENT TIMING?
I CAME BACK TO KILL HIM.
OH. LIKE, METAPHORICALLY? CORPORATE ASSASSINATION, THAT SORT OF THING...?
OKAY... MAYBE WE'RE GETTING AHEAD OF OURSELVES. TAKE ME BACK, WOULD YOU?
TO WHERE?
TO THE VERY BEGINNING... YOU ARE IRON FIST--
NOT YET. THAT CAME LATER.
OKAY. YOU ARE DANIEL RAND, AND YOU ARE TEN YEARS OLD.
IRON FIST? NO, I'M JUST ANOTHER ASSIGNMENT. A FIFTY-THREE MINUTE CURIOSITY WITH CHI-POWERED FISTS, FOLLOWED BY A SMALL PAYCHECK.
AND YOU'RE JUST THREE STEPS OUT OF A JOURNALISM DEGREE, SUBSIDIZED BY MOMMY AND DADDY, AND ENABLED BY A PRETTY FACE.
THERE WAS A TIME I WOULD HAVE ASKED YOU IF YOU WANTED ANOTHER DRINK. OR WATCH THE SUN RISE.
I TELL MYSELF I'M NOT LONELY. I'M JUST ALONE. AND I SHOULD JUST GET UP AND LEAVE.
BUT YOU'RE ASKING QUESTIONS NO ONE ELSE HAS EVER BOTHERED TO ASK.
AR

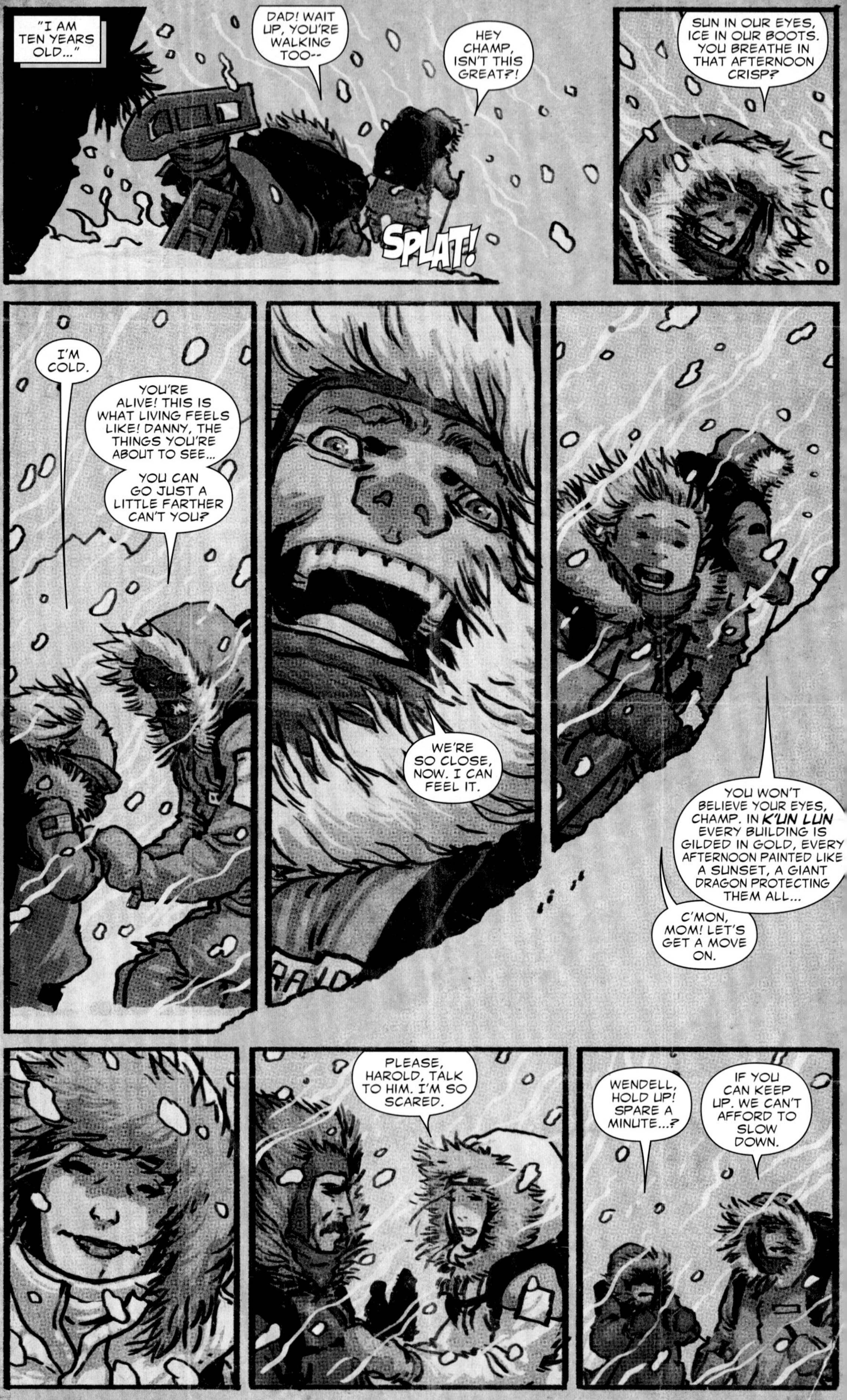
"I AM TEN YEARS OLD..."
DAD! WAIT UP, YOU'RE WALKING TOO--
HEY CHAMP, ISN'T THIS GREAT?!
SPLAT!
SUN IN OUR EYES, ICE IN OUR BOOTS. YOU BREATHE IN THAT AFTERNOON CRISP?
I'M COLD.
YOU'RE ALIVE! THIS IS WHAT LIVING FEELS LIKE! DANNY, THE THINGS YOU'RE ABOUT TO SEE...
YOU CAN GO JUST A LITTLE FARTHER CAN'T YOU?
WE'RE SO CLOSE, NOW. I CAN FEEL IT.
YOU WON'T BELIEVE YOUR EYES, CHAMP. IN K'UN LUN EVERY BUILDING IS GILDED IN GOLD, EVERY AFTERNOON PAINTED LIKE A SUNSET, A GIANT DRAGON PROTECTING THEM ALL...
C'MON, MOM! LET'S GET A MOVE ON.
PLEASE, HAROLD, TALK TO HIM. I'M SO SCARED.
WENDELL, HOLD UP! SPARE A MINUTE...?
IF YOU CAN KEEP UP. WE CAN'T AFFORD TO SLOW DOWN.

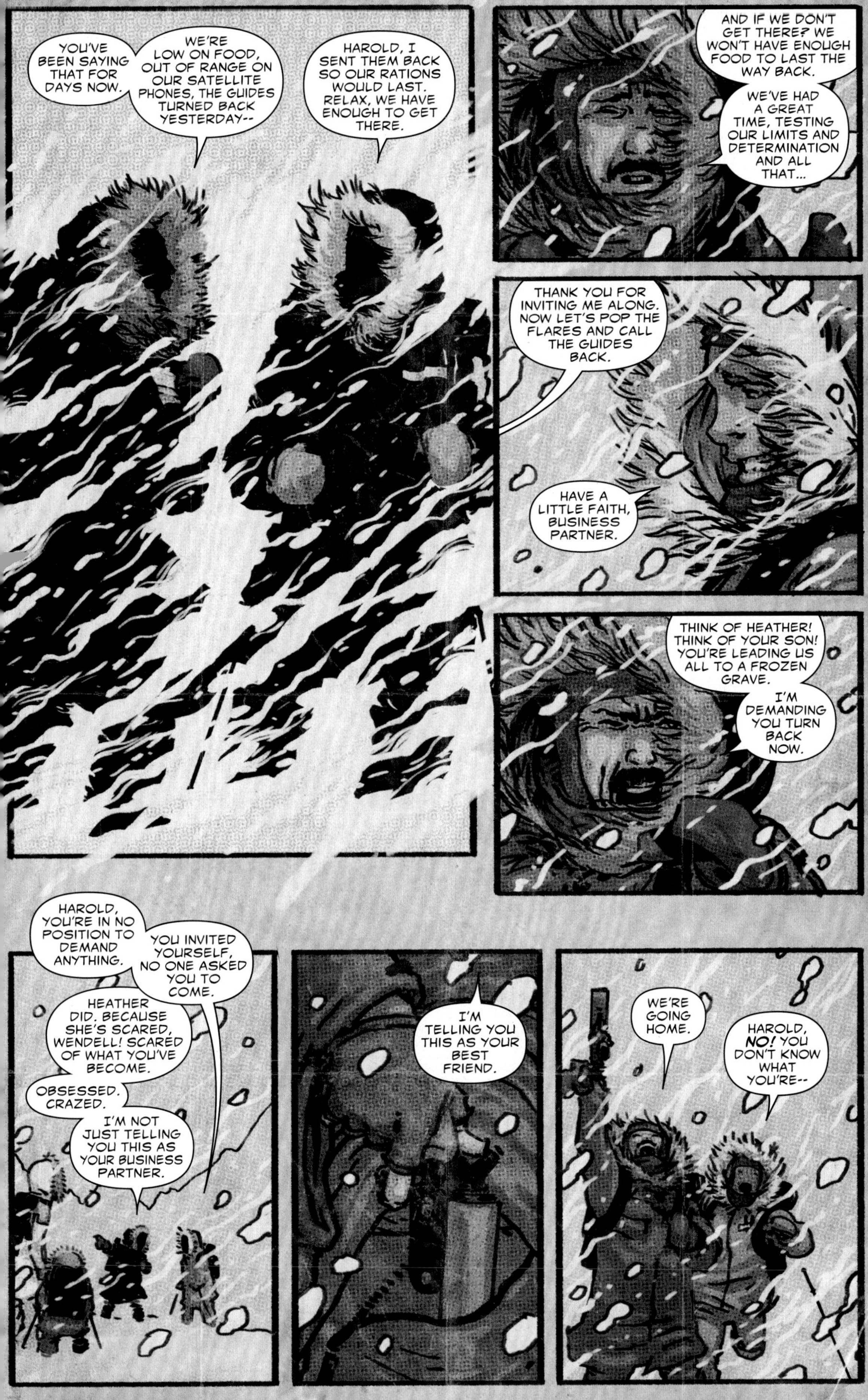
YOU'VE BEEN SAYING THAT FOR DAYS NOW.
WE'RE LOW ON FOOD, OUT OF RANGE ON OUR SATELLITE PHONES, THE GUIDES TURNED BACK YESTERDAY--
HAROLD, I SENT THEM BACK SO OUR RATIONS WOULD LAST. RELAX, WE HAVE ENOUGH TO GET THERE.
AND IF WE DON'T GET THERE? WE WON'T HAVE ENOUGH FOOD TO LAST THE WAY BACK.
WE'VE HAD A GREAT TIME, TESTING OUR LIMITS AND DETERMINATION AND ALL THAT...
THANK YOU FOR INVITING ME ALONG. NOW LET'S POP THE FLARES AND CALL THE GUIDES BACK.
HAVE A LITTLE FAITH, BUSINESS PARTNER.
THINK OF HEATHER! THINK OF YOUR SON! YOU'RE LEADING US ALL TO A FROZEN GRAVE.
I'M DEMANDING YOU TURN BACK NOW.
HAROLD, YOU'RE IN NO POSITION TO DEMAND ANYTHING.
YOU INVITED YOURSELF, NO ONE ASKED YOU TO COME.
HEATHER DID. BECAUSE SHE'S SCARED, WENDELL! SCARED OF WHAT YOU'VE BECOME.
OBSESSED. CRAZED.
I'M NOT JUST TELLING YOU THIS AS YOUR BUSINESS PARTNER.
I'M TELLING YOU THIS AS YOUR BEST FRIEND.
WE'RE GOING HOME.
HAROLD, NO! YOU DON'T KNOW WHAT YOU'RE--

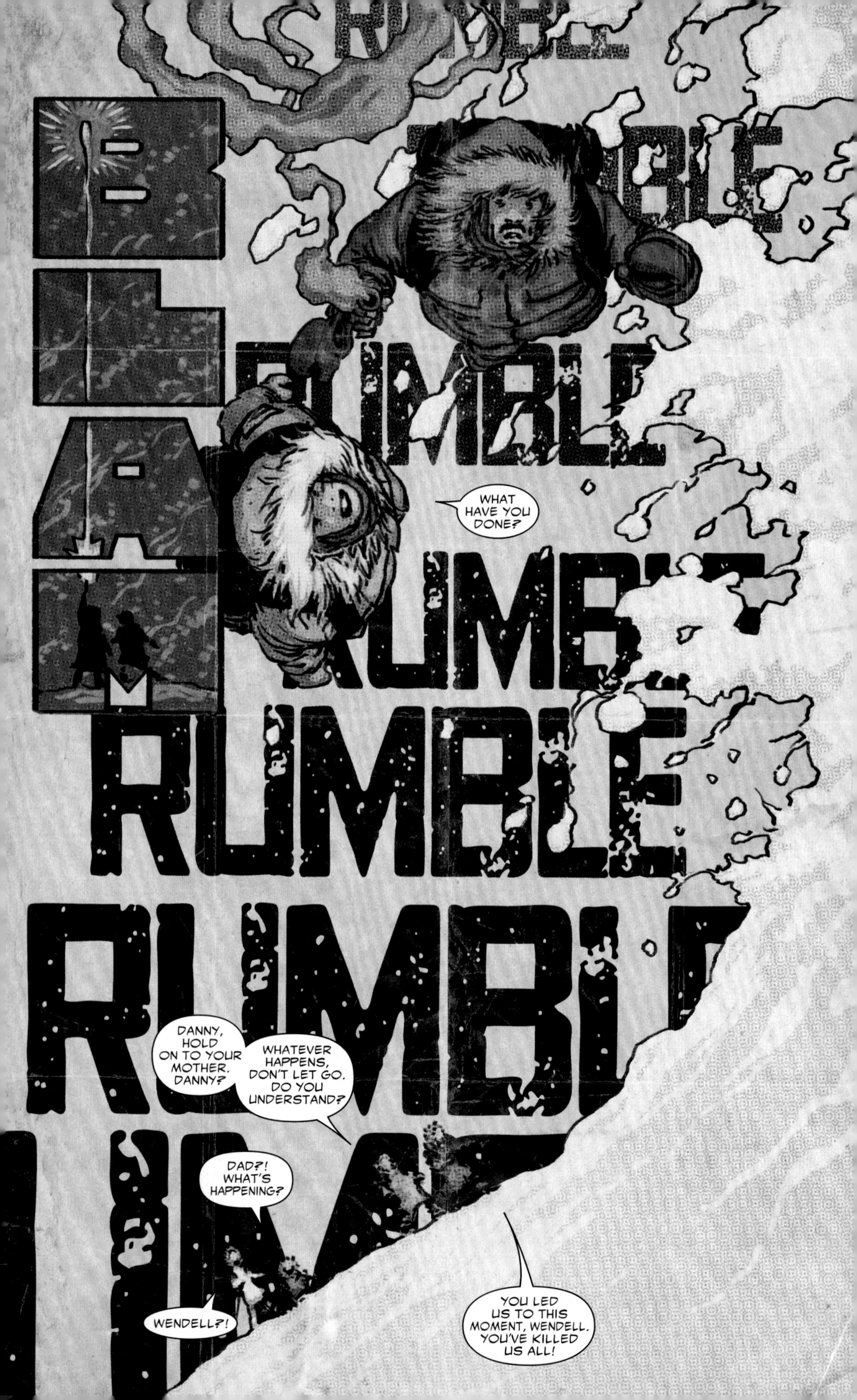
BLAM
WHAT HAVE YOU DONE?
RUMBLE
DANNY, HOLD ON TO YOUR MOTHER. DANNY?
WHATEVER HAPPENS, DON'T LET GO. DO YOU UNDERSTAND?
DAD?! WHAT'S HAPPENING?
WENDELL?!
YOU LED US TO THIS MOMENT, WENDELL. YOU'VE KILLED US ALL!

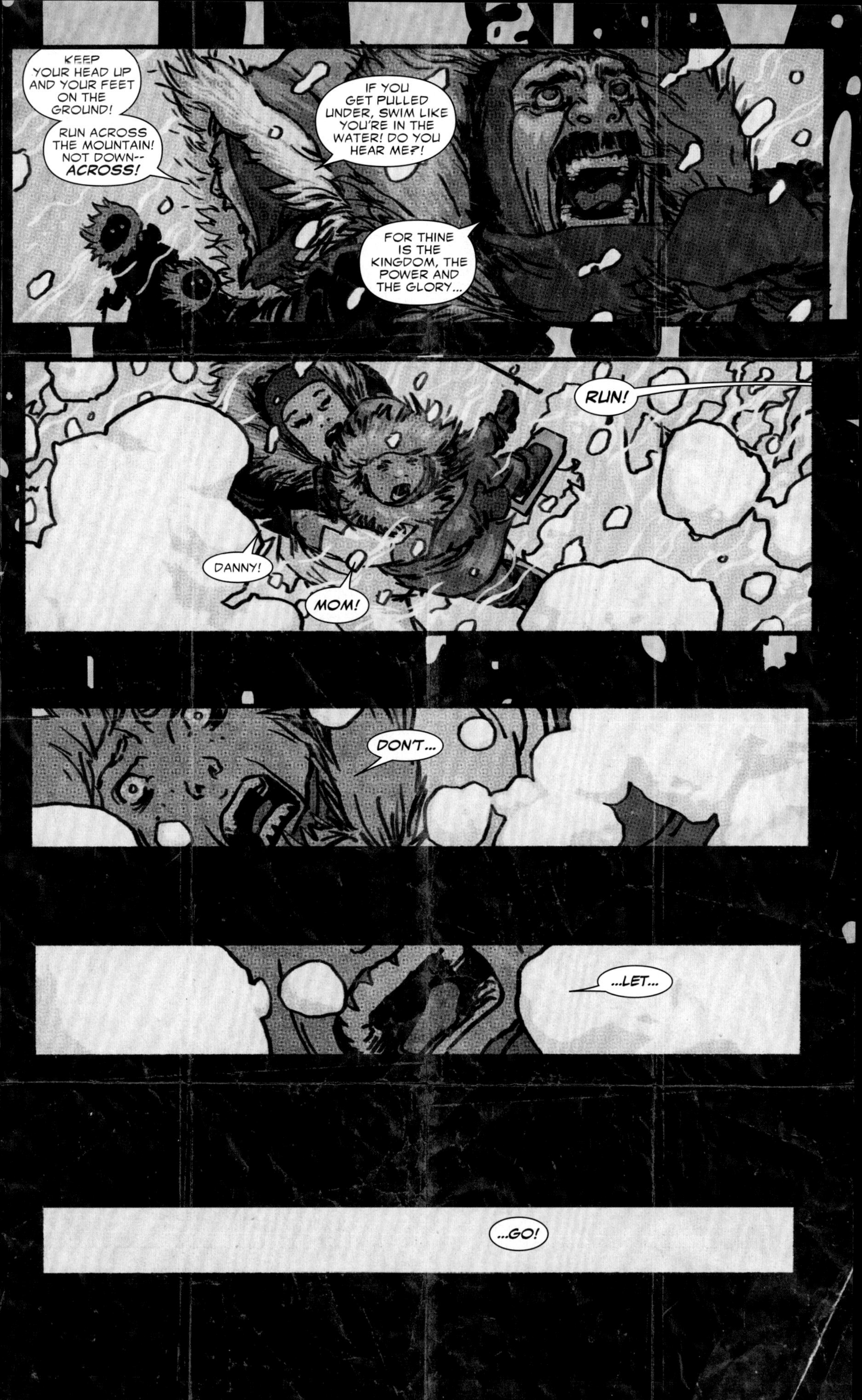
KEEP YOUR HEAD UP AND YOUR FEET ON THE GROUND!
RUN ACROSS THE MOUNTAIN! NOT DOWN-- ACROSS!
IF YOU GET PULLED UNDER, SWIM LIKE YOU'RE IN THE WATER! DO YOU HEAR ME?!
FOR THINE IS THE KINGDOM, THE POWER AND THE GLORY...
RUN!
DANNY!
MOM!
DON'T...
...LET...
...GO!

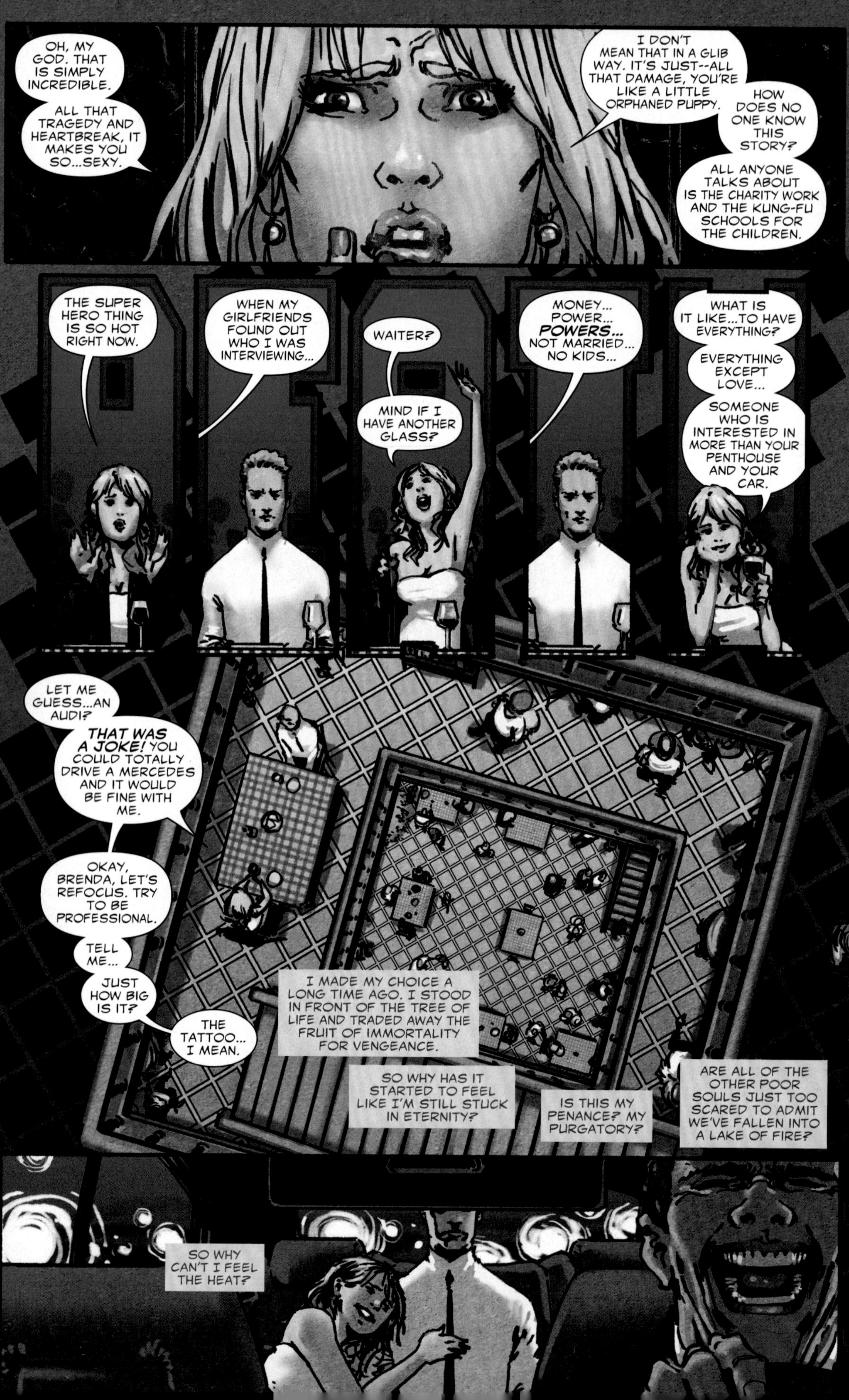
OH, MY GOD. THAT IS SIMPLY INCREDIBLE.
ALL THAT TRAGEDY AND HEARTBREAK, IT MAKES YOU SO...SEXY.
I DON'T MEAN THAT IN A GLIB WAY. IT'S JUST--ALL THAT DAMAGE, YOU'RE LIKE A LITTLE ORPHANED PUPPY.
HOW DOES NO ONE KNOW THIS STORY?
ALL ANYONE TALKS ABOUT IS THE CHARITY WORK AND THE KUNG-FU SCHOOLS FOR THE CHILDREN.
THE SUPER HERO THING IS SO HOT RIGHT NOW.
WHEN MY GIRLFRIENDS FOUND OUT WHO I WAS INTERVIEWING...
WAITER?
MIND IF I HAVE ANOTHER GLASS?
MONEY... POWER... **POWERS...** NOT MARRIED... NO KIDS...
WHAT IS IT LIKE...TO HAVE EVERYTHING?
EVERYTHING EXCEPT LOVE...
SOMEONE WHO IS INTERESTED IN MORE THAN YOUR PENTHOUSE AND YOUR CAR.
LET ME GUESS...AN AUDI?
THAT WAS A JOKE! YOU COULD TOTALLY DRIVE A MERCEDES AND IT WOULD BE FINE WITH ME.
OKAY, BRENDA, LET'S REFOCUS. TRY TO BE PROFESSIONAL.
TELL ME...
JUST HOW BIG IS IT?
THE TATTOO... I MEAN.
I MADE MY CHOICE A LONG TIME AGO. I STOOD IN FRONT OF THE TREE OF LIFE AND TRADED AWAY THE FRUIT OF IMMORTALITY FOR VENGEANCE.
SO WHY HAS IT STARTED TO FEEL LIKE I'M STILL STUCK IN ETERNITY?
IS THIS MY PENANCE? MY PURGATORY?
ARE ALL OF THE OTHER POOR SOULS JUST TOO SCARED TO ADMIT WE'VE FALLEN INTO A LAKE OF FIRE?
SO WHY CAN'T I FEEL THE HEAT?

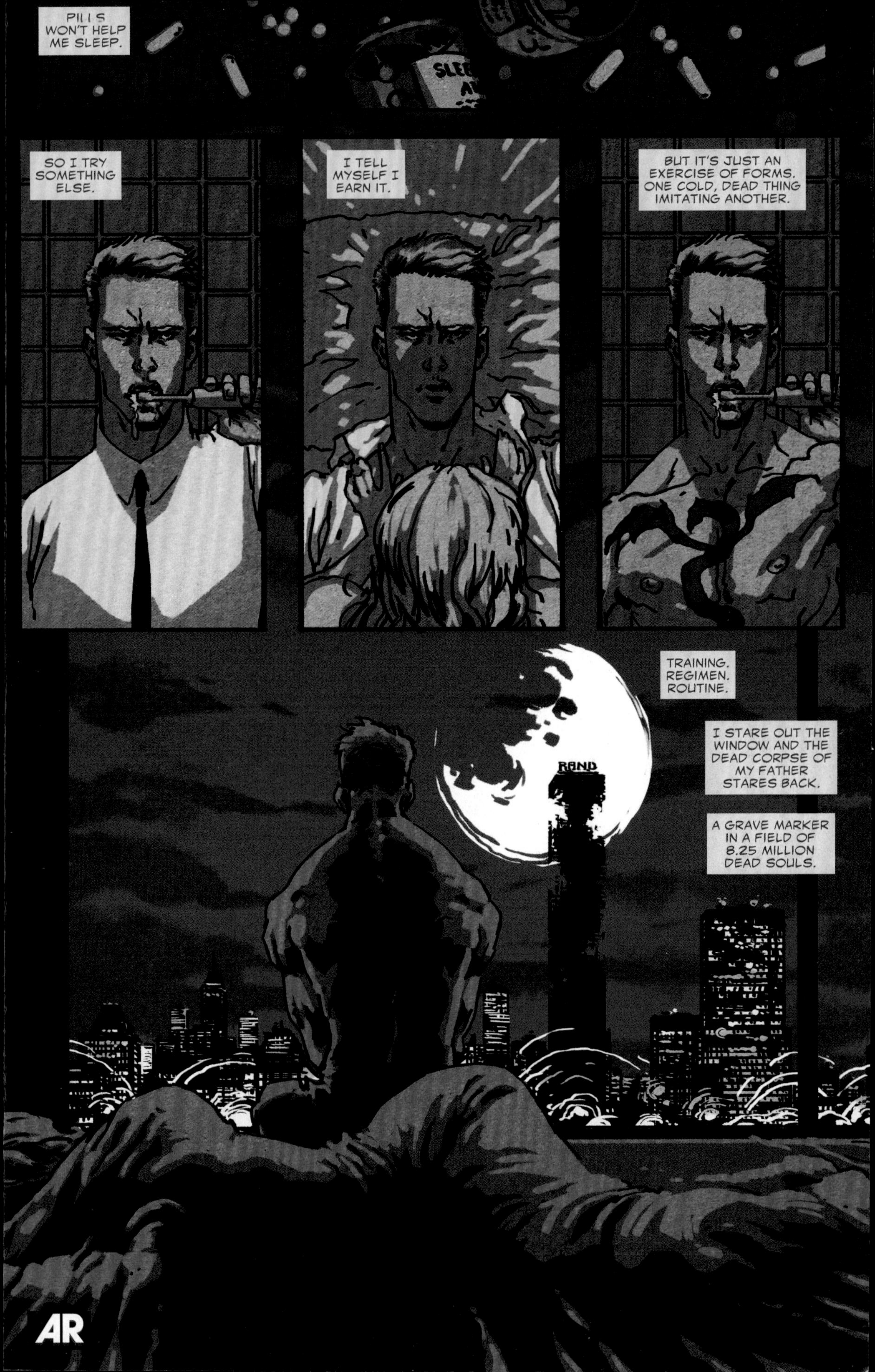
PILLS WON'T HELP ME SLEEP.
SO I TRY SOMETHING ELSE.
I TELL MYSELF I EARN IT.
BUT IT'S JUST AN EXERCISE OF FORMS. ONE COLD, DEAD THING IMITATING ANOTHER.
TRAINING. REGIMEN. ROUTINE.
RAND
I STARE OUT THE WINDOW AND THE DEAD CORPSE OF MY FATHER STARES BACK.
A GRAVE MARKER IN A FIELD OF 8.25 MILLION DEAD SOULS.
AR

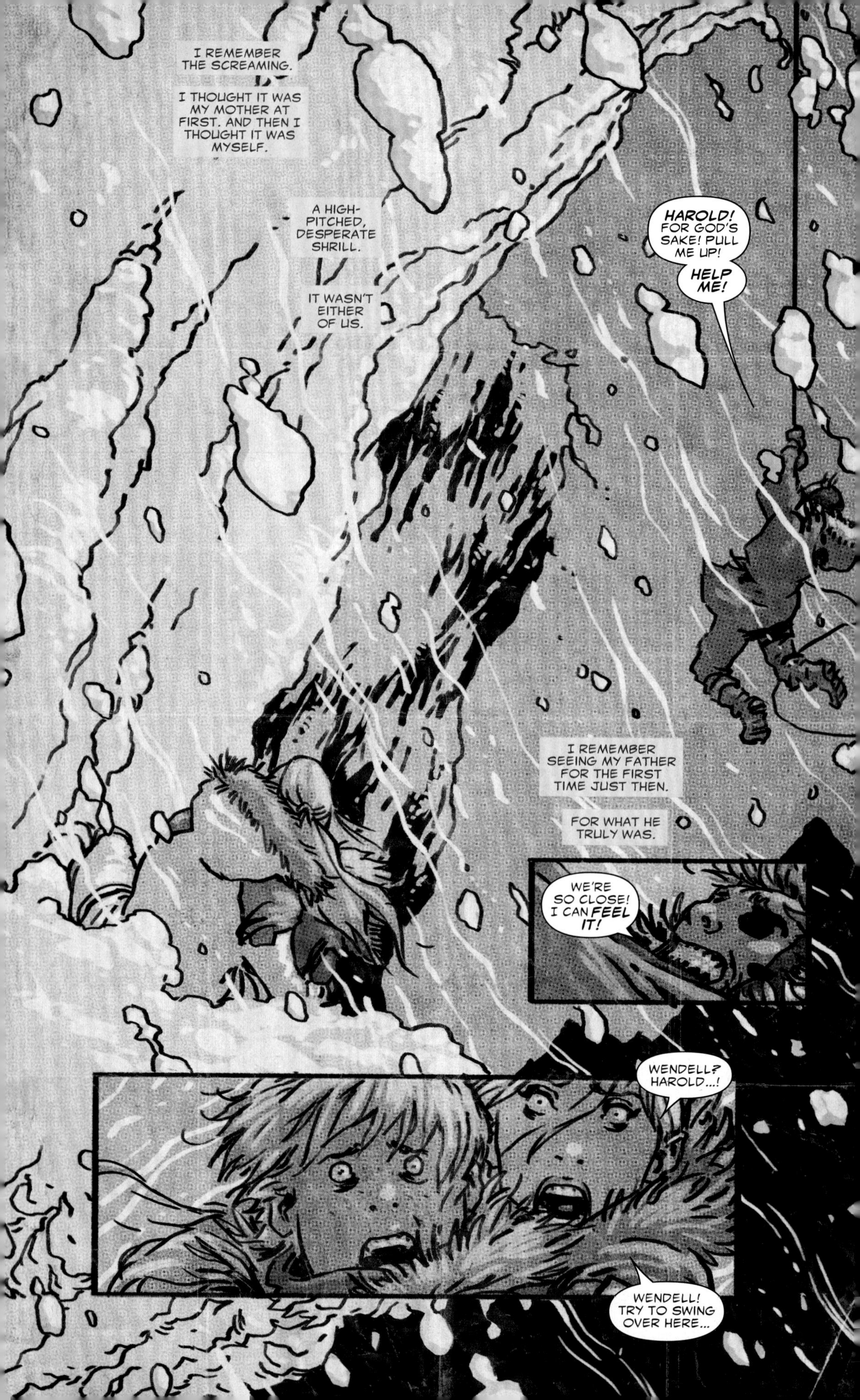
I REMEMBER THE SCREAMING.
I THOUGHT IT WAS MY MOTHER AT FIRST. AND THEN I THOUGHT IT WAS MYSELF.
A HIGH-PITCHED, DESPERATE SHRILL.
IT WASN'T EITHER OF US.
HAROLD! FOR GOD'S SAKE! PULL ME UP!
HELP ME!
I REMEMBER SEEING MY FATHER FOR THE FIRST TIME JUST THEN.
FOR WHAT HE TRULY WAS.
WE'RE SO CLOSE! I CAN FEEL IT!
WENDELL? HAROLD...!
WENDELL! TRY TO SWING OVER HERE...

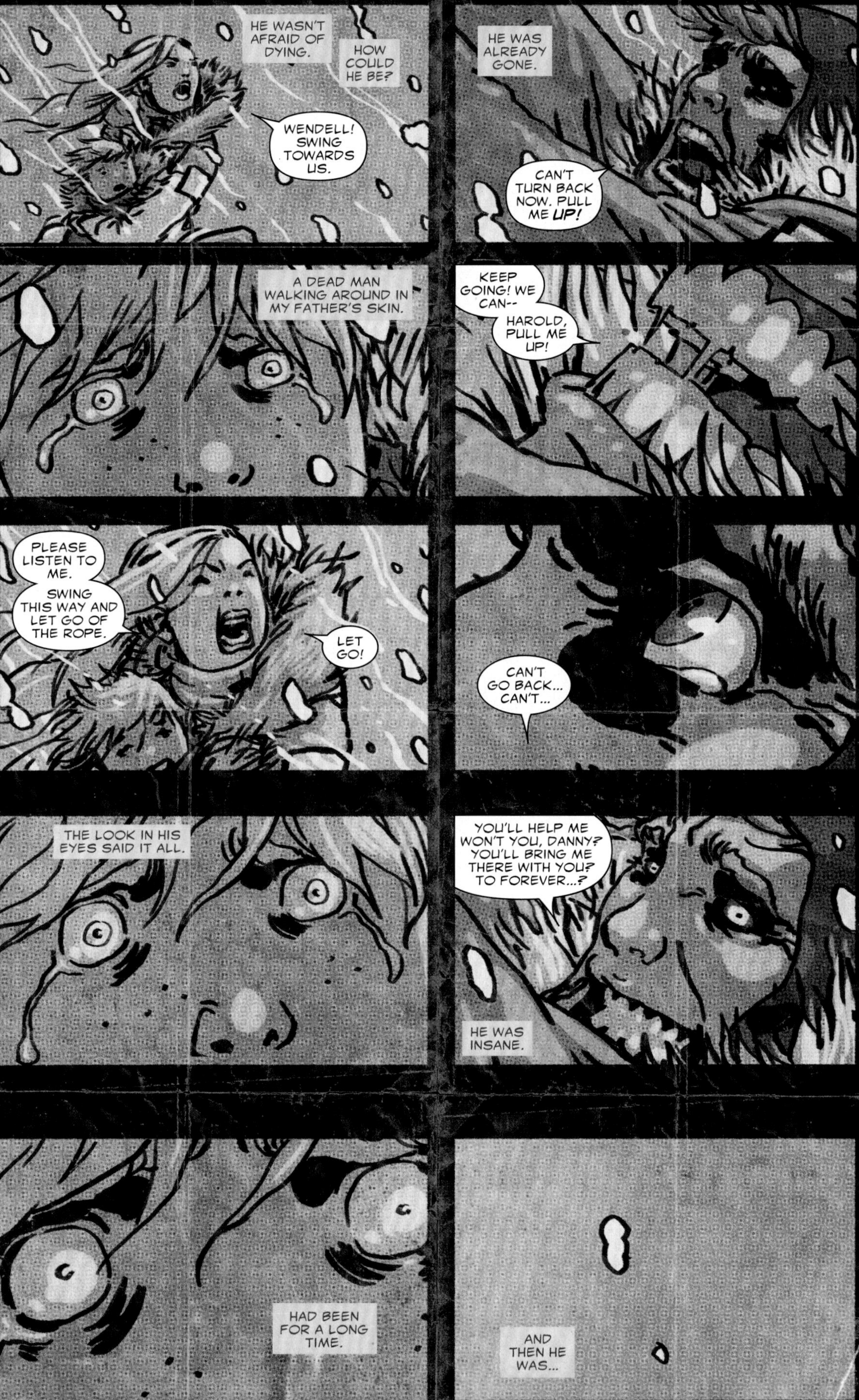
HE WASN'T AFRAID OF DYING.
HOW COULD HE BE?
WENDELL! SWING TOWARDS US.
HE WAS ALREADY GONE.
CAN'T TURN BACK NOW. PULL ME UP!
A DEAD MAN WALKING AROUND IN MY FATHER'S SKIN.
KEEP GOING! WE CAN--
HAROLD, PULL ME UP!
PLEASE LISTEN TO ME.
SWING THIS WAY AND LET GO OF THE ROPE.
LET GO!
CAN'T GO BACK... CAN'T...
THE LOOK IN HIS EYES SAID IT ALL.
YOU'LL HELP ME WON'T YOU, DANNY? YOU'LL BRING ME THERE WITH YOU? TO FOREVER...?
HE WAS INSANE.
HAD BEEN FOR A LONG TIME.
AND THEN HE WAS...

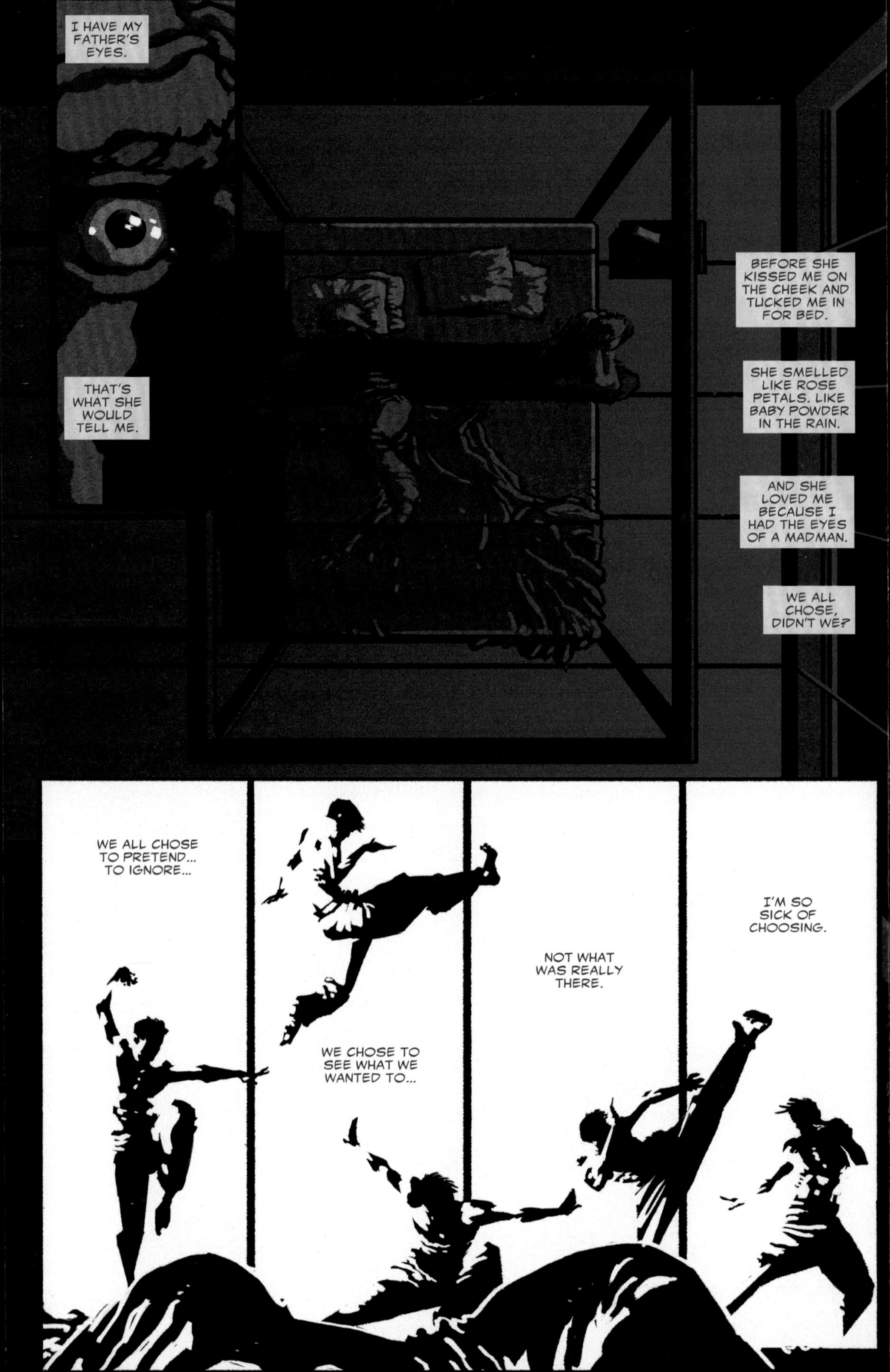
I HAVE MY FATHER'S EYES.
THAT'S WHAT SHE WOULD TELL ME.
BEFORE SHE KISSED ME ON THE CHEEK AND TUCKED ME IN FOR BED.
SHE SMELLED LIKE ROSE PETALS. LIKE BABY POWDER IN THE RAIN.
AND SHE LOVED ME BECAUSE I HAD THE EYES OF A MADMAN.
WE ALL CHOSE, DIDN'T WE?
WE ALL CHOSE TO PRETEND... TO IGNORE...
WE CHOSE TO SEE WHAT WE WANTED TO...
NOT WHAT WAS REALLY THERE.
I'M SO SICK OF CHOOSING.

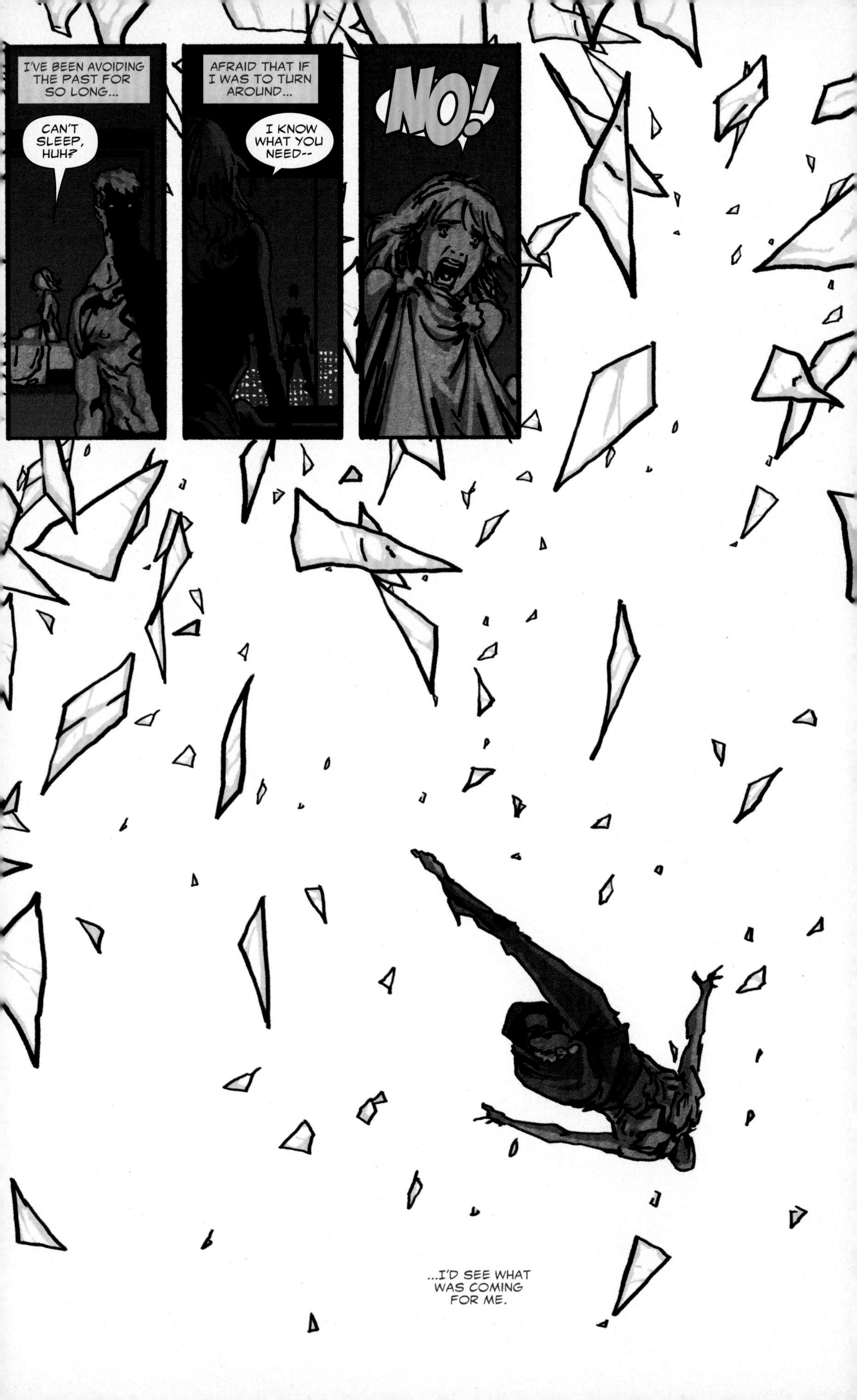
I'VE BEEN AVOIDING THE PAST FOR SO LONG...
CAN'T SLEEP, HUH?
AFRAID THAT IF I WAS TO TURN AROUND...
I KNOW WHAT YOU NEED--
NO!
...I'D SEE WHAT WAS COMING FOR ME.

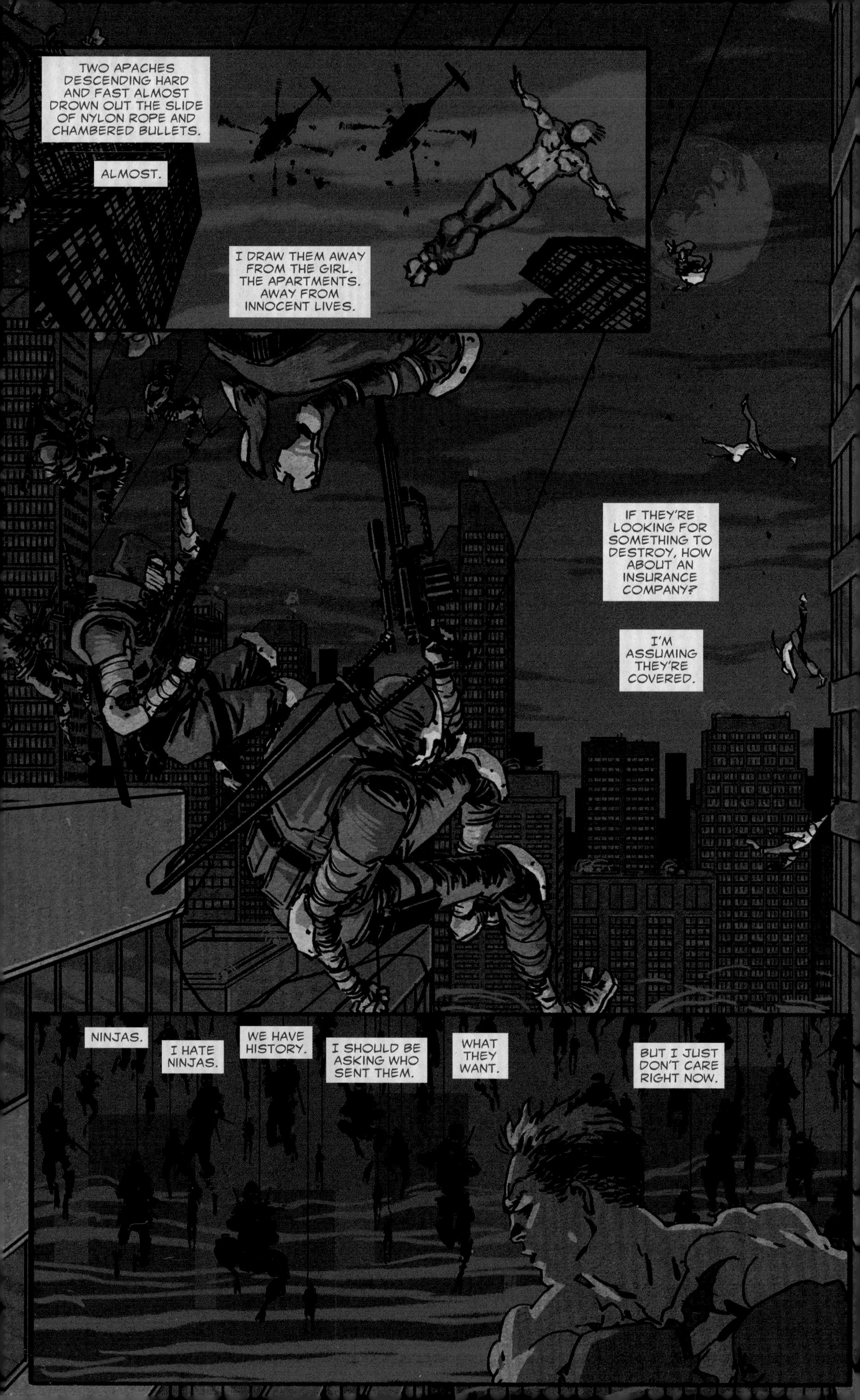
TWO APACHES DESCENDING HARD AND FAST ALMOST DROWN OUT THE SLIDE OF NYLON ROPE AND CHAMBERED BULLETS.
ALMOST.
I DRAW THEM AWAY FROM THE GIRL. THE APARTMENTS. AWAY FROM INNOCENT LIVES.
IF THEY'RE LOOKING FOR SOMETHING TO DESTROY, HOW ABOUT AN INSURANCE COMPANY?
I'M ASSUMING THEY'RE COVERED.
NINJAS.
I HATE NINJAS.
WE HAVE HISTORY.
I SHOULD BE ASKING WHO SENT THEM.
WHAT THEY WANT.
BUT I JUST DON'T CARE RIGHT NOW.

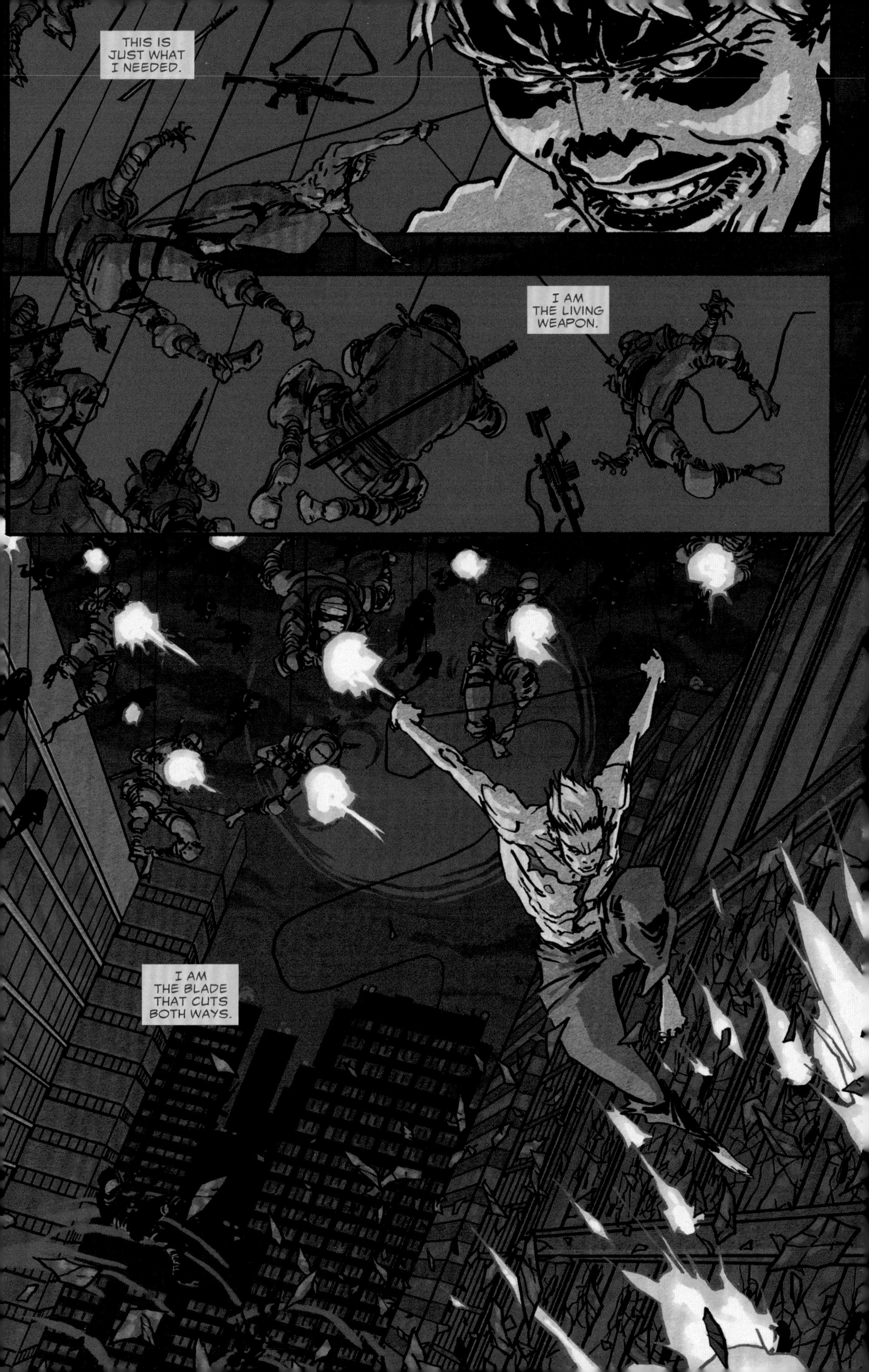
THIS IS JUST WHAT I NEEDED.
I AM THE LIVING WEAPON.
I AM THE BLADE THAT CUTS BOTH WAYS.

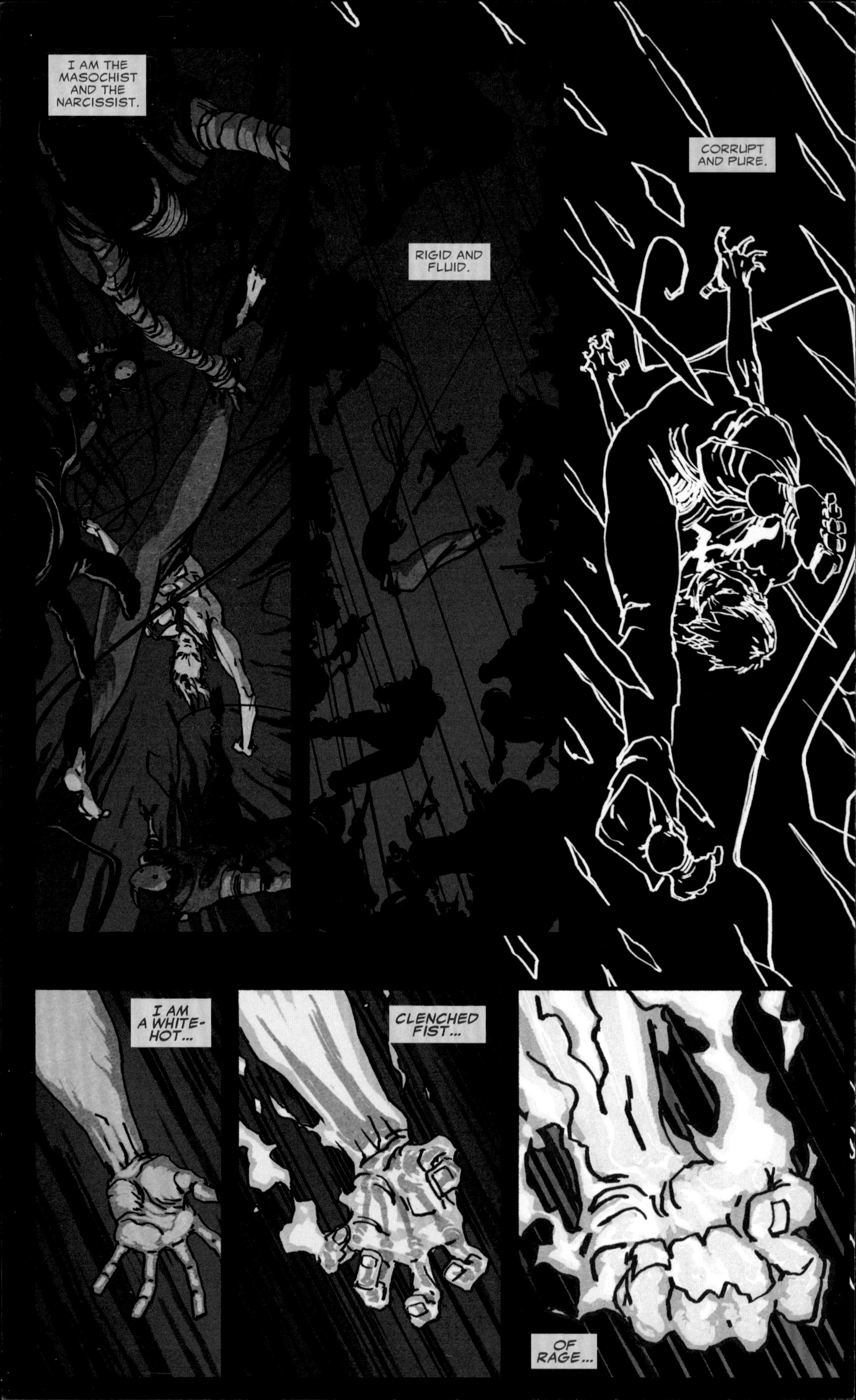
I AM THE MASOCHIST AND THE NARCISSIST.
RIGID AND FLUID.
CORRUPT AND PURE.
I AM A WHITE-HOT...
CLENCHED FIST...
OF RAGE...

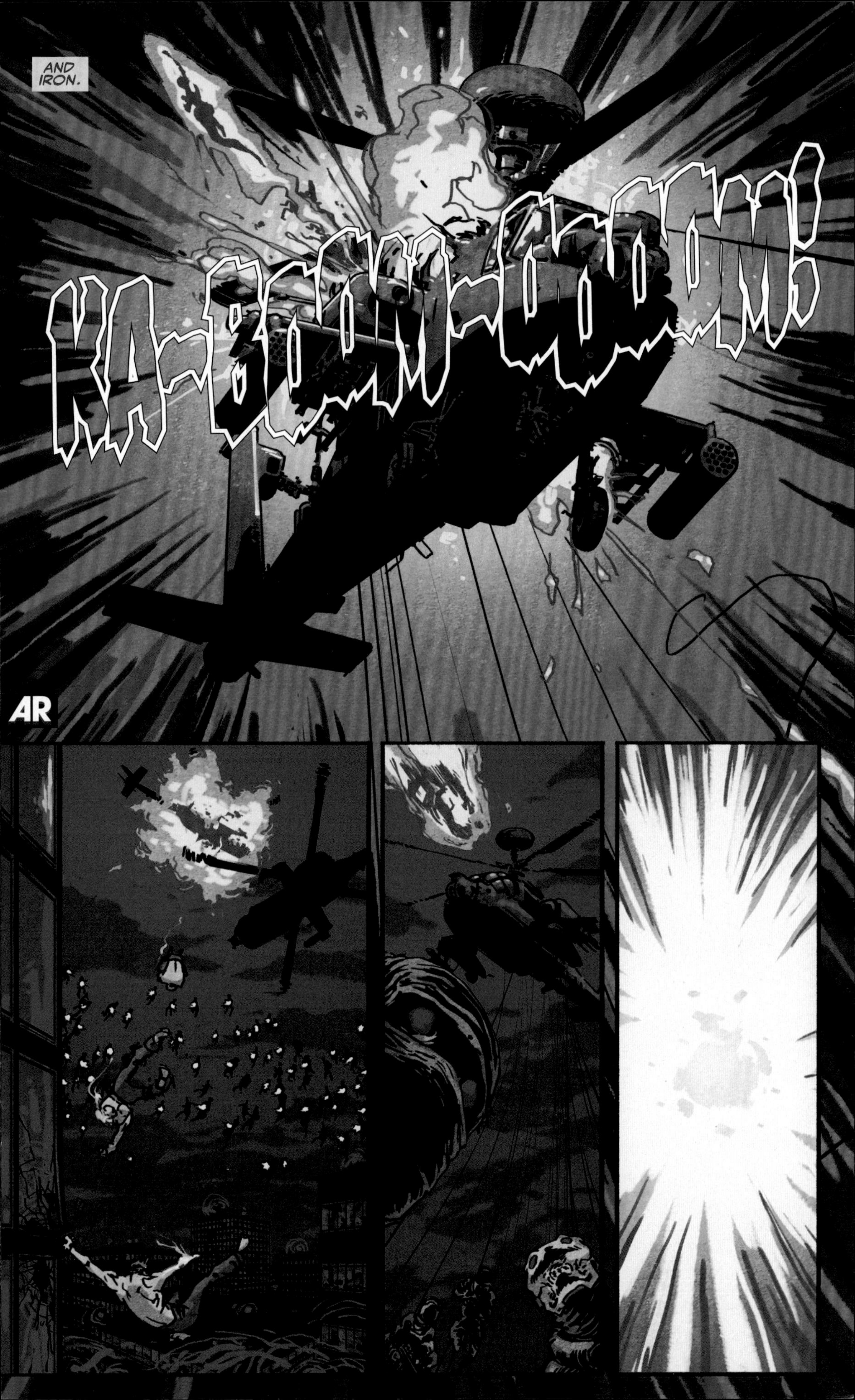
AND IRON.
KA-BOOM-BOOOM!

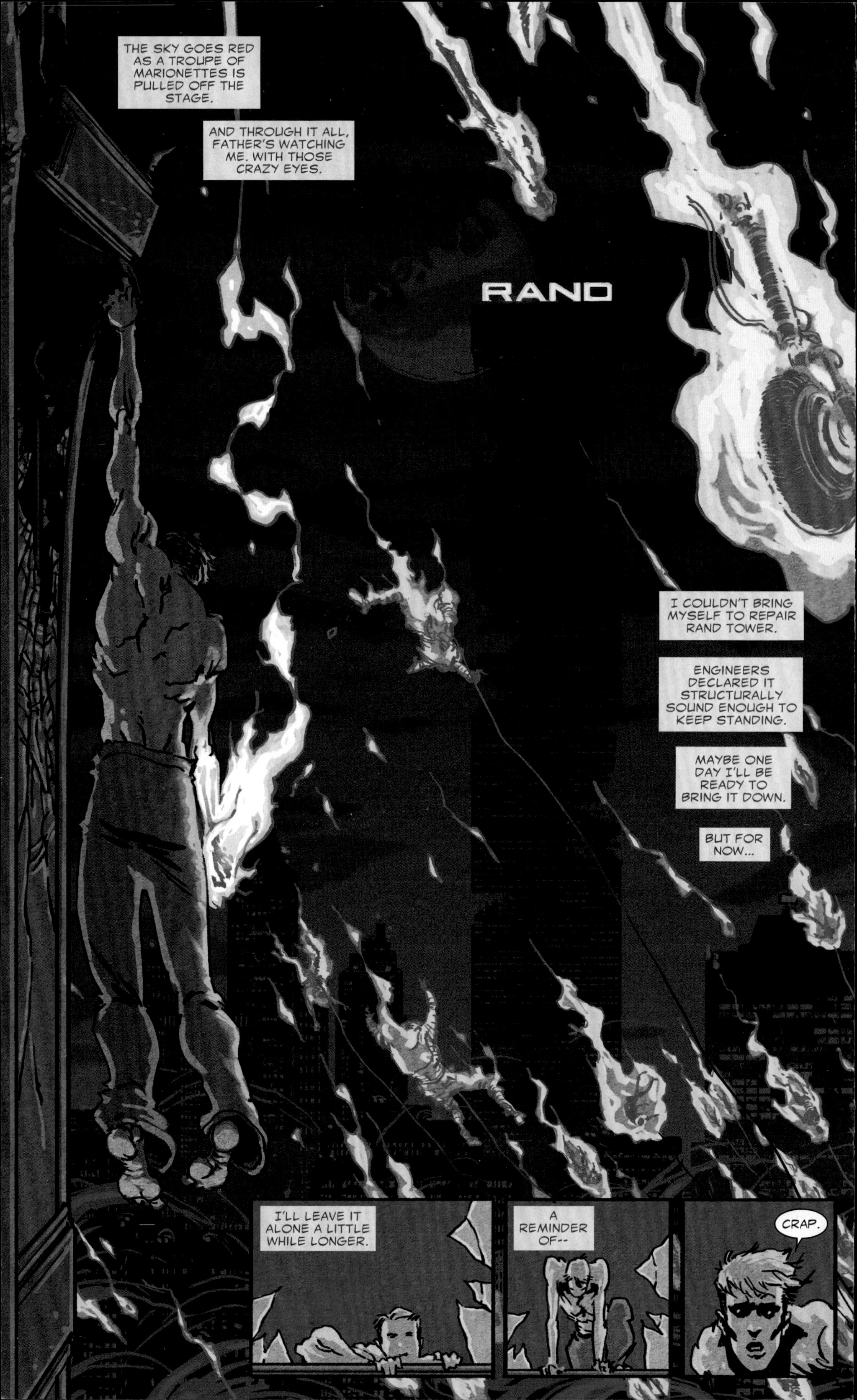
THE SKY GOES RED AS A TROUPE OF MARIONETTES IS PULLED OFF THE STAGE.
AND THROUGH IT ALL, FATHER'S WATCHING ME. WITH THOSE CRAZY EYES.
RAND
I COULDN'T BRING MYSELF TO REPAIR RAND TOWER.
ENGINEERS DECLARED IT STRUCTURALLY SOUND ENOUGH TO KEEP STANDING.
MAYBE ONE DAY I'LL BE READY TO BRING IT DOWN.
BUT FOR NOW...
I'LL LEAVE IT ALONE A LITTLE WHILE LONGER.
A REMINDER OF--
CRAP.

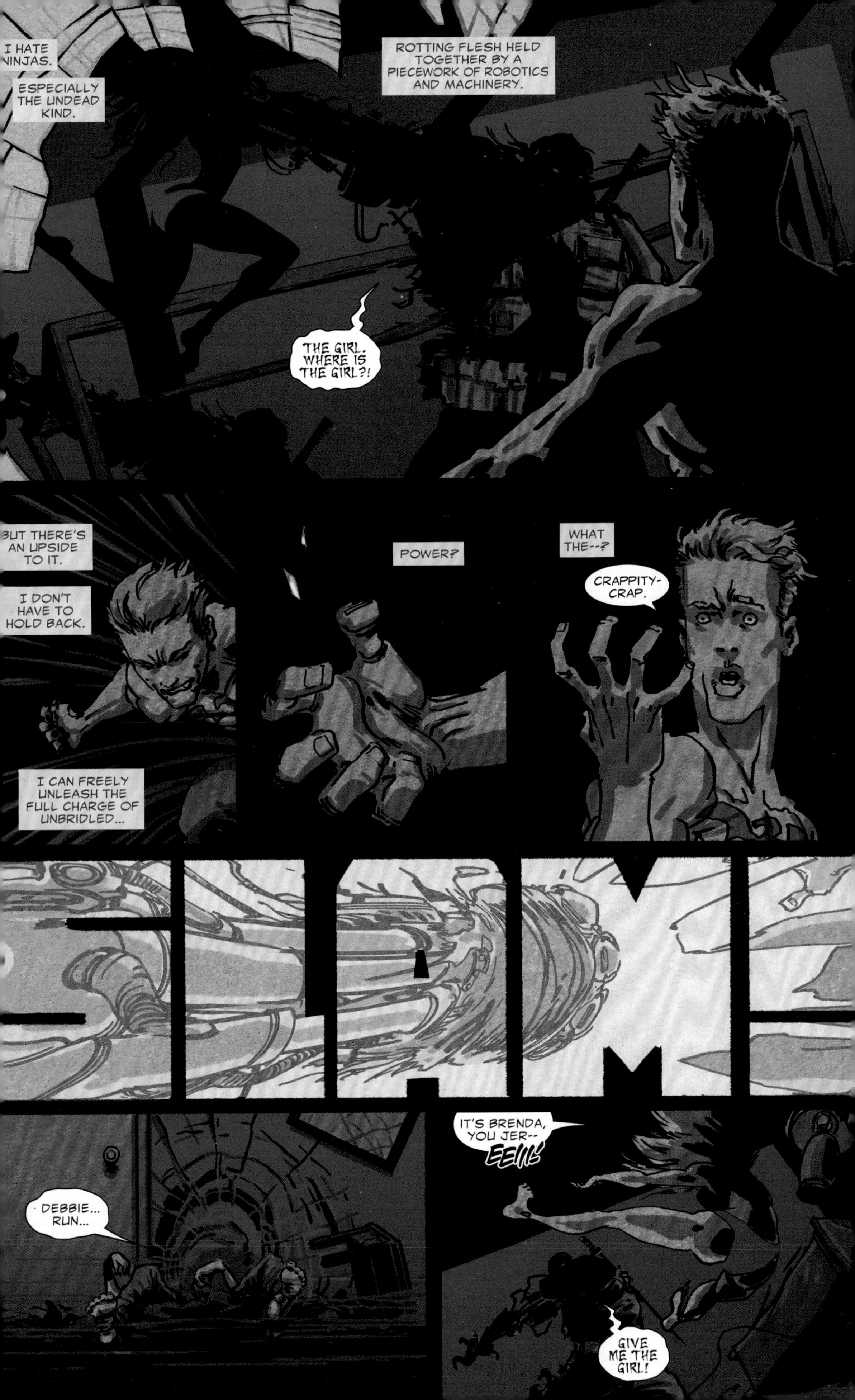
I HATE NINJAS.
ESPECIALLY THE UNDEAD KIND.
ROTTING FLESH HELD TOGETHER BY A PIECEWORK OF ROBOTICS AND MACHINERY.
THE GIRL. WHERE IS THE GIRL?!
BUT THERE'S AN UPSIDE TO IT.
I DON'T HAVE TO HOLD BACK.
I CAN FREELY UNLEASH THE FULL CHARGE OF UNBRIDLED...
POWER?
WHAT THE--?
CRAPPITY-CRAP.
SLAM
DEBBIE... RUN...
IT'S BRENDA, YOU JER--
EEIII!
GIVE ME THE GIRL!

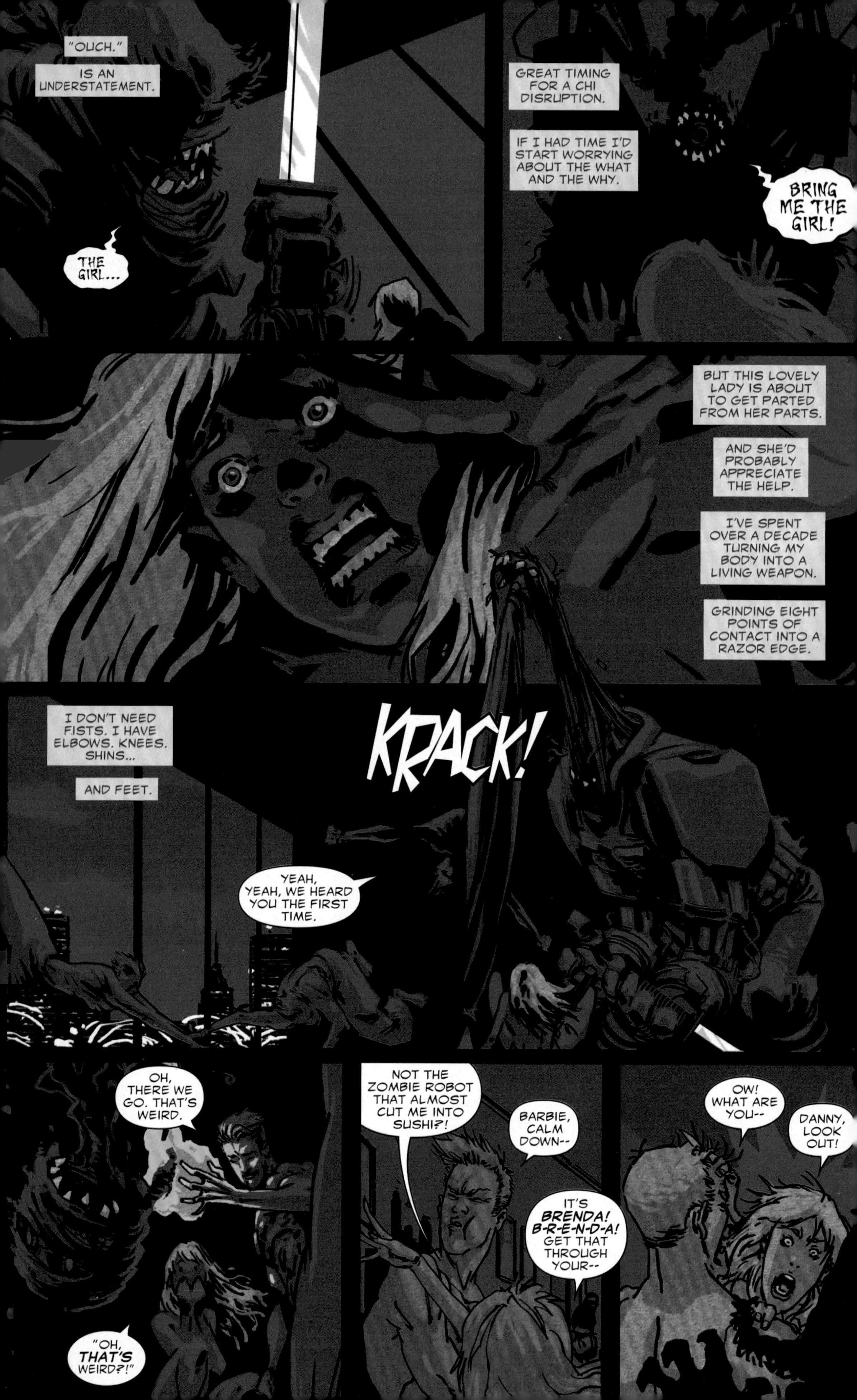
"OUCH."
IS AN UNDERSTATEMENT.
THE GIRL...
GREAT TIMING FOR A CHI DISRUPTION.
IF I HAD TIME I'D START WORRYING ABOUT THE WHAT AND THE WHY.
BRING ME THE GIRL!
BUT THIS LOVELY LADY IS ABOUT TO GET PARTED FROM HER PARTS.
AND SHE'D PROBABLY APPRECIATE THE HELP.
I'VE SPENT OVER A DECADE TURNING MY BODY INTO A LIVING WEAPON.
GRINDING EIGHT POINTS OF CONTACT INTO A RAZOR EDGE.
I DON'T NEED FISTS. I HAVE ELBOWS. KNEES. SHINS...
AND FEET.
KRACK!
YEAH, YEAH, WE HEARD YOU THE FIRST TIME.
OH, THERE WE GO. THAT'S WEIRD.
"OH, THAT'S WEIRD?!"
NOT THE ZOMBIE ROBOT THAT ALMOST CUT ME INTO SUSHI?!
BARBIE, CALM DOWN--
IT'S BRENDA! B-R-E-N-D-A! GET THAT THROUGH YOUR--
OW! WHAT ARE YOU--
DANNY, LOOK OUT!

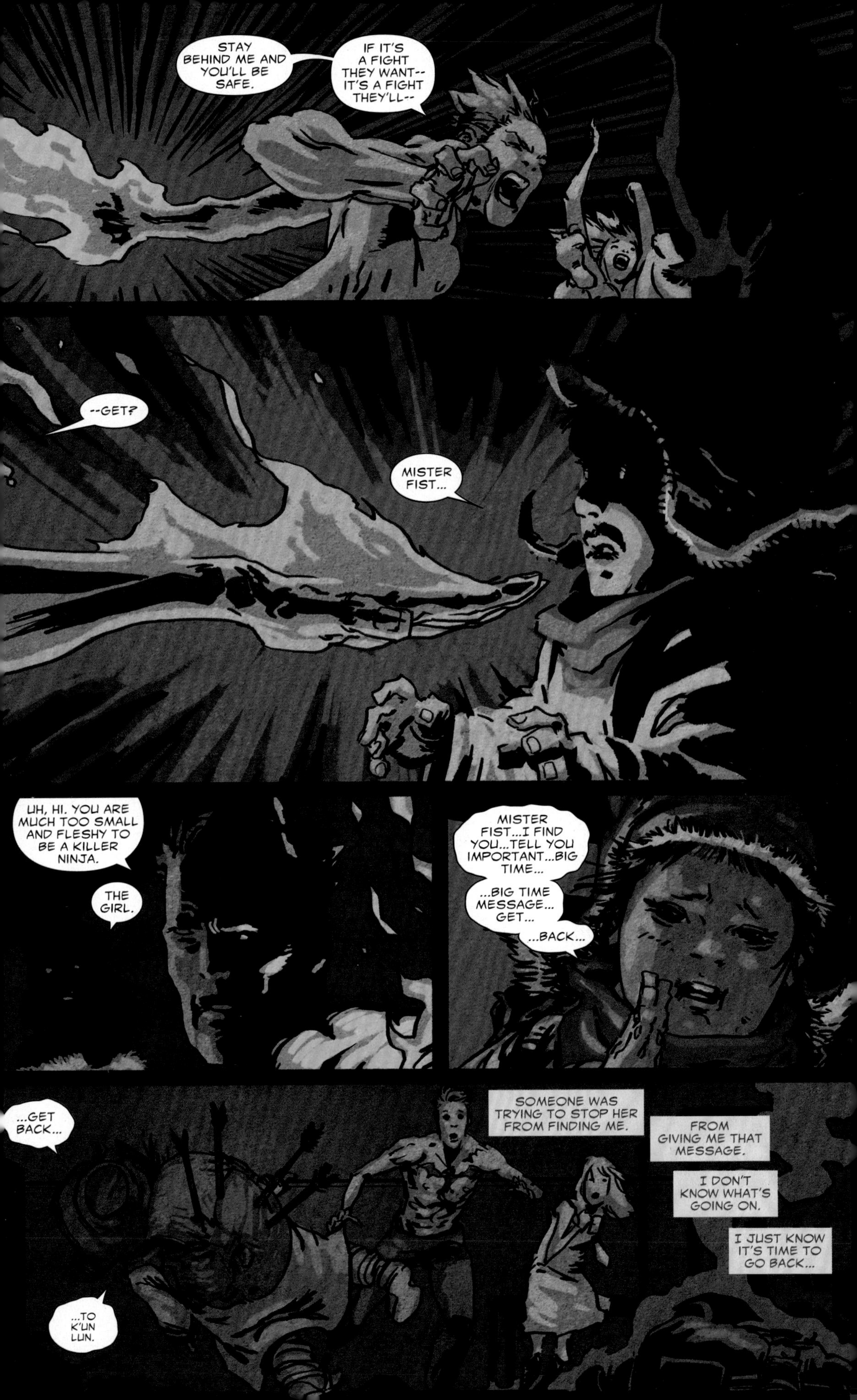
STAY BEHIND ME AND YOU'LL BE SAFE.
IF IT'S A FIGHT THEY WANT-- IT'S A FIGHT THEY'LL--
--GET?
MISTER FIST...
UH, HI. YOU ARE MUCH TOO SMALL AND FLESHY TO BE A KILLER NINJA.
THE GIRL.
MISTER FIST...I FIND YOU...TELL YOU IMPORTANT...BIG TIME...
...BIG TIME MESSAGE... GET...
...BACK...
...GET BACK...
SOMEONE WAS TRYING TO STOP HER FROM FINDING ME.
FROM GIVING ME THAT MESSAGE.
I DON'T KNOW WHAT'S GOING ON.
I JUST KNOW IT'S TIME TO GO BACK...
...TO K'UN LUN.

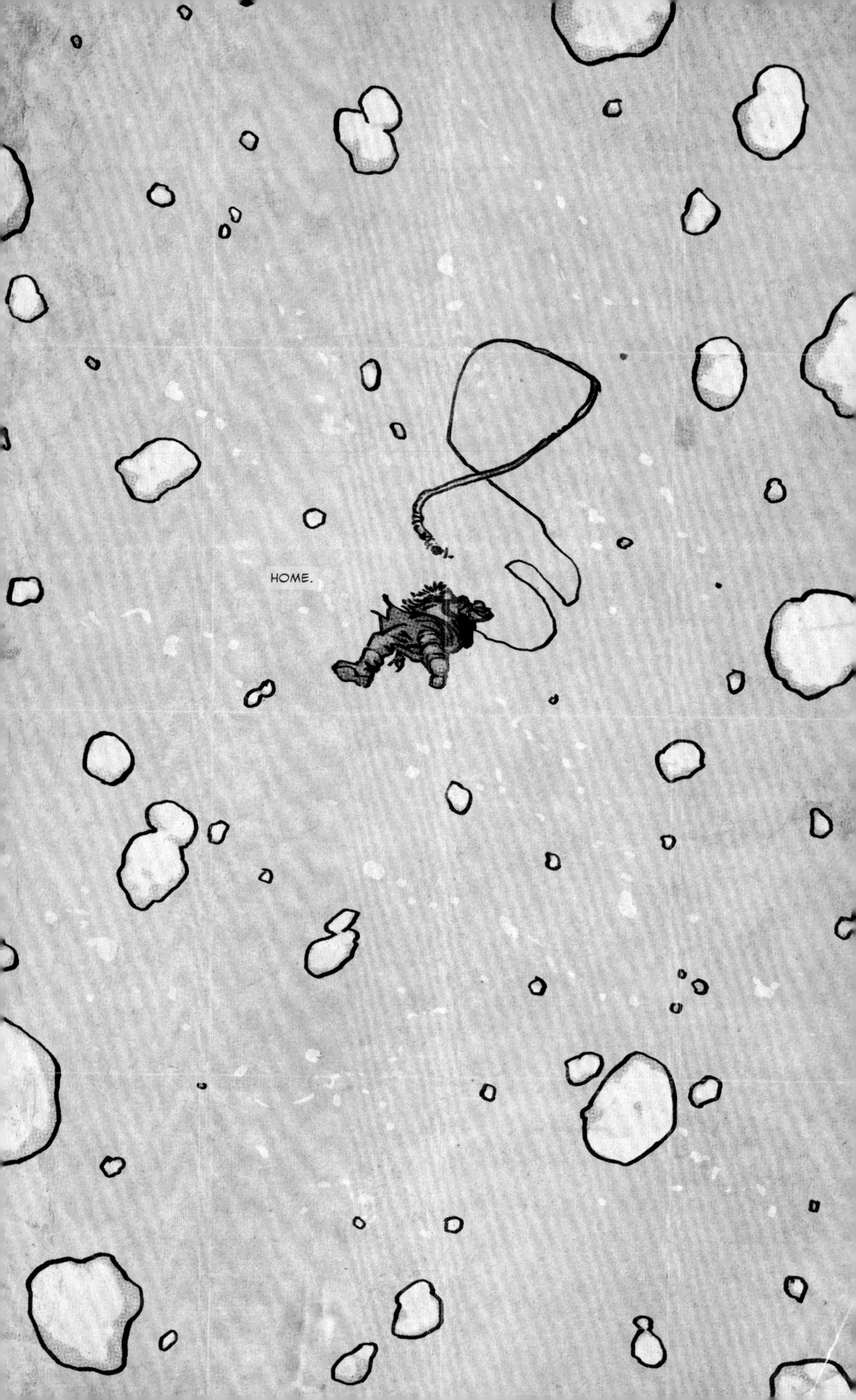
HOME.

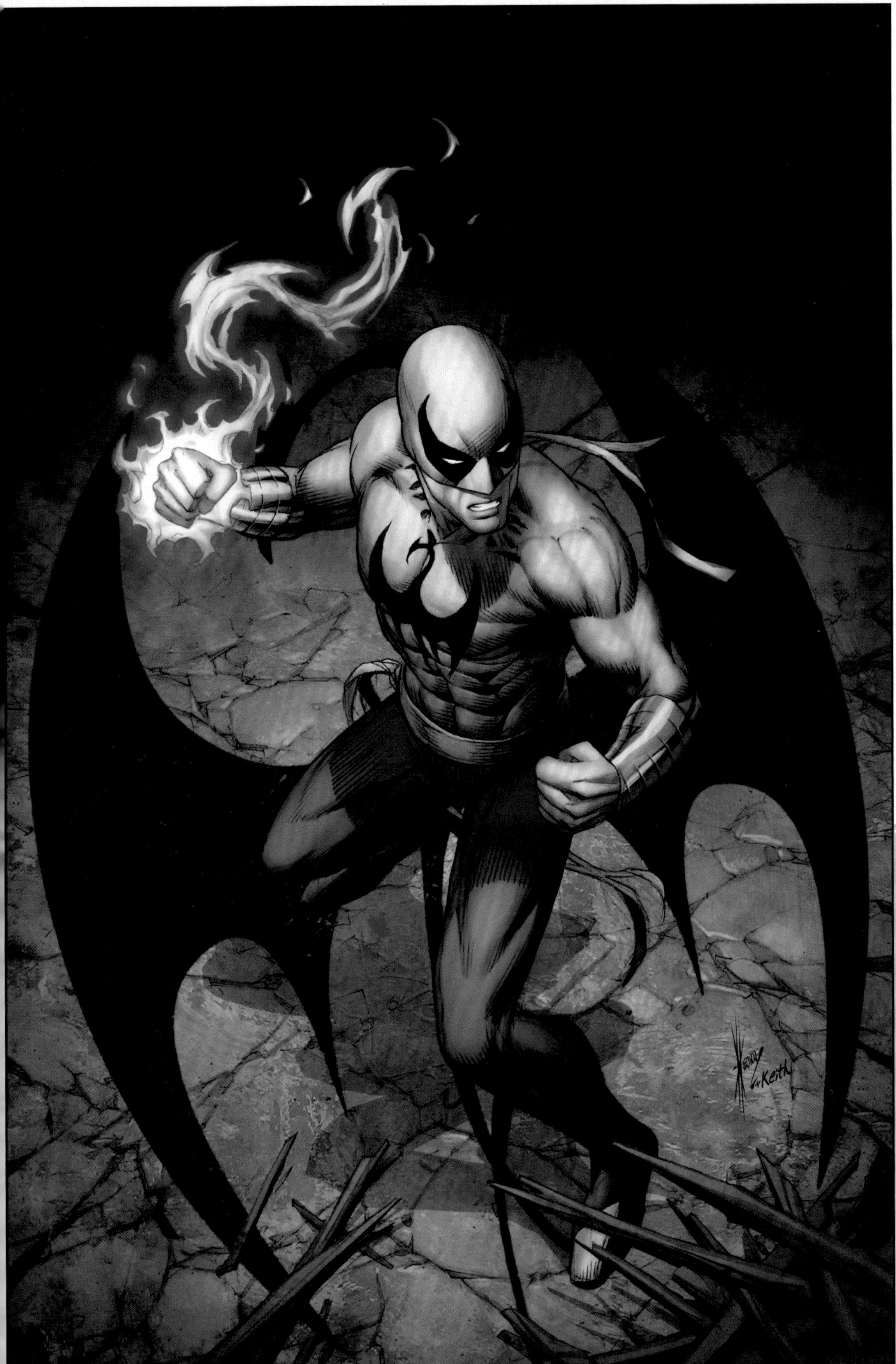

IRON FIST: THE LIVING WEAPON #1 VARIANT
BY DALE KEOWN & JASON KEITH

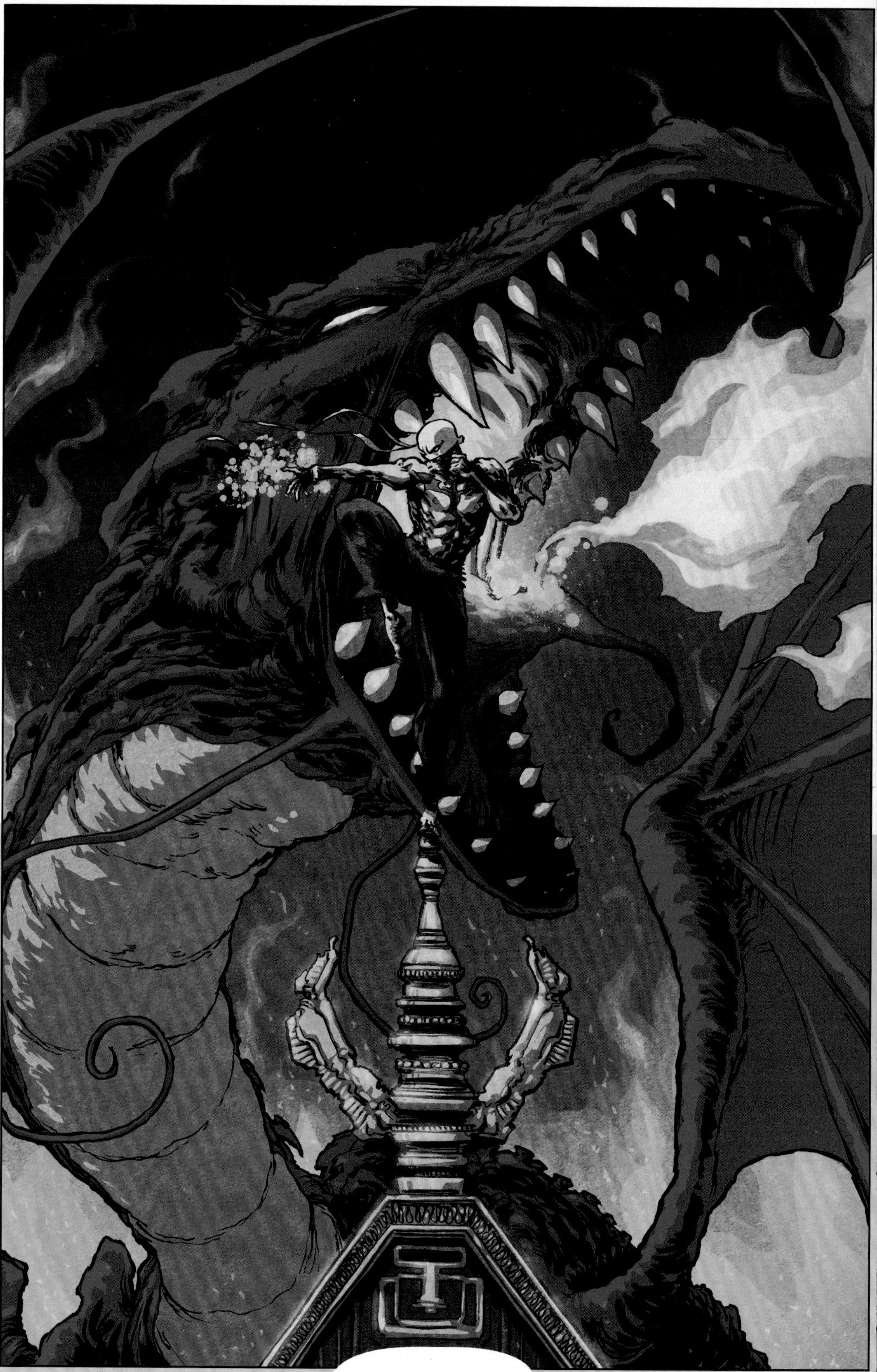

2

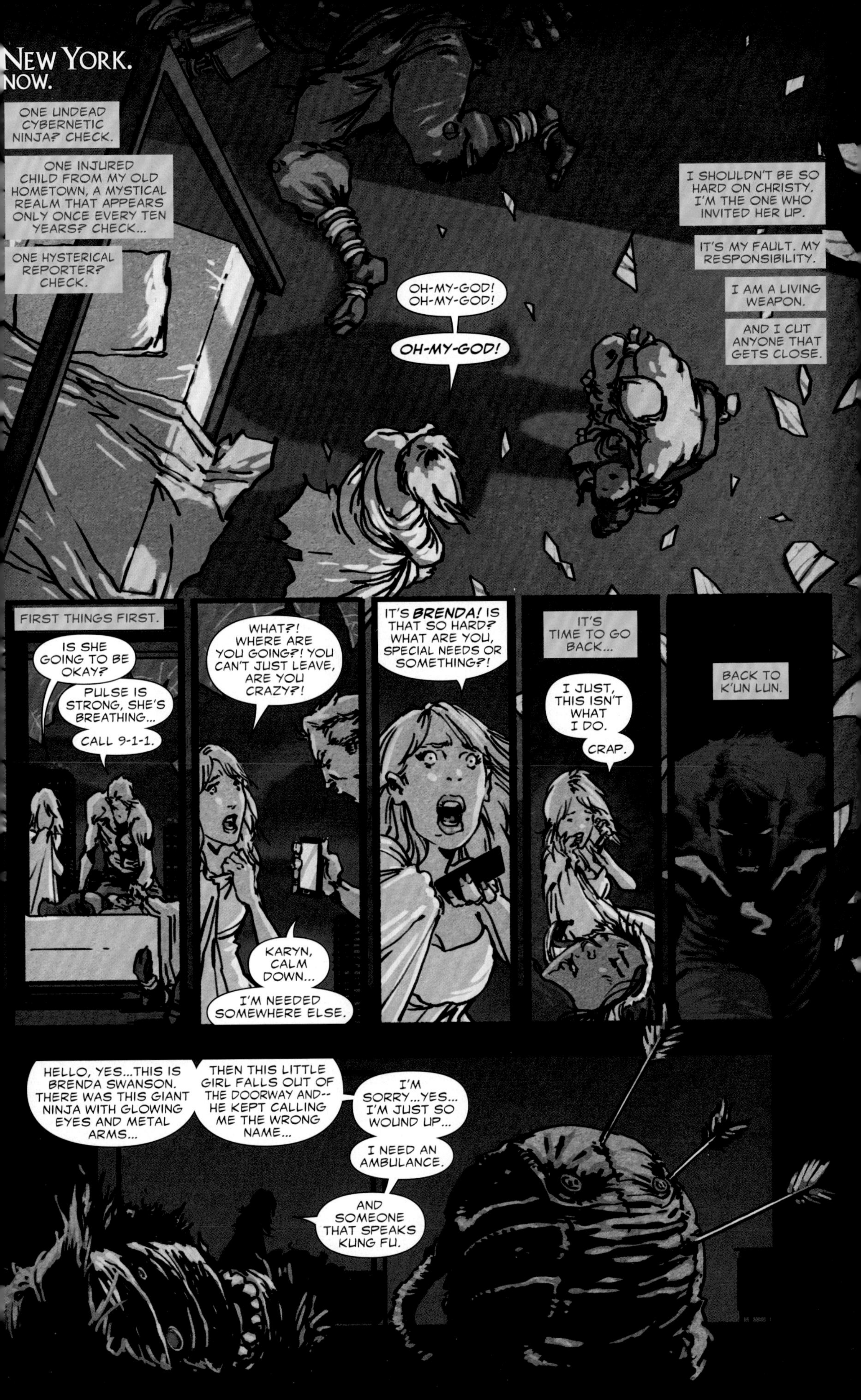

NEW YORK.
NOW.
ONE UNDEAD CYBERNETIC NINJA? CHECK.
ONE INJURED CHILD FROM MY OLD HOMETOWN, A MYSTICAL REALM THAT APPEARS ONLY ONCE EVERY TEN YEARS? CHECK...
ONE HYSTERICAL REPORTER? CHECK.
OH-MY-GOD! OH-MY-GOD!
OH-MY-GOD!
I SHOULDN'T BE SO HARD ON CHRISTY. I'M THE ONE WHO INVITED HER UP.
IT'S MY FAULT. MY RESPONSIBILITY.
I AM A LIVING WEAPON.
AND I CUT ANYONE THAT GETS CLOSE.
FIRST THINGS FIRST.
IS SHE GOING TO BE OKAY?
PULSE IS STRONG, SHE'S BREATHING...
CALL 9-1-1.
WHAT?! WHERE ARE YOU GOING?! YOU CAN'T JUST LEAVE, ARE YOU CRAZY?!
KARYN, CALM DOWN...
I'M NEEDED SOMEWHERE ELSE.
IT'S BRENDA! IS THAT SO HARD? WHAT ARE YOU, SPECIAL NEEDS OR SOMETHING?!
IT'S TIME TO GO BACK...
I JUST, THIS ISN'T WHAT I DO.
CRAP.
BACK TO K'UN LUN.
HELLO, YES...THIS IS BRENDA SWANSON. THERE WAS THIS GIANT NINJA WITH GLOWING EYES AND METAL ARMS...
THEN THIS LITTLE GIRL FALLS OUT OF THE DOORWAY AND-- HE KEPT CALLING ME THE WRONG NAME...
I'M SORRY...YES... I'M JUST SO WOUND UP...
I NEED AN AMBULANCE.
AND SOMEONE THAT SPEAKS KUNG FU.

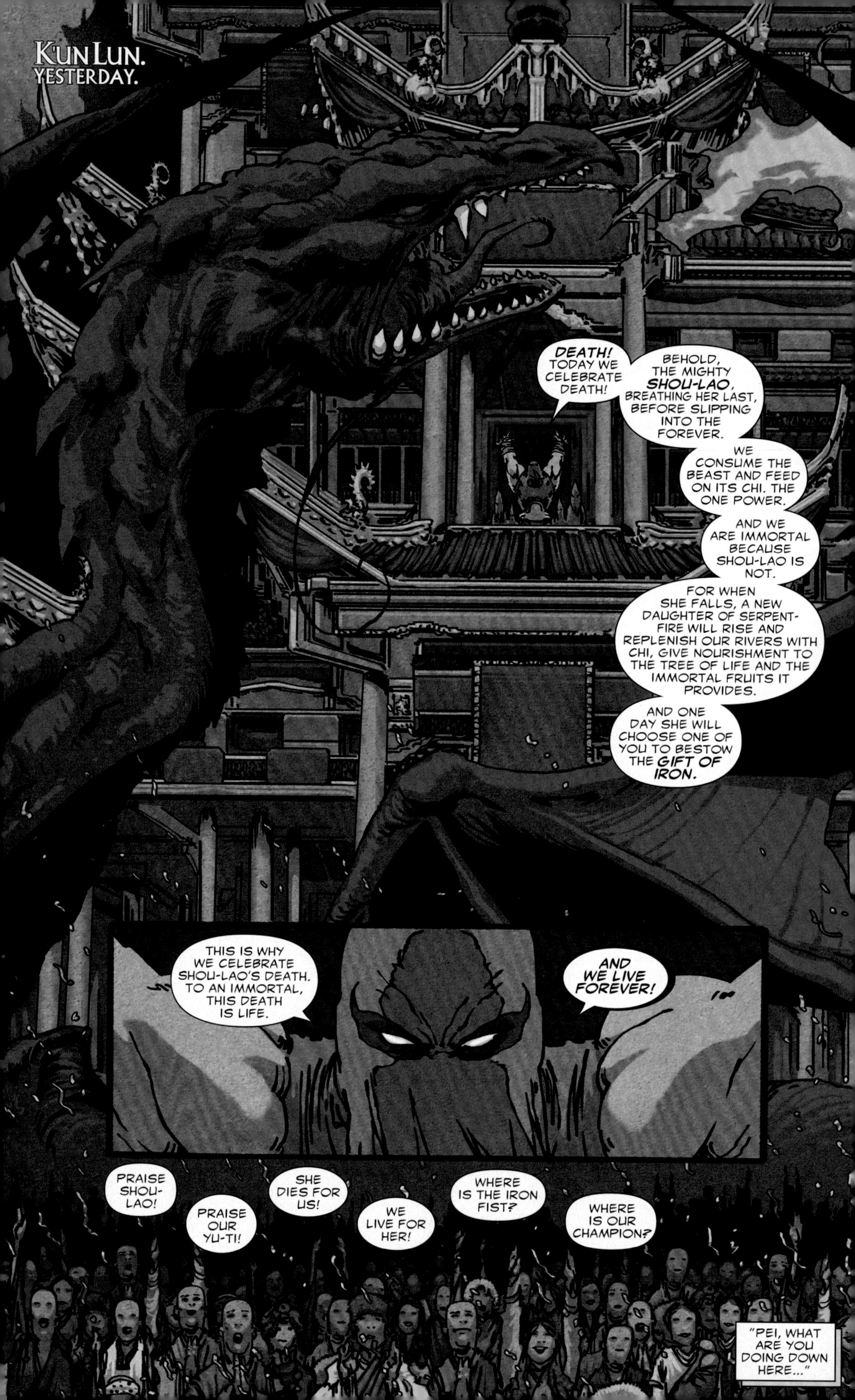
K'UN LUN.
YESTERDAY.
DEATH! TODAY WE CELEBRATE DEATH!
BEHOLD, THE MIGHTY SHOU-LAO, BREATHING HER LAST, BEFORE SLIPPING INTO THE FOREVER.
WE CONSUME THE BEAST AND FEED ON ITS CHI. THE ONE POWER.
AND WE ARE IMMORTAL BECAUSE SHOU-LAO IS NOT.
FOR WHEN SHE FALLS, A NEW DAUGHTER OF SERPENT-FIRE WILL RISE AND REPLENISH OUR RIVERS WITH CHI, GIVE NOURISHMENT TO THE TREE OF LIFE AND THE IMMORTAL FRUITS IT PROVIDES.
AND ONE DAY SHE WILL CHOOSE ONE OF YOU TO BESTOW THE GIFT OF IRON.
THIS IS WHY WE CELEBRATE SHOU-LAO'S DEATH. TO AN IMMORTAL, THIS DEATH IS LIFE.
AND WE LIVE FOREVER!
PRAISE SHOU-LAO!
PRAISE OUR YU-TI!
SHE DIES FOR US!
WE LIVE FOR HER!
WHERE IS THE IRON FIST?
WHERE IS OUR CHAMPION?
"PEI, WHAT ARE YOU DOING DOWN HERE..."

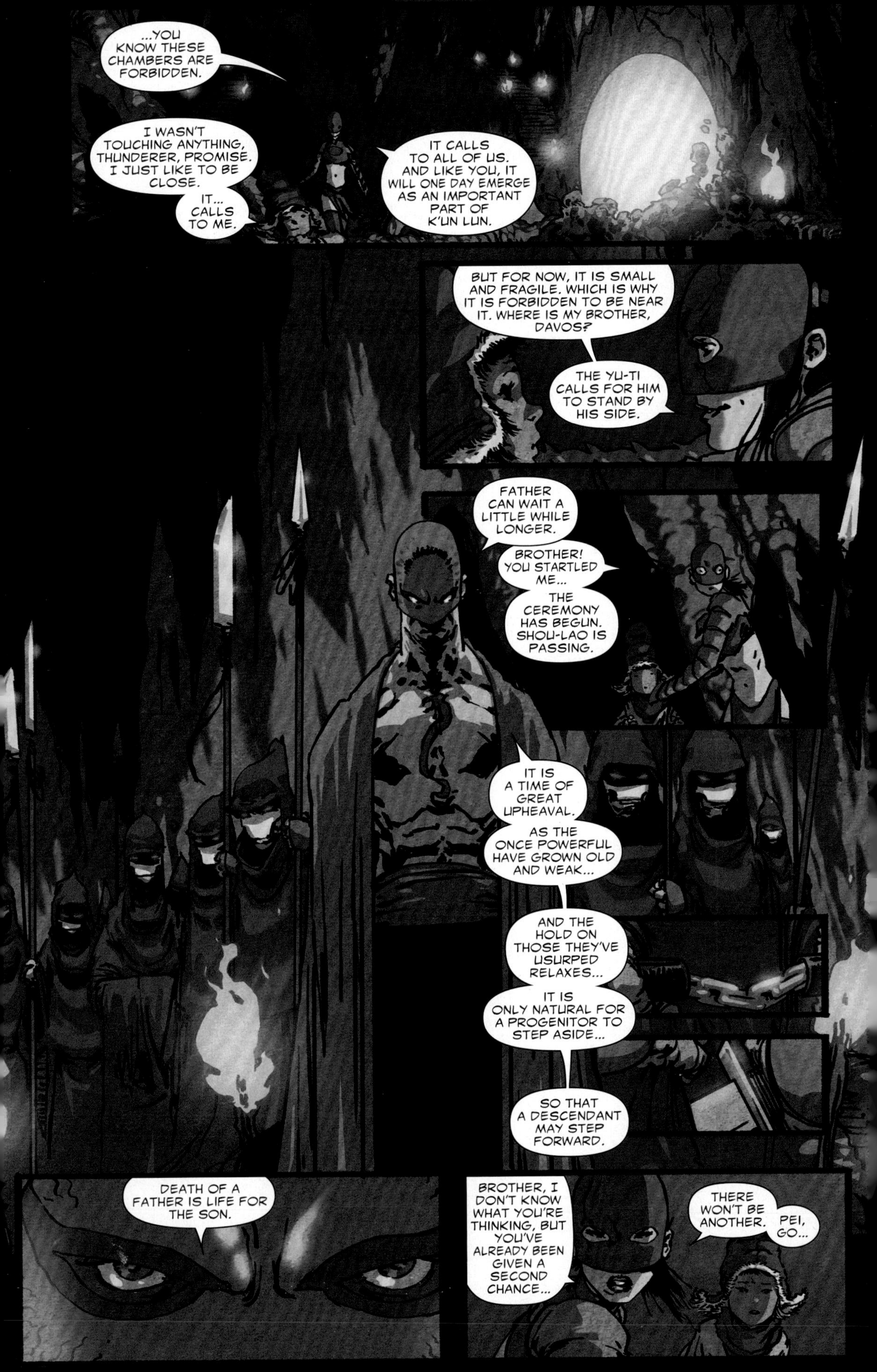

...YOU KNOW THESE CHAMBERS ARE FORBIDDEN.
I WASN'T TOUCHING ANYTHING, THUNDERER, PROMISE. I JUST LIKE TO BE CLOSE.
IT... CALLS TO ME.
IT CALLS TO ALL OF US. AND LIKE YOU, IT WILL ONE DAY EMERGE AS AN IMPORTANT PART OF K'UN LUN.
BUT FOR NOW, IT IS SMALL AND FRAGILE. WHICH IS WHY IT IS FORBIDDEN TO BE NEAR IT. WHERE IS MY BROTHER, DAVOS?
THE YU-TI CALLS FOR HIM TO STAND BY HIS SIDE.
FATHER CAN WAIT A LITTLE WHILE LONGER.
BROTHER! YOU STARTLED ME...
THE CEREMONY HAS BEGUN. SHOU-LAO IS PASSING.
IT IS A TIME OF GREAT UPHEAVAL.
AS THE ONCE POWERFUL HAVE GROWN OLD AND WEAK...
AND THE HOLD ON THOSE THEY'VE USURPED RELAXES...
IT IS ONLY NATURAL FOR A PROGENITOR TO STEP ASIDE...
SO THAT A DESCENDANT MAY STEP FORWARD.
DEATH OF A FATHER IS LIFE FOR THE SON.
BROTHER, I DON'T KNOW WHAT YOU'RE THINKING, BUT YOU'VE ALREADY BEEN GIVEN A SECOND CHANCE...
THERE WON'T BE ANOTHER.
PEI, GO...

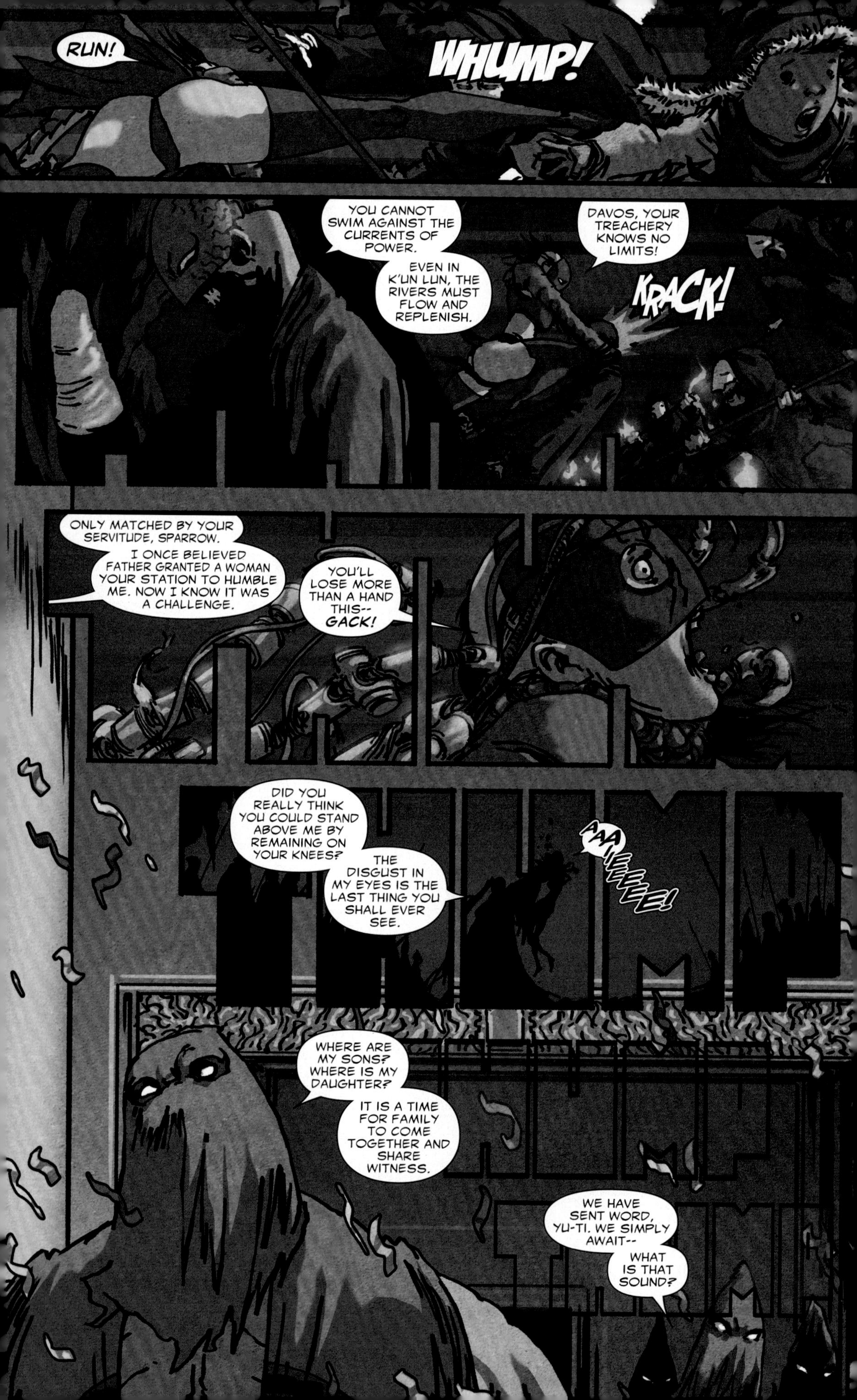
RUN!
WHUMP!
YOU CANNOT SWIM AGAINST THE CURRENTS OF POWER.
EVEN IN K'UN LUN, THE RIVERS MUST FLOW AND REPLENISH.
DAVOS, YOUR TREACHERY KNOWS NO LIMITS!
KRACK!
ONLY MATCHED BY YOUR SERVITUDE, SPARROW.
I ONCE BELIEVED FATHER GRANTED A WOMAN YOUR STATION TO HUMBLE ME. NOW I KNOW IT WAS A CHALLENGE.
YOU'LL LOSE MORE THAN A HAND THIS-- GACK!
DID YOU REALLY THINK YOU COULD STAND ABOVE ME BY REMAINING ON YOUR KNEES?
THE DISGUST IN MY EYES IS THE LAST THING YOU SHALL EVER SEE.
AAAIEEEEE!
WHERE ARE MY SONS? WHERE IS MY DAUGHTER?
IT IS A TIME FOR FAMILY TO COME TOGETHER AND SHARE WITNESS.
WE HAVE SENT WORD, YU-TI. WE SIMPLY AWAIT--
WHAT IS THAT SOUND?

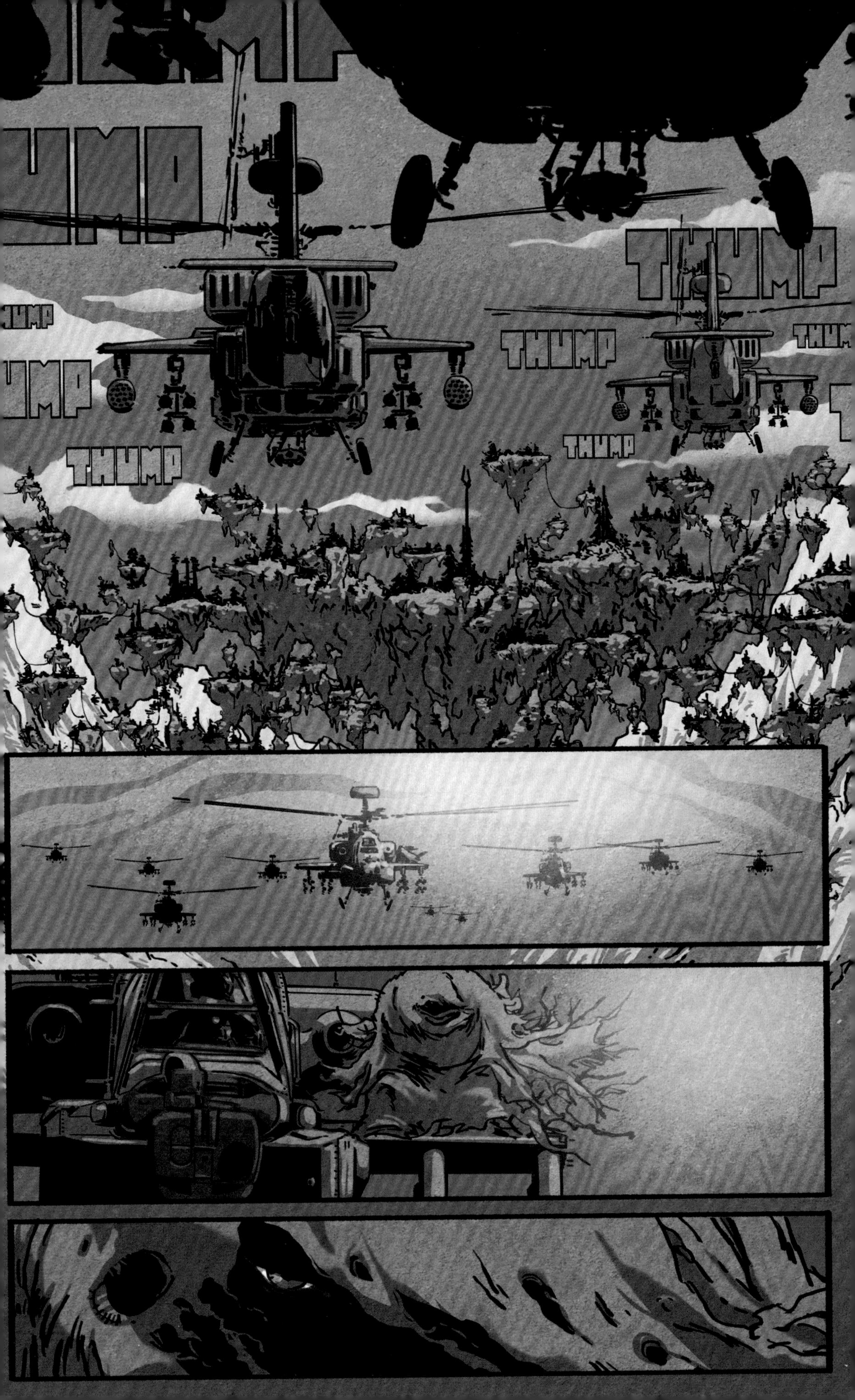
THUMP
THUMP
THUMP
THUMP

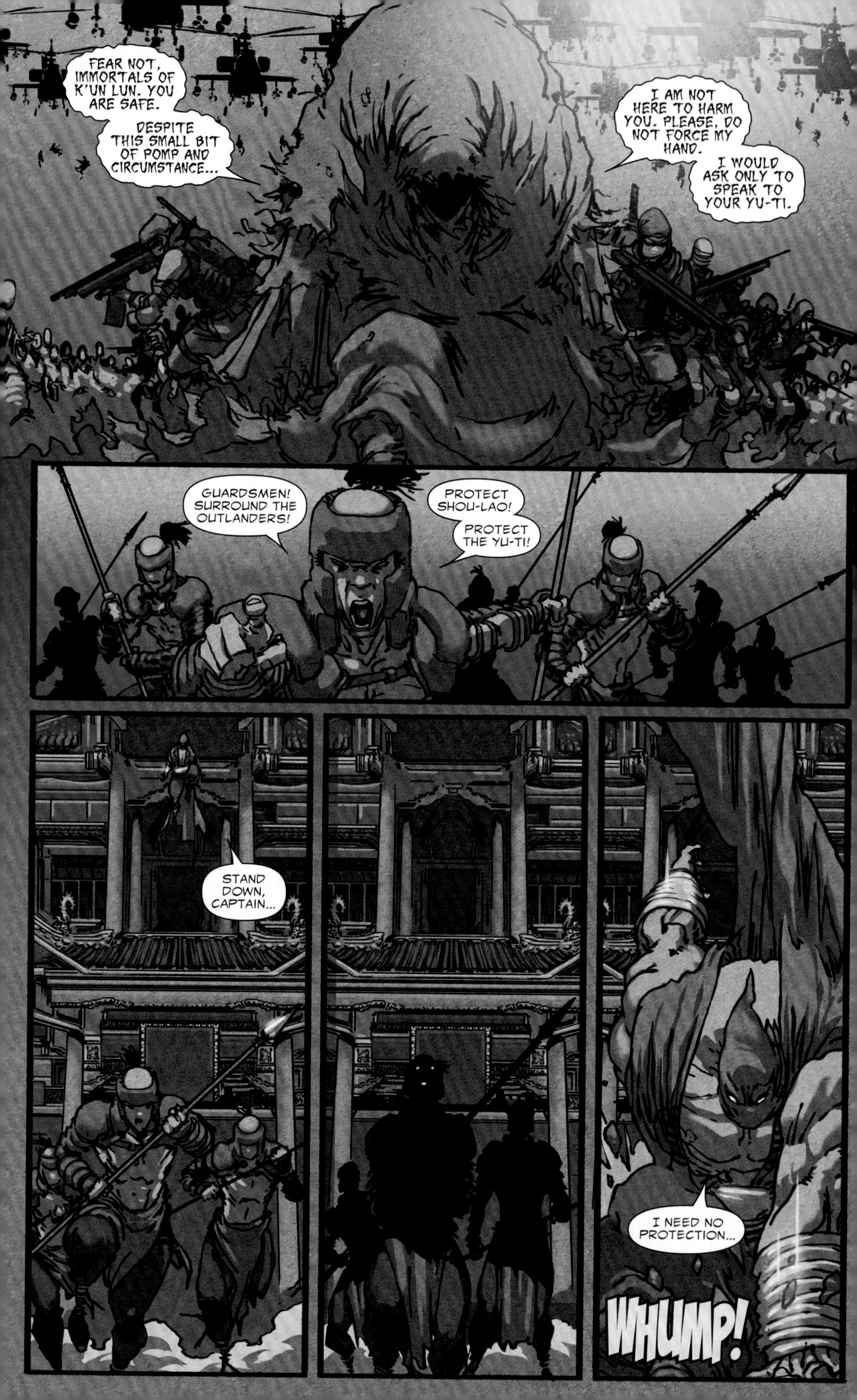
FEAR NOT, IMMORTALS OF K'UN LUN. YOU ARE SAFE.
DESPITE THIS SMALL BIT OF POMP AND CIRCUMSTANCE...
I AM NOT HERE TO HARM YOU. PLEASE, DO NOT FORCE MY HAND.
I WOULD ASK ONLY TO SPEAK TO YOUR YU-TI.
GUARDSMEN! SURROUND THE OUTLANDERS!
PROTECT SHOU-LAO!
PROTECT THE YU-TI!
STAND DOWN, CAPTAIN...
I NEED NO PROTECTION...
WHUMP!

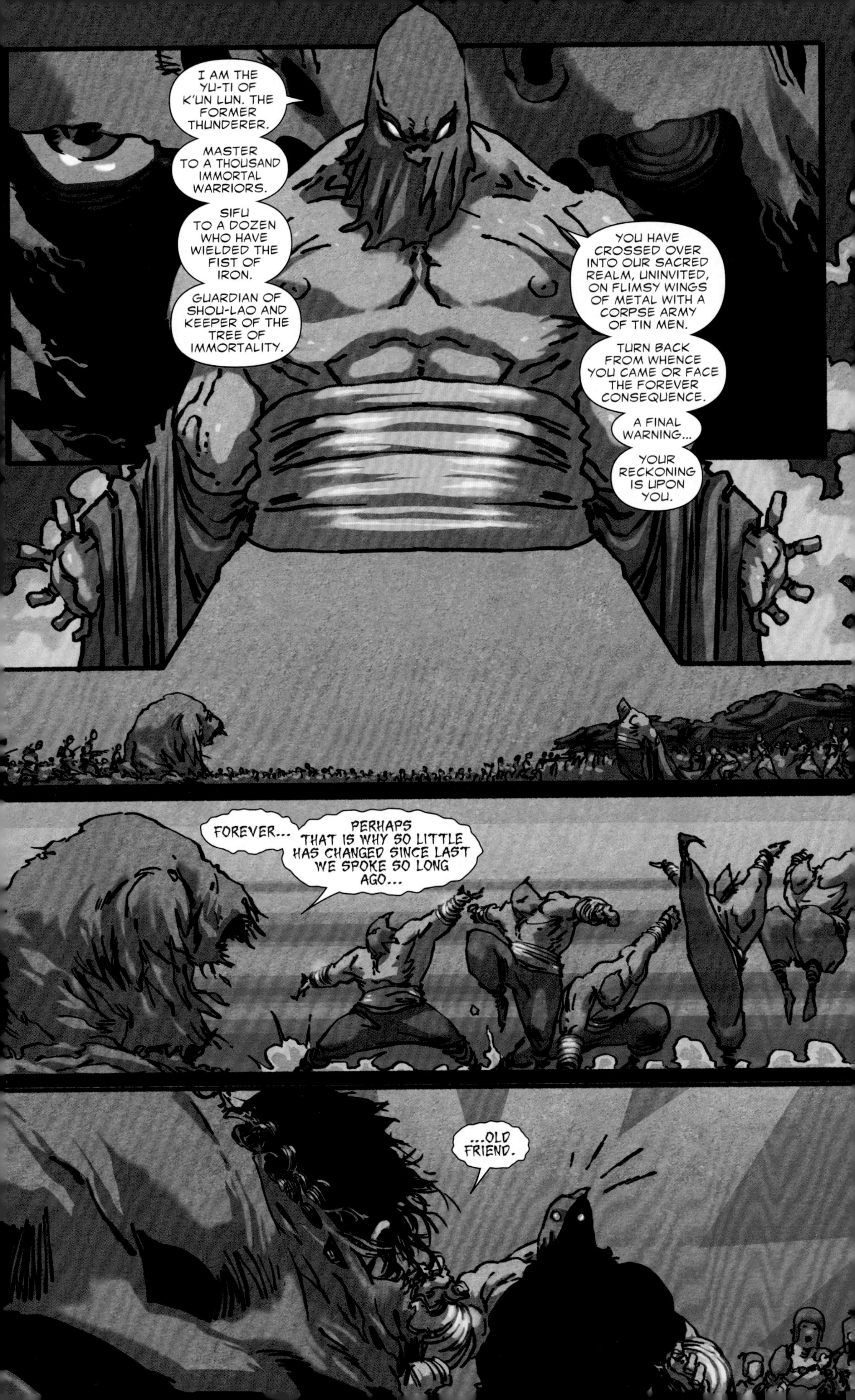
I AM THE YU-TI OF K'UN LUN. THE FORMER THUNDERER.
MASTER TO A THOUSAND IMMORTAL WARRIORS.
SIFU TO A DOZEN WHO HAVE WIELDED THE FIST OF IRON.
GUARDIAN OF SHOU-LAO AND KEEPER OF THE TREE OF IMMORTALITY.
YOU HAVE CROSSED OVER INTO OUR SACRED REALM, UNINVITED, ON FLIMSY WINGS OF METAL WITH A CORPSE ARMY OF TIN MEN.
TURN BACK FROM WHENCE YOU CAME OR FACE THE FOREVER CONSEQUENCE.
A FINAL WARNING...
YOUR RECKONING IS UPON YOU.
FOREVER...
PERHAPS THAT IS WHY SO LITTLE HAS CHANGED SINCE LAST WE SPOKE SO LONG AGO...
...OLD FRIEND.

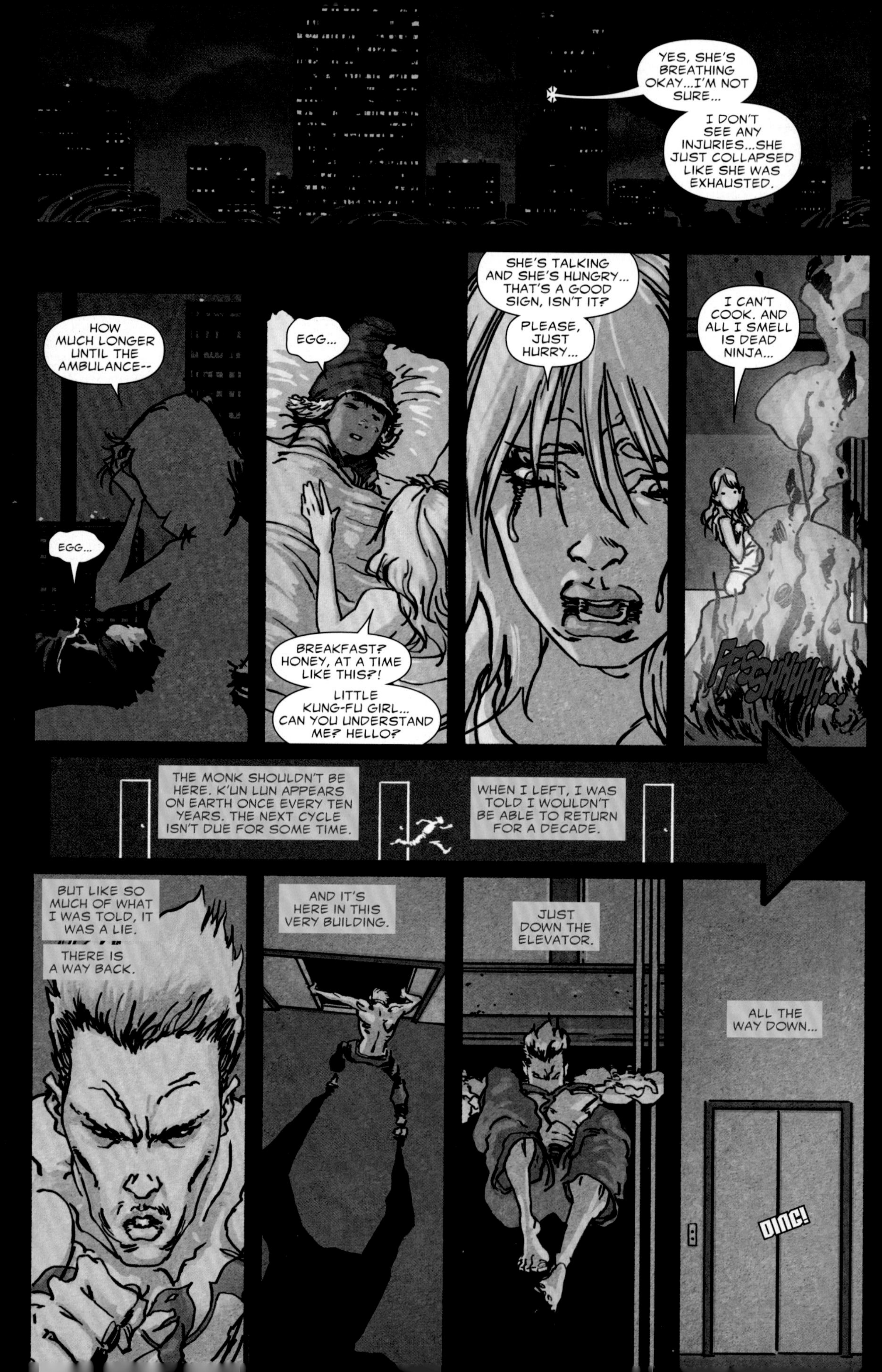

YES, SHE'S BREATHING OKAY...I'M NOT SURE...
I DON'T SEE ANY INJURIES...SHE JUST COLLAPSED LIKE SHE WAS EXHAUSTED.
HOW MUCH LONGER UNTIL THE AMBULANCE--
EGG...
EGG...
BREAKFAST? HONEY, AT A TIME LIKE THIS?!
LITTLE KUNG-FU GIRL... CAN YOU UNDERSTAND ME? HELLO?
SHE'S TALKING AND SHE'S HUNGRY... THAT'S A GOOD SIGN, ISN'T IT?
PLEASE, JUST HURRY...
I CAN'T COOK. AND ALL I SMELL IS DEAD NINJA...
PFSSHHHH...
THE MONK SHOULDN'T BE HERE. K'UN LUN APPEARS ON EARTH ONCE EVERY TEN YEARS. THE NEXT CYCLE ISN'T DUE FOR SOME TIME.
WHEN I LEFT, I WAS TOLD I WOULDN'T BE ABLE TO RETURN FOR A DECADE.
BUT LIKE SO MUCH OF WHAT I WAS TOLD, IT WAS A LIE.
THERE IS A WAY BACK.
AND IT'S HERE IN THIS VERY BUILDING.
JUST DOWN THE ELEVATOR.
ALL THE WAY DOWN...
DING!

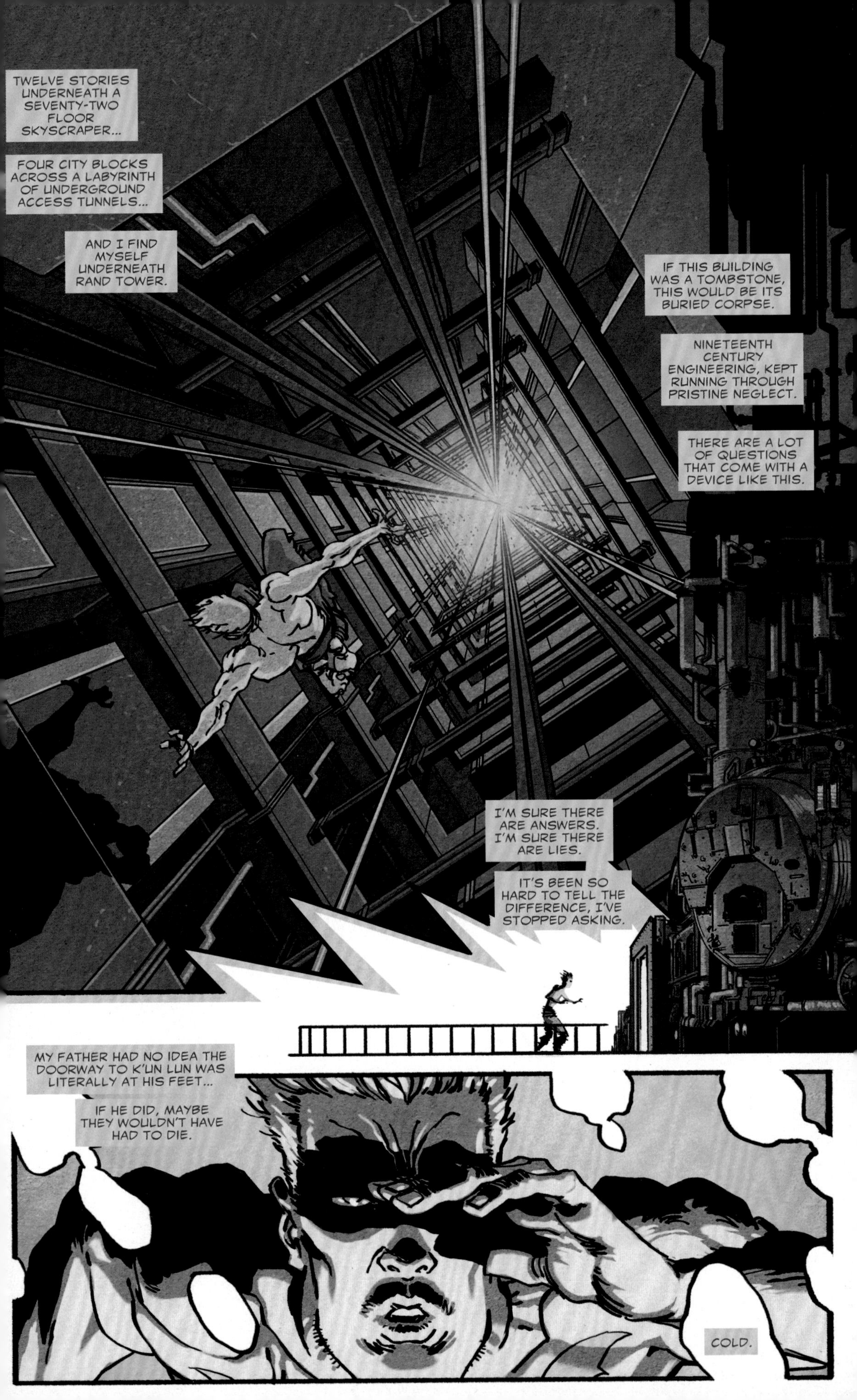
TWELVE STORIES UNDERNEATH A SEVENTY-TWO FLOOR SKYSCRAPER...
FOUR CITY BLOCKS ACROSS A LABYRINTH OF UNDERGROUND ACCESS TUNNELS...
AND I FIND MYSELF UNDERNEATH RAND TOWER.
IF THIS BUILDING WAS A TOMBSTONE, THIS WOULD BE ITS BURIED CORPSE.
NINETEENTH CENTURY ENGINEERING, KEPT RUNNING THROUGH PRISTINE NEGLECT.
THERE ARE A LOT OF QUESTIONS THAT COME WITH A DEVICE LIKE THIS.
I'M SURE THERE ARE ANSWERS. I'M SURE THERE ARE LIES.
IT'S BEEN SO HARD TO TELL THE DIFFERENCE, I'VE STOPPED ASKING.
MY FATHER HAD NO IDEA THE DOORWAY TO K'UN LUN WAS LITERALLY AT HIS FEET...
IF HE DID, MAYBE THEY WOULDN'T HAVE HAD TO DIE.
COLD.

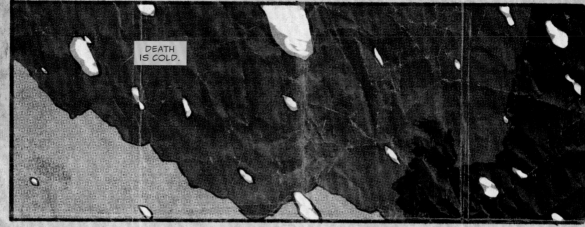

DEATH IS COLD.

HEATHER...?

HEATHER, YOU'RE ALIVE!

THANK GOD.

WAIT RIGHT THERE...

I'LL THROW YOU A LINE.

I WAS SO WORRIED ABOUT YOU.

ARE YOU HURT? ANYTHING BROKEN?

IF WE HURRY, WE CAN DIG IN FOR THE NIGHT, THEN MAKE IT BACK TO BASE CAMP IN A DAY OR TWO.

WE SHOULD HAVE ENOUGH RATIONS TO LAST THE TRIP BACK, NOW THAT THERE'S ONLY THE THREE OF US...

HAROLD... WHAT HAVE YOU DONE?

THE ROPE... WENDELL DIDN'T LET GO...

YOU DID.

I DON'T KNOW WHAT YOU THINK YOU SAW, HEATHER...

YOU'RE EXHAUSTED, DISTRESSED, WE ALL ARE--

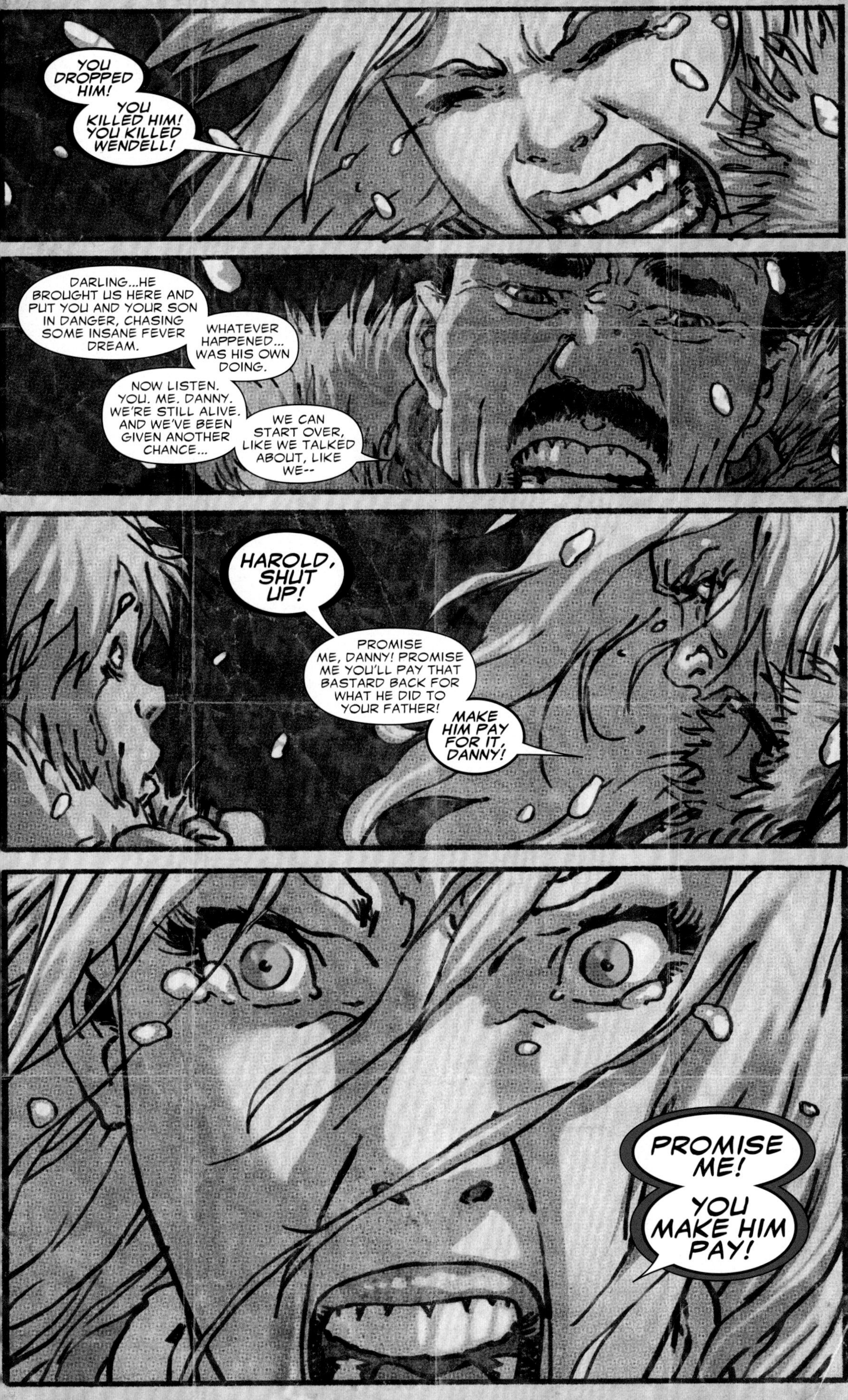
YOU DROPPED HIM!
YOU KILLED HIM! YOU KILLED WENDELL!
DARLING...HE BROUGHT US HERE AND PUT YOU AND YOUR SON IN DANGER, CHASING SOME INSANE FEVER DREAM.
WHATEVER HAPPENED... WAS HIS OWN DOING.
NOW LISTEN. YOU. ME. DANNY. WE'RE STILL ALIVE. AND WE'VE BEEN GIVEN ANOTHER CHANCE...
WE CAN START OVER, LIKE WE TALKED ABOUT, LIKE WE--
HAROLD, SHUT UP!
PROMISE ME, DANNY! PROMISE ME YOU'LL PAY THAT BASTARD BACK FOR WHAT HE DID TO YOUR FATHER!
MAKE HIM PAY FOR IT, DANNY!
PROMISE ME!
YOU MAKE HIM PAY!

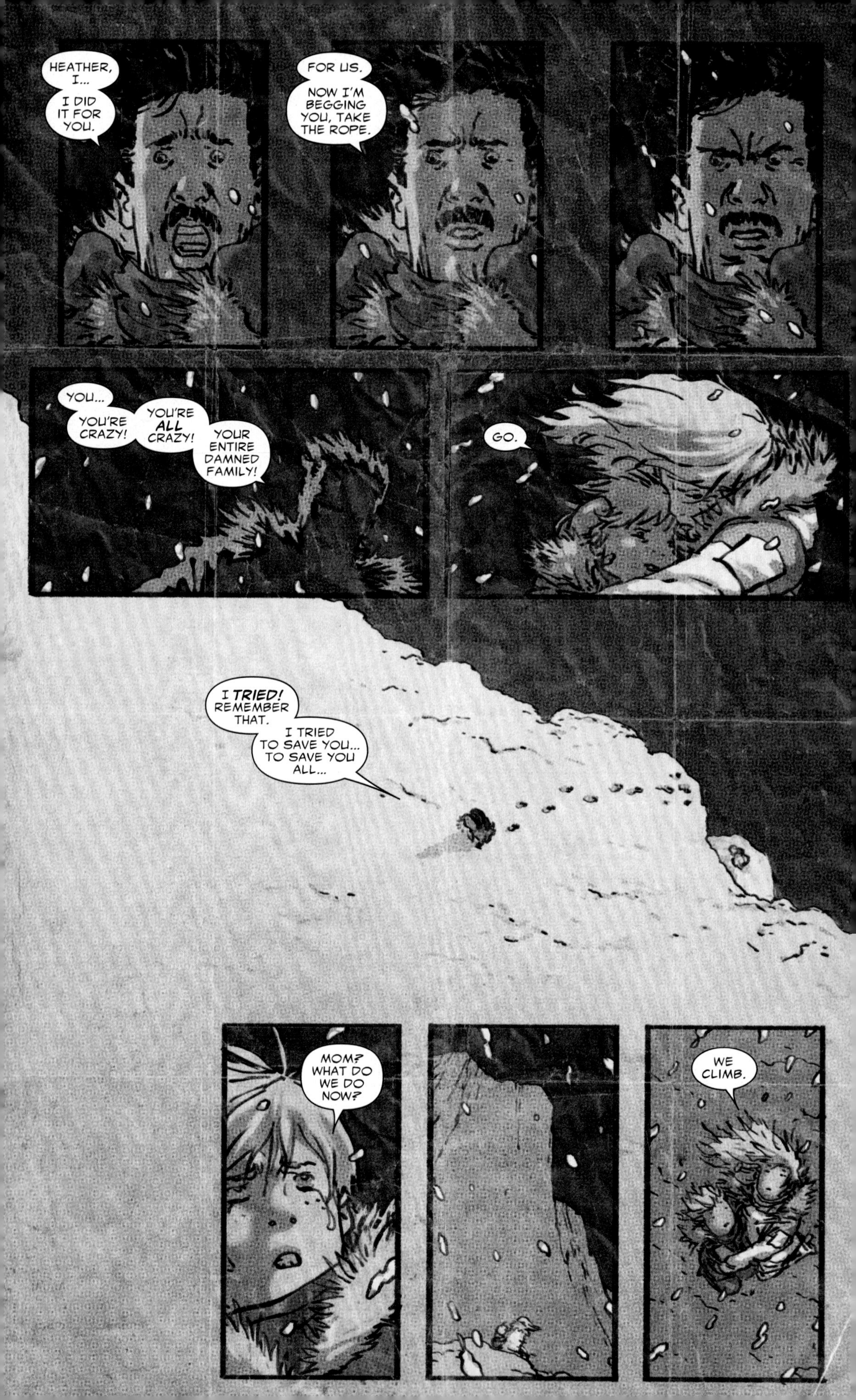
HEATHER, I...
I DID IT FOR YOU.
FOR US.
NOW I'M BEGGING YOU, TAKE THE ROPE.
YOU...
YOU'RE CRAZY!
YOU'RE ALL CRAZY!
YOUR ENTIRE DAMNED FAMILY!
GO.
I TRIED! REMEMBER THAT.
I TRIED TO SAVE YOU... TO SAVE YOU ALL...
MOM? WHAT DO WE DO NOW?
WE CLIMB.

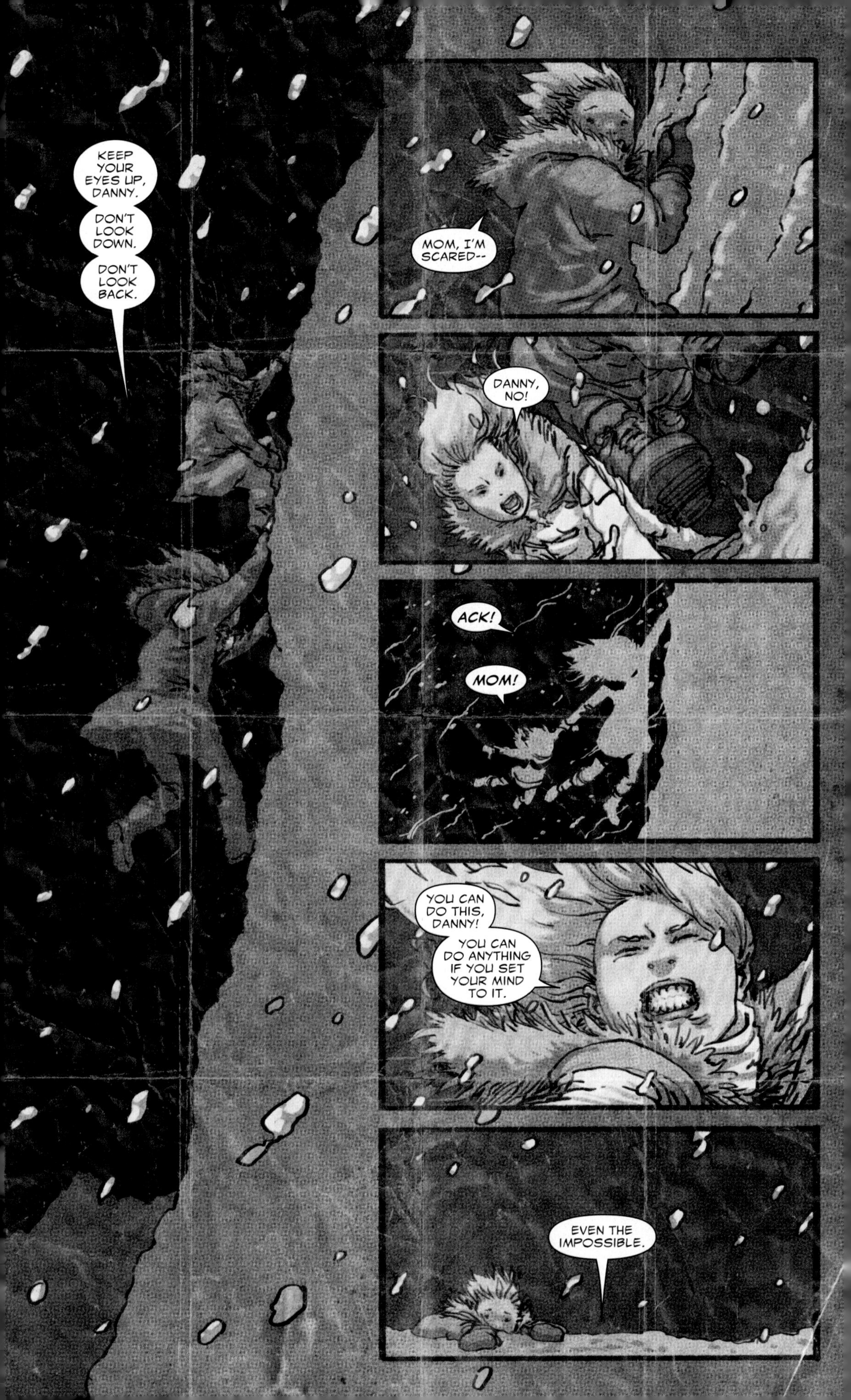
KEEP YOUR EYES UP, DANNY.
DON'T LOOK DOWN.
DON'T LOOK BACK.
MOM, I'M SCARED--
DANNY, NO!
ACK!
MOM!
YOU CAN DO THIS, DANNY!
YOU CAN DO ANYTHING IF YOU SET YOUR MIND TO IT.
EVEN THE IMPOSSIBLE.

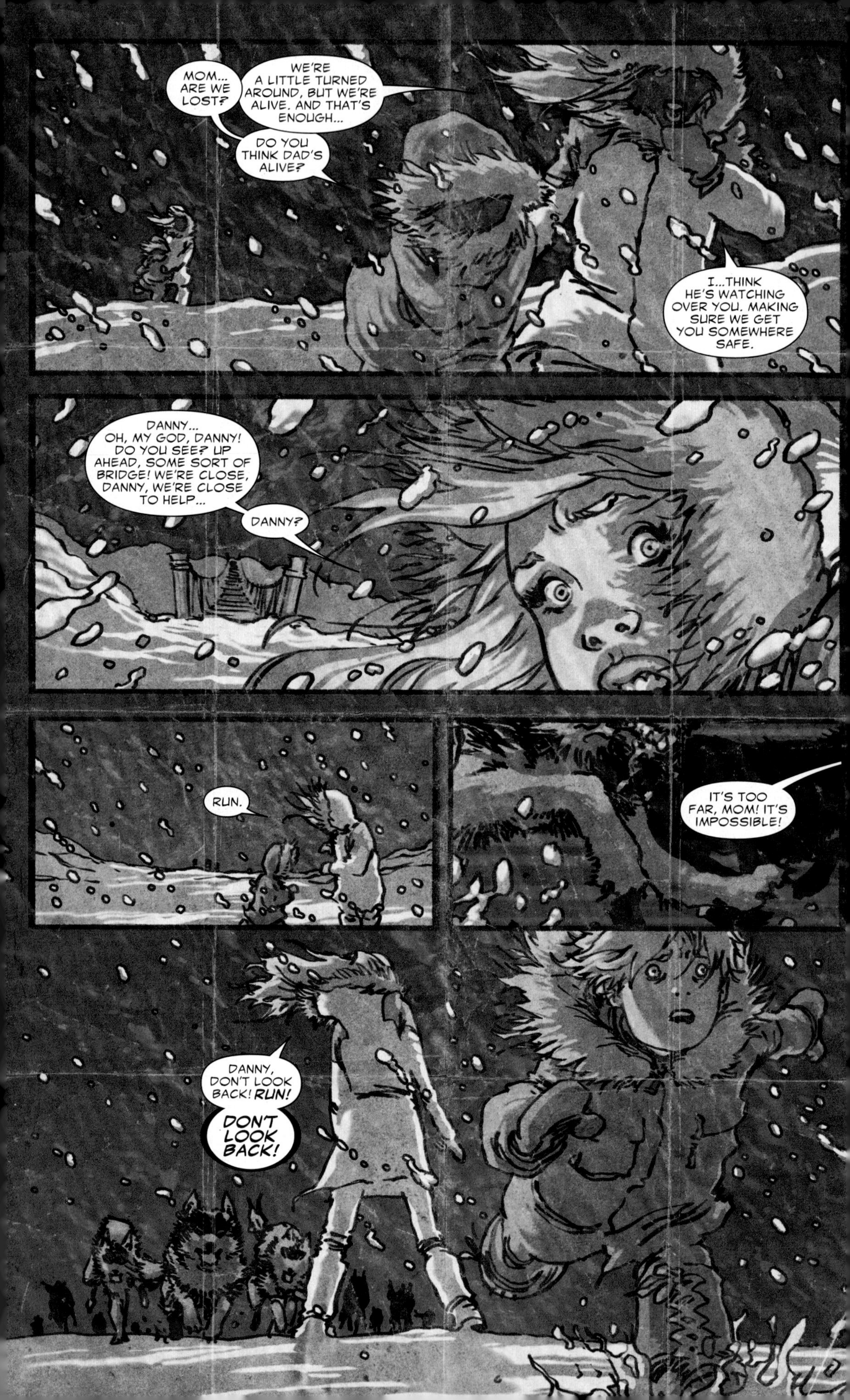
MOM... ARE WE LOST?
WE'RE A LITTLE TURNED AROUND, BUT WE'RE ALIVE. AND THAT'S ENOUGH...
DO YOU THINK DAD'S ALIVE?
I...THINK HE'S WATCHING OVER YOU. MAKING SURE WE GET YOU SOMEWHERE SAFE.
DANNY... OH, MY GOD, DANNY! DO YOU SEE? UP AHEAD, SOME SORT OF BRIDGE! WE'RE CLOSE, DANNY, WE'RE CLOSE TO HELP...
DANNY?
RUN.
IT'S TOO FAR, MOM! IT'S IMPOSSIBLE!
DANNY, DON'T LOOK BACK! RUN!
DON'T LOOK BACK!

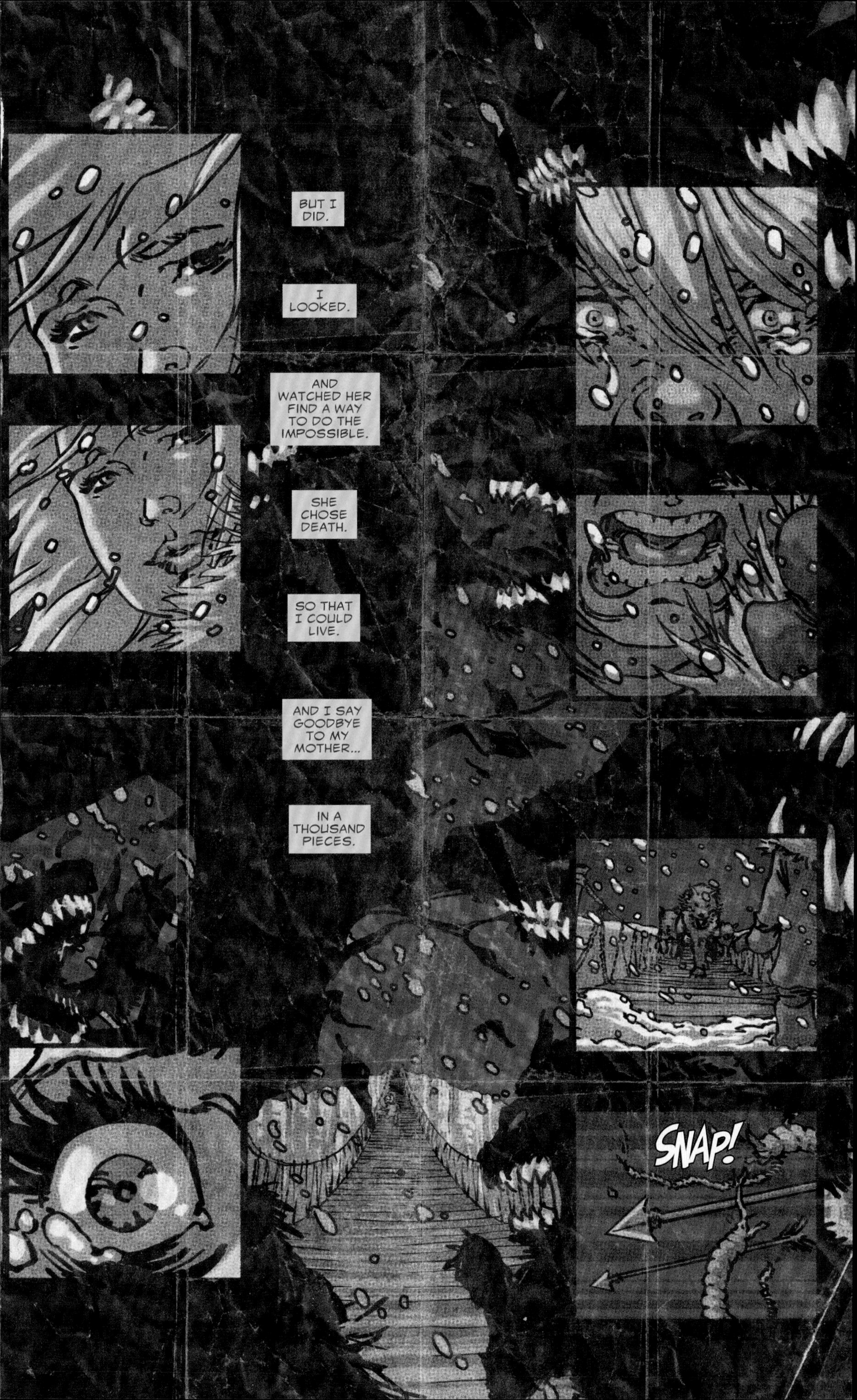
BUT I DID.
I LOOKED.
AND WATCHED HER FIND A WAY TO DO THE IMPOSSIBLE.
SHE CHOSE DEATH.
SO THAT I COULD LIVE.
AND I SAY GOODBYE TO MY MOTHER...
IN A THOUSAND PIECES.
SNAP!

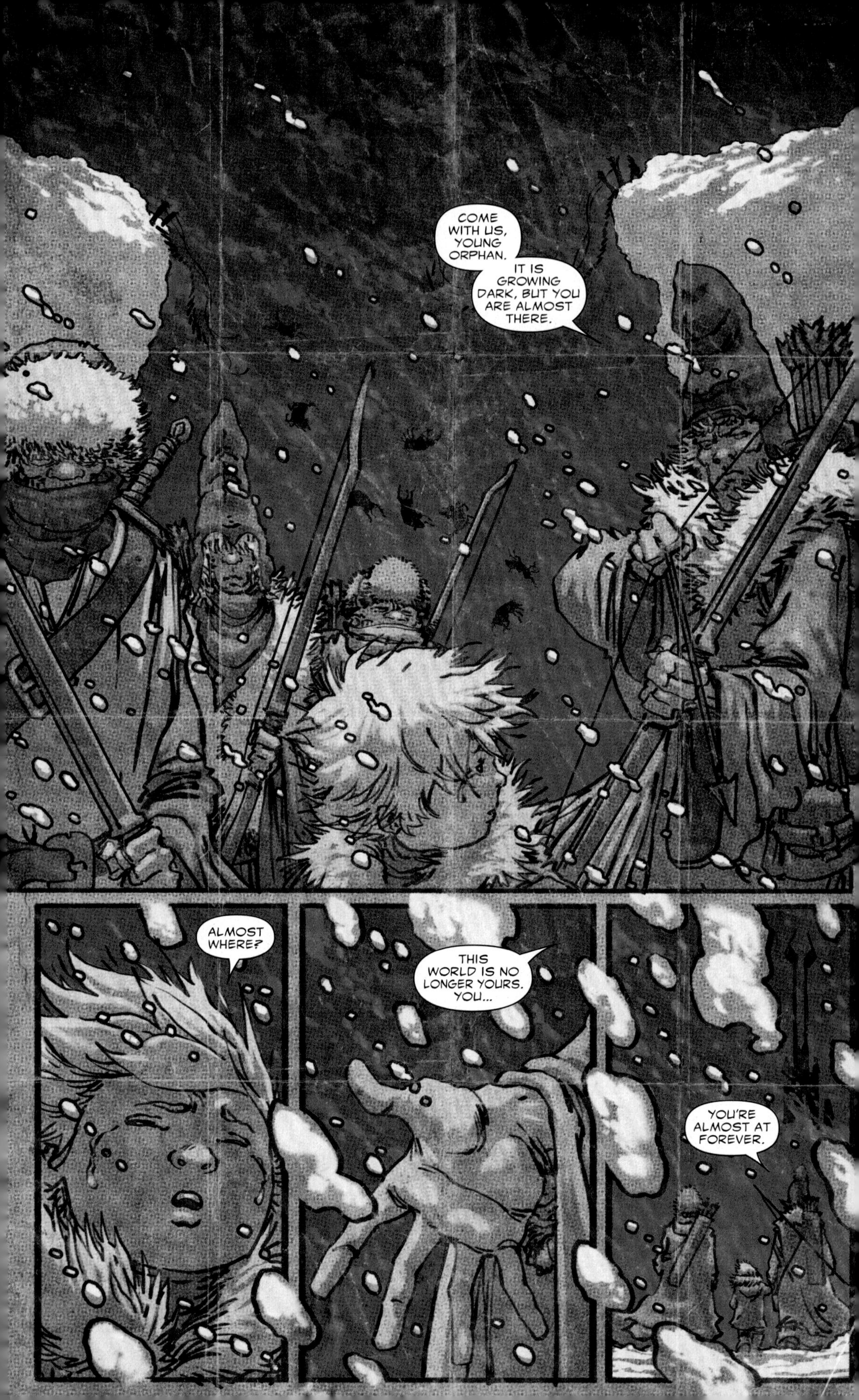
COME WITH US, YOUNG ORPHAN.
IT IS GROWING DARK, BUT YOU ARE ALMOST THERE.
ALMOST WHERE?
THIS WORLD IS NO LONGER YOURS. YOU...
YOU'RE ALMOST AT FOREVER.

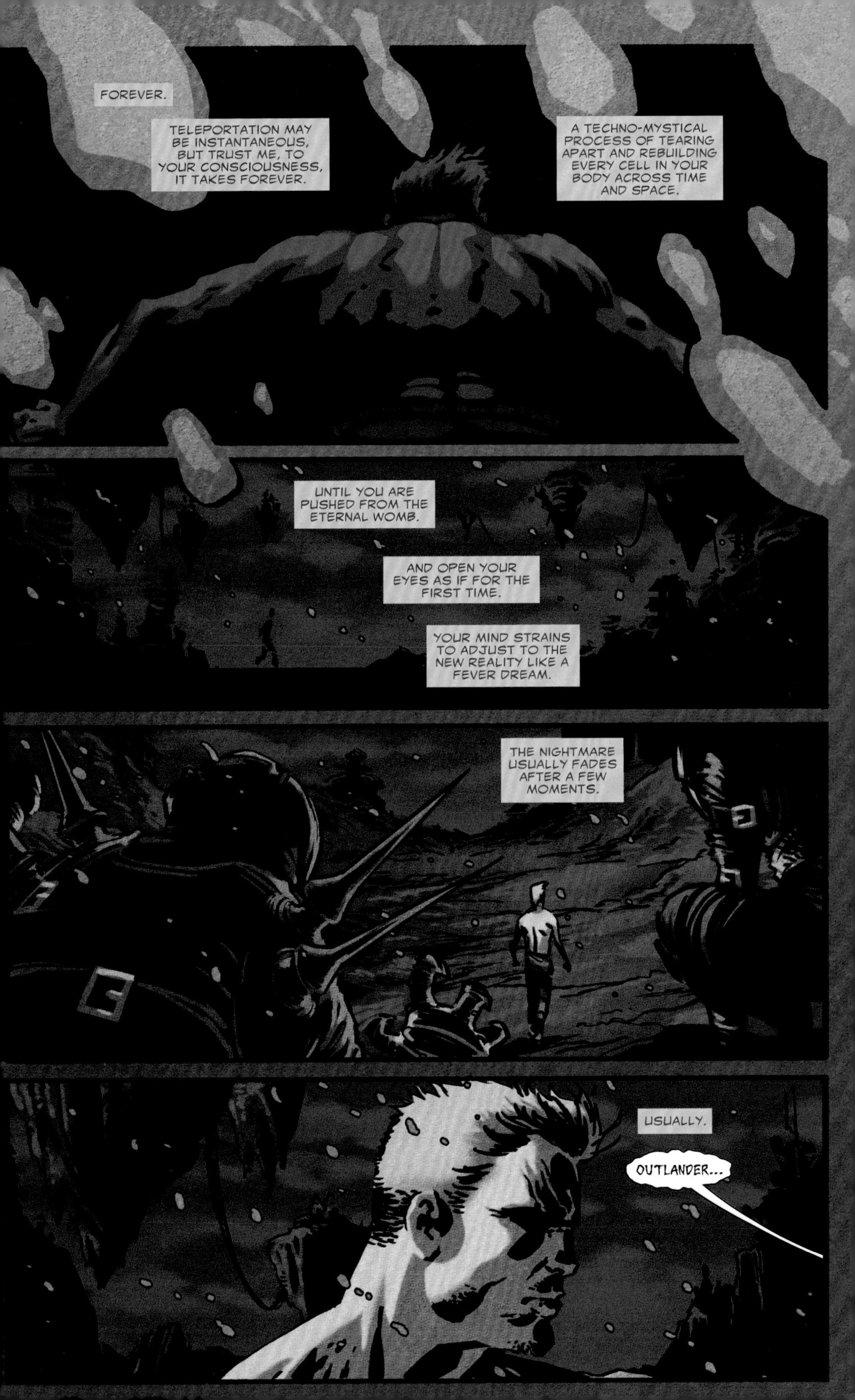
FOREVER.
TELEPORTATION MAY BE INSTANTANEOUS, BUT TRUST ME, TO YOUR CONSCIOUSNESS, IT TAKES FOREVER.
A TECHNO-MYSTICAL PROCESS OF TEARING APART AND REBUILDING EVERY CELL IN YOUR BODY ACROSS TIME AND SPACE.
UNTIL YOU ARE PUSHED FROM THE ETERNAL WOMB.
AND OPEN YOUR EYES AS IF FOR THE FIRST TIME.
YOUR MIND STRAINS TO ADJUST TO THE NEW REALITY LIKE A FEVER DREAM.
THE NIGHTMARE USUALLY FADES AFTER A FEW MOMENTS.
USUALLY.
OUTLANDER...

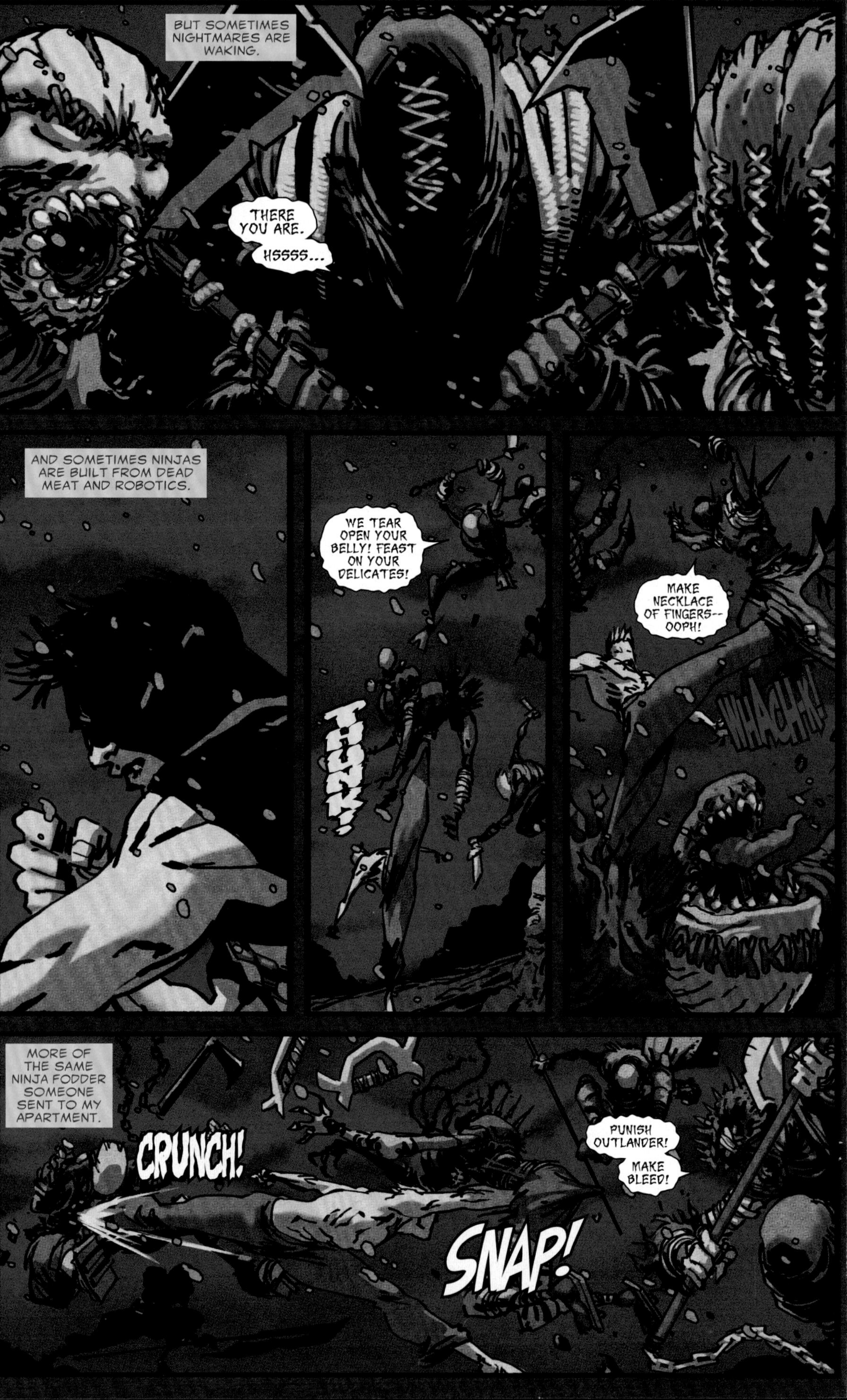
BUT SOMETIMES NIGHTMARES ARE WAKING.
THERE YOU ARE.
HSSSS...
AND SOMETIMES NINJAS ARE BUILT FROM DEAD MEAT AND ROBOTICS.
WE TEAR OPEN YOUR BELLY! FEAST ON YOUR DELICATES!
MAKE NECKLACE OF FINGERS-- OOPH!
MORE OF THE SAME NINJA FODDER SOMEONE SENT TO MY APARTMENT.
CRUNCH!
PUNISH OUTLANDER!
MAKE BLEED!
SNAP!

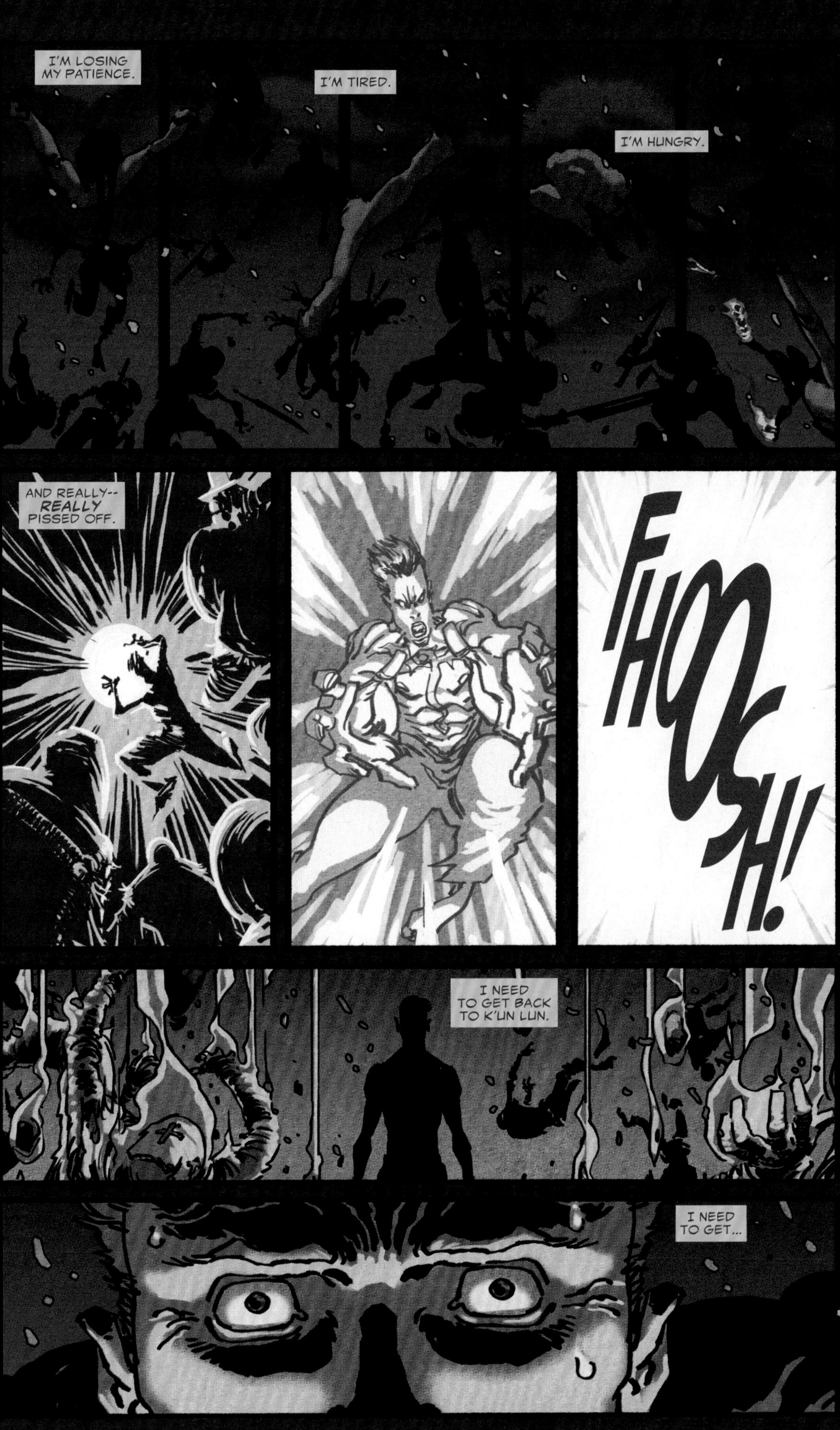
I'M LOSING MY PATIENCE.
I'M TIRED.
I'M HUNGRY.
AND REALLY-- REALLY PISSED OFF.
FHOOSH!
I NEED TO GET BACK TO K'UN LUN.
I NEED TO GET...

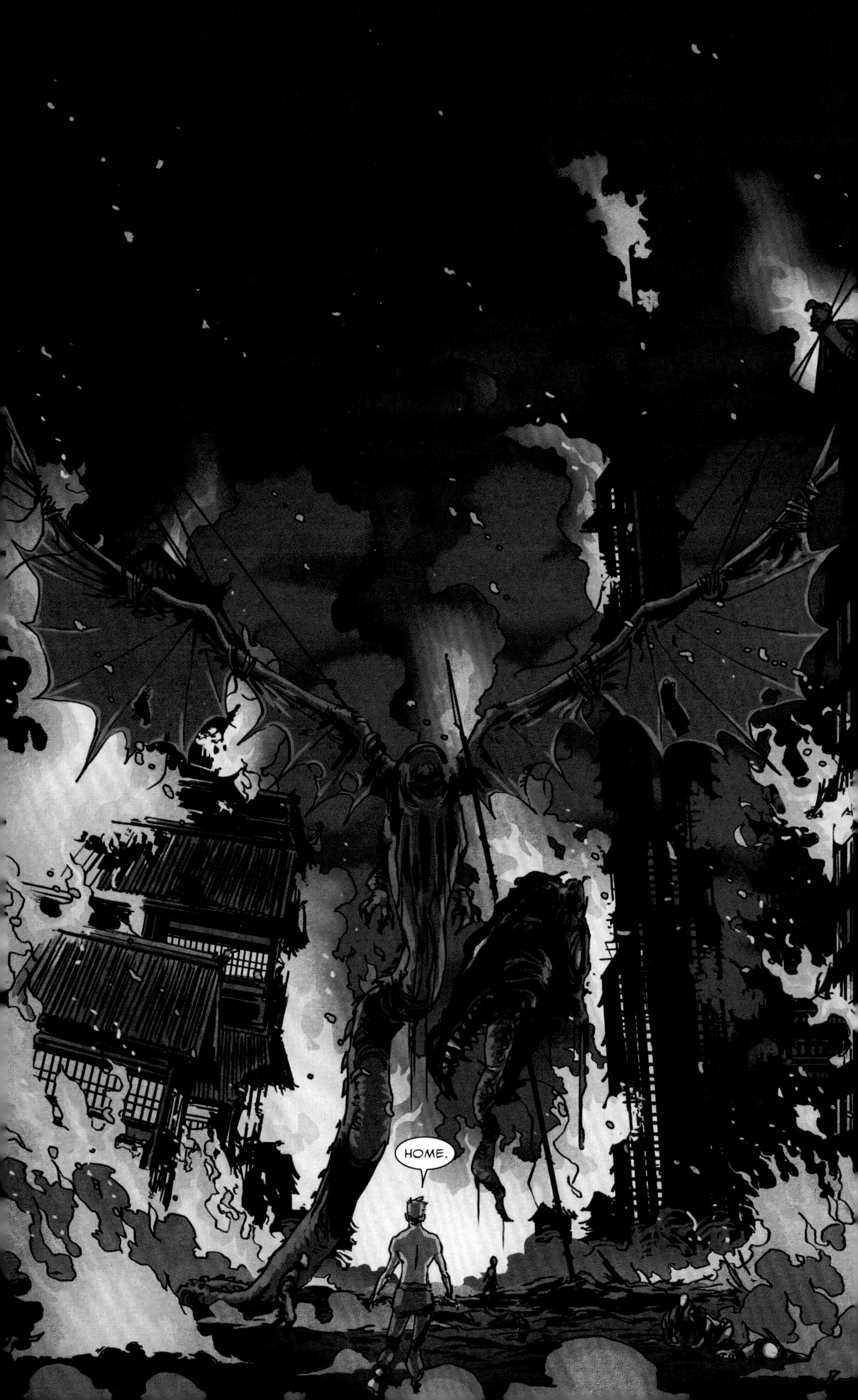
HOME.

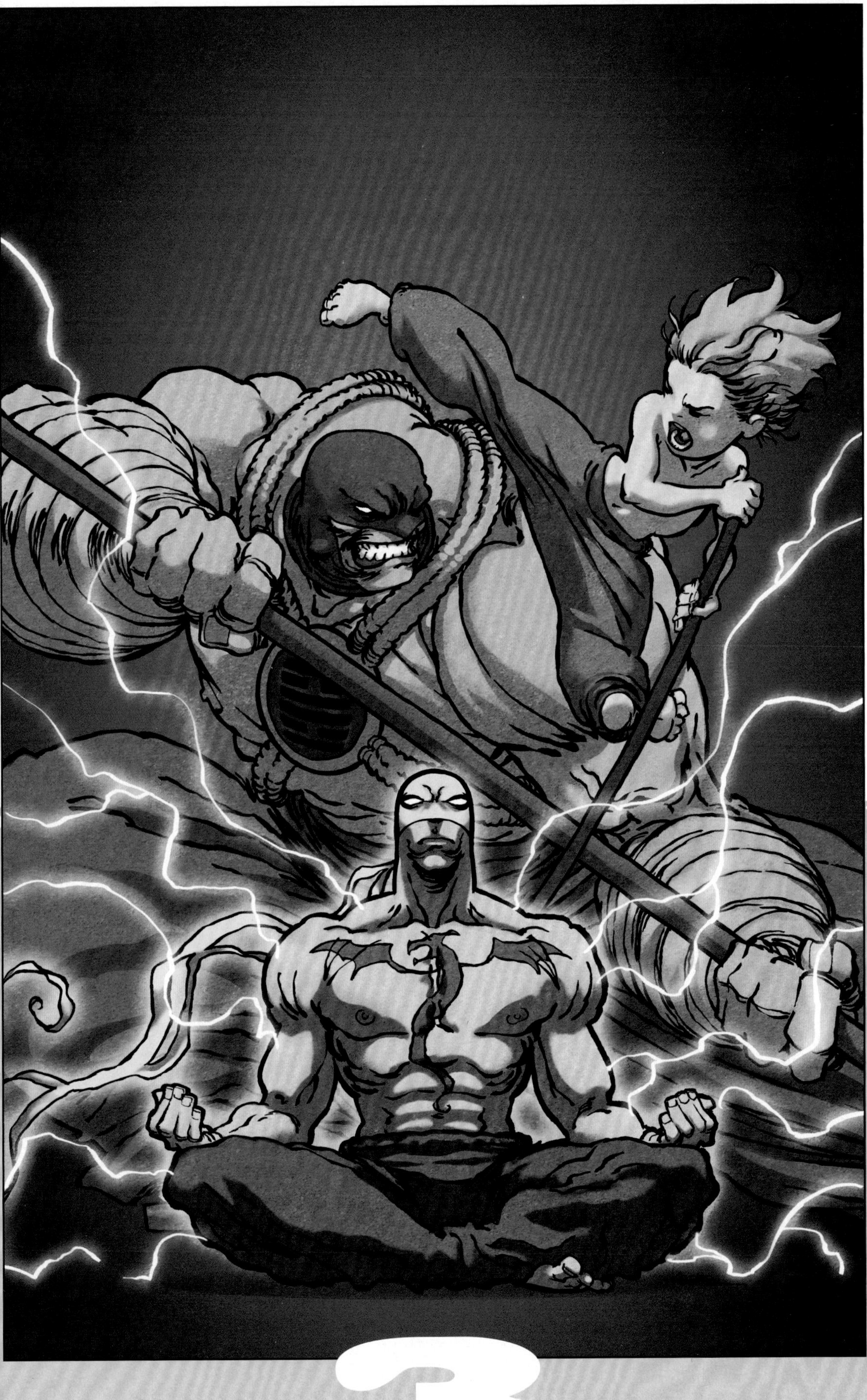

3

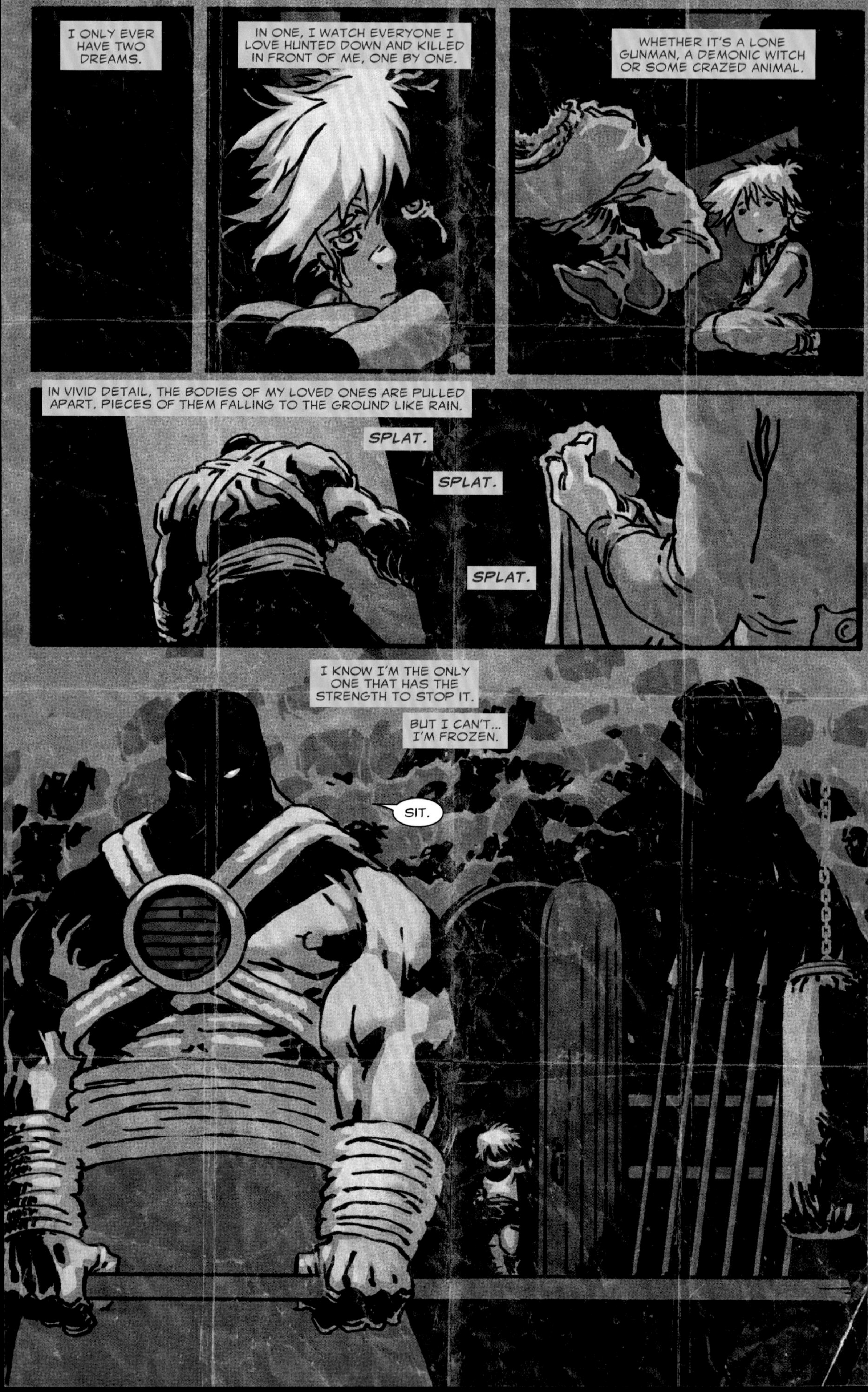
I ONLY EVER HAVE TWO DREAMS.
IN ONE, I WATCH EVERYONE I LOVE HUNTED DOWN AND KILLED IN FRONT OF ME, ONE BY ONE.
WHETHER IT'S A LONE GUNMAN, A DEMONIC WITCH OR SOME CRAZED ANIMAL.
IN VIVID DETAIL, THE BODIES OF MY LOVED ONES ARE PULLED APART. PIECES OF THEM FALLING TO THE GROUND LIKE RAIN.
SPLAT.
SPLAT.
SPLAT.
I KNOW I'M THE ONLY ONE THAT HAS THE STRENGTH TO STOP IT.
BUT I CAN'T... I'M FROZEN.
SIT.

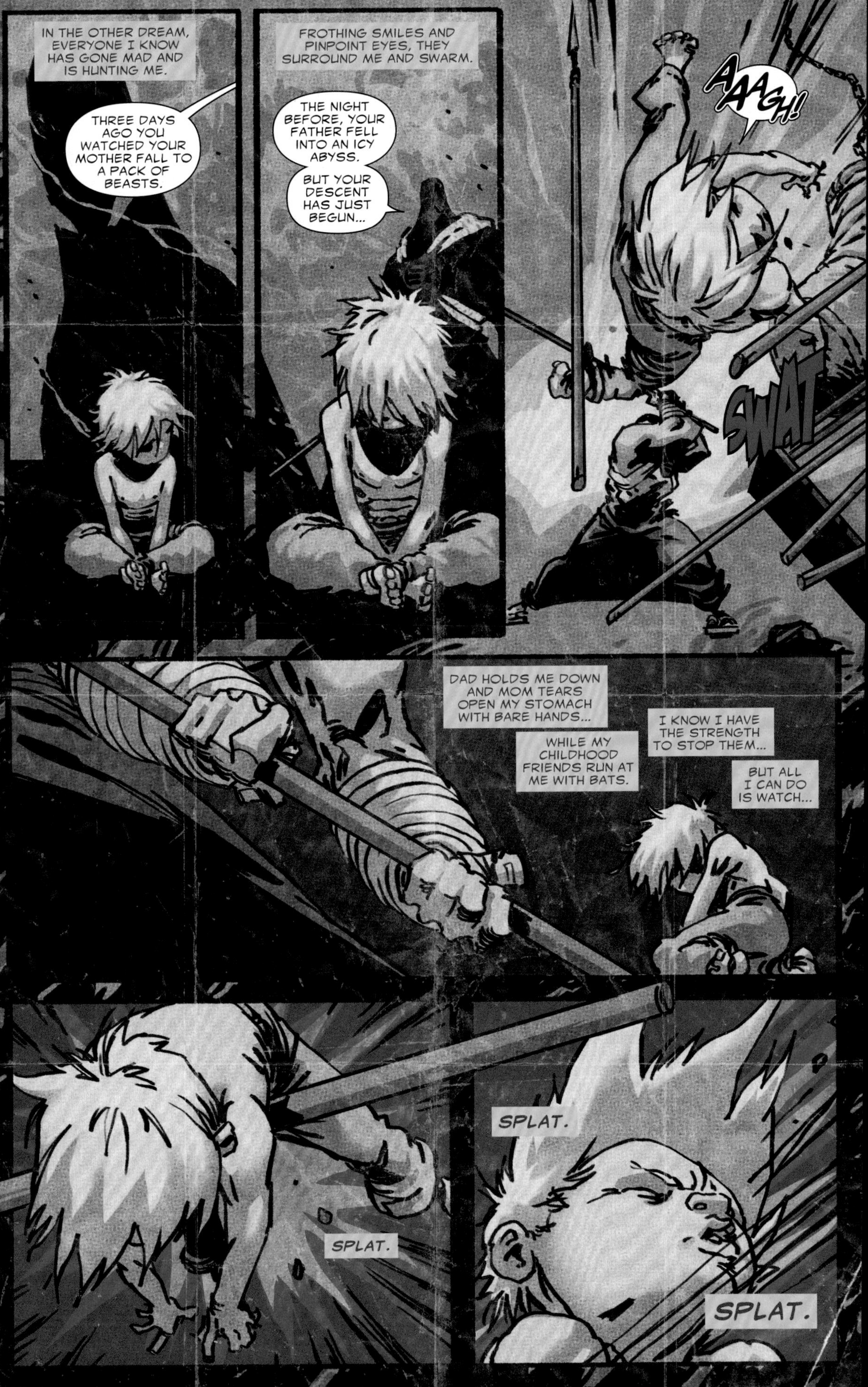
IN THE OTHER DREAM, EVERYONE I KNOW HAS GONE MAD AND IS HUNTING ME.
THREE DAYS AGO YOU WATCHED YOUR MOTHER FALL TO A PACK OF BEASTS.
FROTHING SMILES AND PINPOINT EYES, THEY SURROUND ME AND SWARM.
THE NIGHT BEFORE, YOUR FATHER FELL INTO AN ICY ABYSS.
BUT YOUR DESCENT HAS JUST BEGUN...
AAAGH!
SWAT
DAD HOLDS ME DOWN AND MOM TEARS OPEN MY STOMACH WITH BARE HANDS...
WHILE MY CHILDHOOD FRIENDS RUN AT ME WITH BATS.
I KNOW I HAVE THE STRENGTH TO STOP THEM...
BUT ALL I CAN DO IS WATCH...
SPLAT.
SPLAT.
SPLAT.

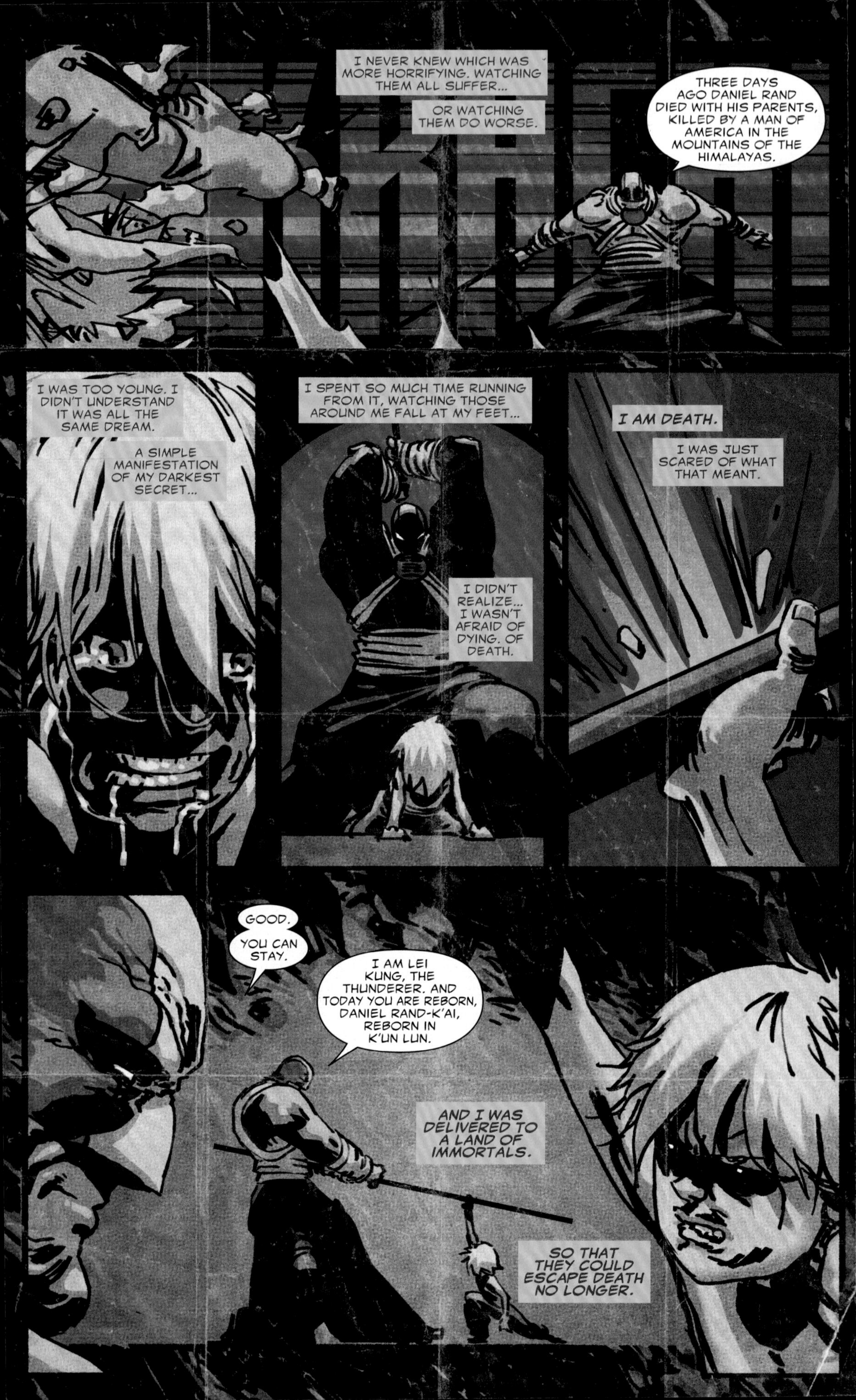
I NEVER KNEW WHICH WAS MORE HORRIFYING. WATCHING THEM ALL SUFFER...
OR WATCHING THEM DO WORSE.
THREE DAYS AGO DANIEL RAND DIED WITH HIS PARENTS, KILLED BY A MAN OF AMERICA IN THE MOUNTAINS OF THE HIMALAYAS.
I WAS TOO YOUNG. I DIDN'T UNDERSTAND IT WAS ALL THE SAME DREAM.
A SIMPLE MANIFESTATION OF MY DARKEST SECRET...
I SPENT SO MUCH TIME RUNNING FROM IT, WATCHING THOSE AROUND ME FALL AT MY FEET...
I DIDN'T REALIZE... I WASN'T AFRAID OF DYING. OF DEATH.
I AM DEATH.
I WAS JUST SCARED OF WHAT THAT MEANT.
GOOD.
YOU CAN STAY.
I AM LEI KUNG, THE THUNDERER. AND TODAY YOU ARE REBORN, DANIEL RAND-K'AI, REBORN IN K'UN LUN.
AND I WAS DELIVERED TO A LAND OF IMMORTALS.
SO THAT THEY COULD ESCAPE DEATH NO LONGER.

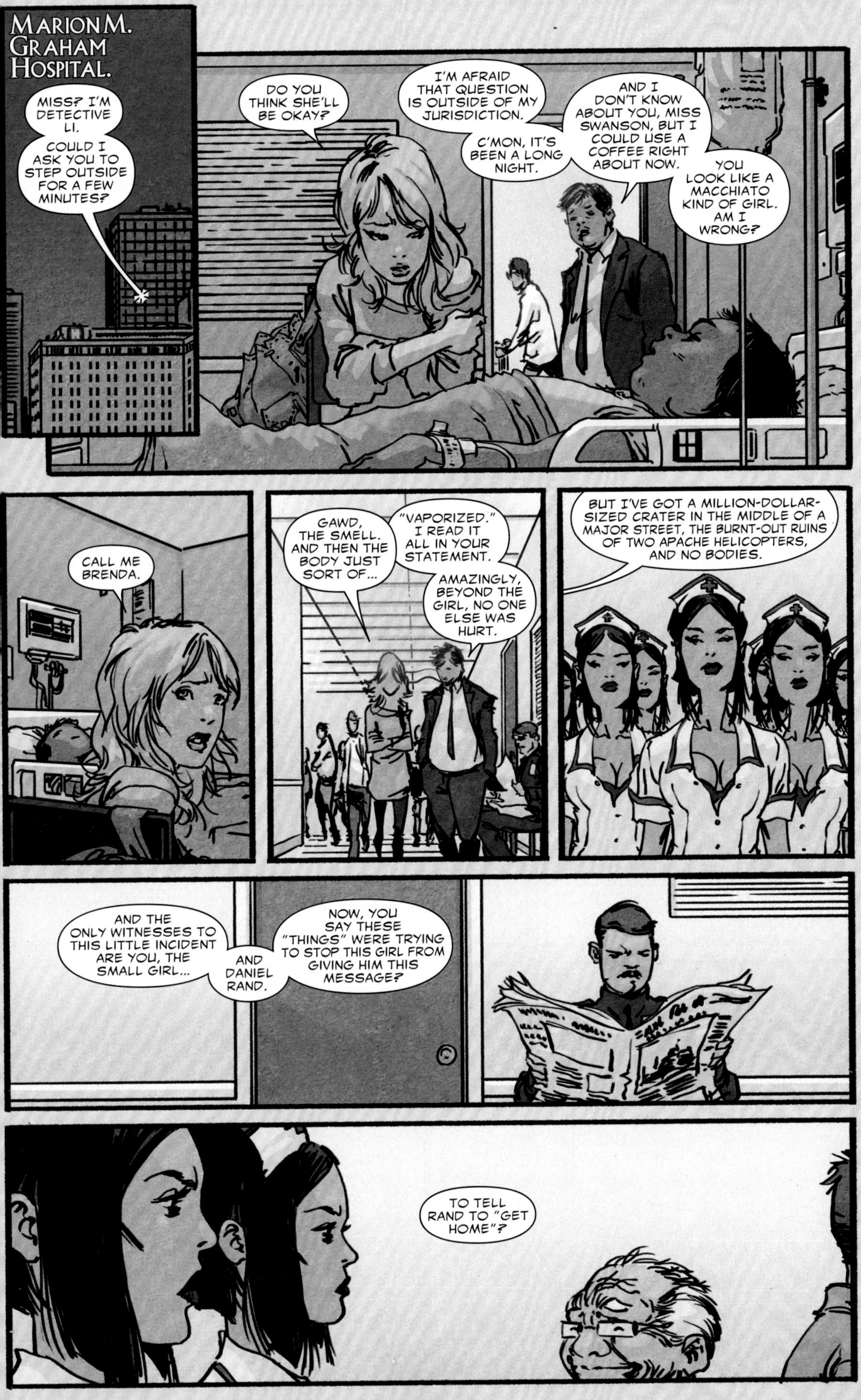
Marion M. Graham Hospital.
MISS? I'M DETECTIVE LI.
COULD I ASK YOU TO STEP OUTSIDE FOR A FEW MINUTES?
DO YOU THINK SHE'LL BE OKAY?
I'M AFRAID THAT QUESTION IS OUTSIDE OF MY JURISDICTION.
C'MON, IT'S BEEN A LONG NIGHT.
AND I DON'T KNOW ABOUT YOU, MISS SWANSON, BUT I COULD USE A COFFEE RIGHT ABOUT NOW.
YOU LOOK LIKE A MACCHIATO KIND OF GIRL. AM I WRONG?
CALL ME BRENDA.
GAWD, THE SMELL. AND THEN THE BODY JUST SORT OF...
"VAPORIZED." I READ IT ALL IN YOUR STATEMENT.
AMAZINGLY, BEYOND THE GIRL, NO ONE ELSE WAS HURT.
BUT I'VE GOT A MILLION-DOLLAR-SIZED CRATER IN THE MIDDLE OF A MAJOR STREET, THE BURNT-OUT RUINS OF TWO APACHE HELICOPTERS, AND NO BODIES.
AND THE ONLY WITNESSES TO THIS LITTLE INCIDENT ARE YOU, THE SMALL GIRL...
AND DANIEL RAND.
NOW, YOU SAY THESE "THINGS" WERE TRYING TO STOP THIS GIRL FROM GIVING HIM THIS MESSAGE?
TO TELL RAND TO "GET HOME"?

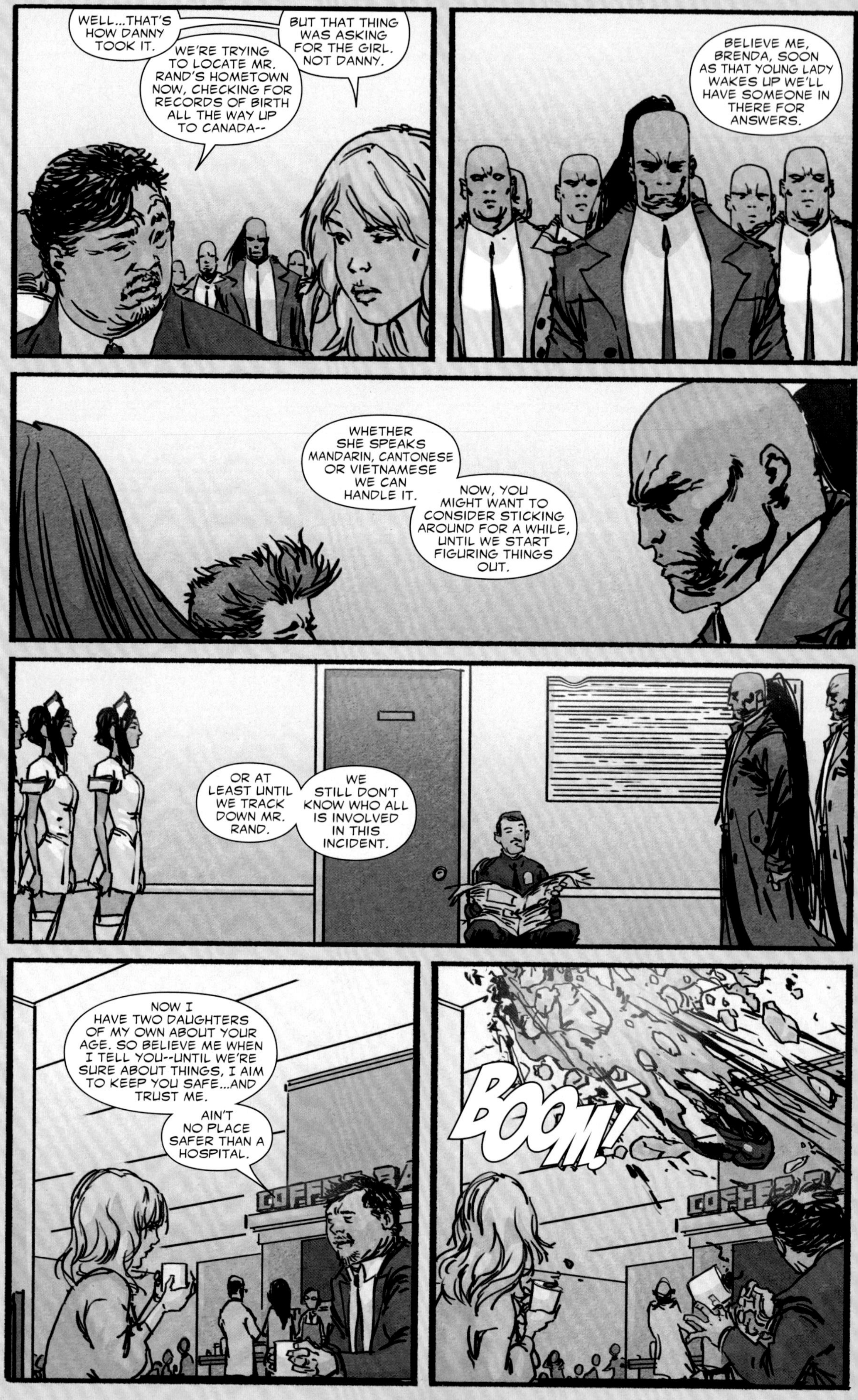
WELL...THAT'S HOW DANNY TOOK IT.
BUT THAT THING WAS ASKING FOR THE GIRL. NOT DANNY.
WE'RE TRYING TO LOCATE MR. RAND'S HOMETOWN NOW, CHECKING FOR RECORDS OF BIRTH ALL THE WAY UP TO CANADA--
BELIEVE ME, BRENDA, SOON AS THAT YOUNG LADY WAKES UP WE'LL HAVE SOMEONE IN THERE FOR ANSWERS.
WHETHER SHE SPEAKS MANDARIN, CANTONESE OR VIETNAMESE WE CAN HANDLE IT.
NOW, YOU MIGHT WANT TO CONSIDER STICKING AROUND FOR A WHILE, UNTIL WE START FIGURING THINGS OUT.
OR AT LEAST UNTIL WE TRACK DOWN MR. RAND.
WE STILL DON'T KNOW WHO ALL IS INVOLVED IN THIS INCIDENT.
NOW I HAVE TWO DAUGHTERS OF MY OWN ABOUT YOUR AGE. SO BELIEVE ME WHEN I TELL YOU--UNTIL WE'RE SURE ABOUT THINGS, I AIM TO KEEP YOU SAFE...AND TRUST ME.
AIN'T NO PLACE SAFER THAN A HOSPITAL.
BOOM!

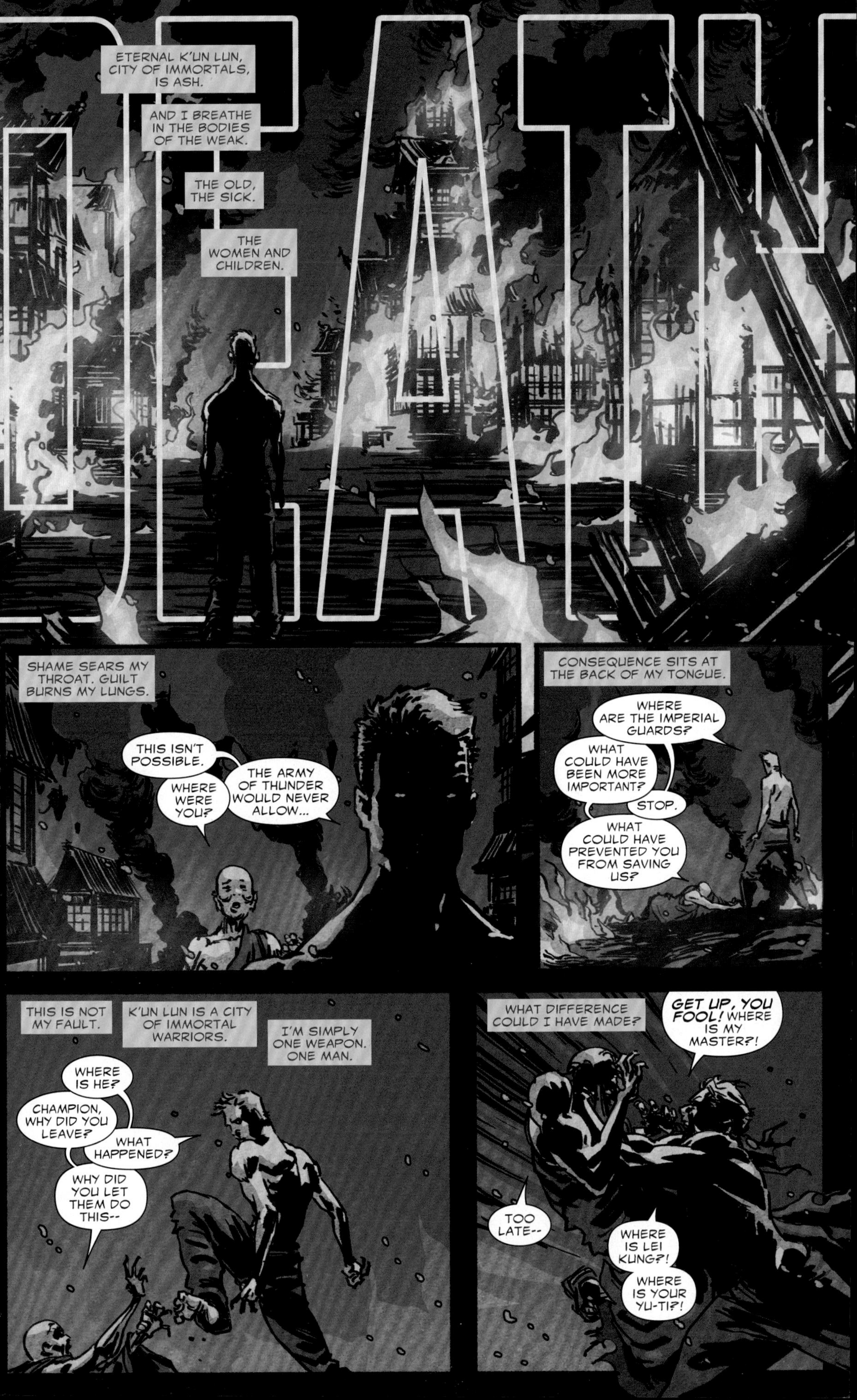
DEATH
ETERNAL K'UN LUN, CITY OF IMMORTALS, IS ASH.
AND I BREATHE IN THE BODIES OF THE WEAK.
THE OLD, THE SICK.
THE WOMEN AND CHILDREN.
SHAME SEARS MY THROAT. GUILT BURNS MY LUNGS.
THIS ISN'T POSSIBLE.
WHERE WERE YOU?
THE ARMY OF THUNDER WOULD NEVER ALLOW...
CONSEQUENCE SITS AT THE BACK OF MY TONGUE.
WHERE ARE THE IMPERIAL GUARDS?
WHAT COULD HAVE BEEN MORE IMPORTANT?
STOP.
WHAT COULD HAVE PREVENTED YOU FROM SAVING US?
THIS IS NOT MY FAULT.
K'UN LUN IS A CITY OF IMMORTAL WARRIORS.
I'M SIMPLY ONE WEAPON. ONE MAN.
WHERE IS HE?
CHAMPION, WHY DID YOU LEAVE?
WHAT HAPPENED?
WHY DID YOU LET THEM DO THIS--
WHAT DIFFERENCE COULD I HAVE MADE?
GET UP, YOU FOOL! WHERE IS MY MASTER?!
TOO LATE--
WHERE IS LEI KUNG?!
WHERE IS YOUR YU-TI?!

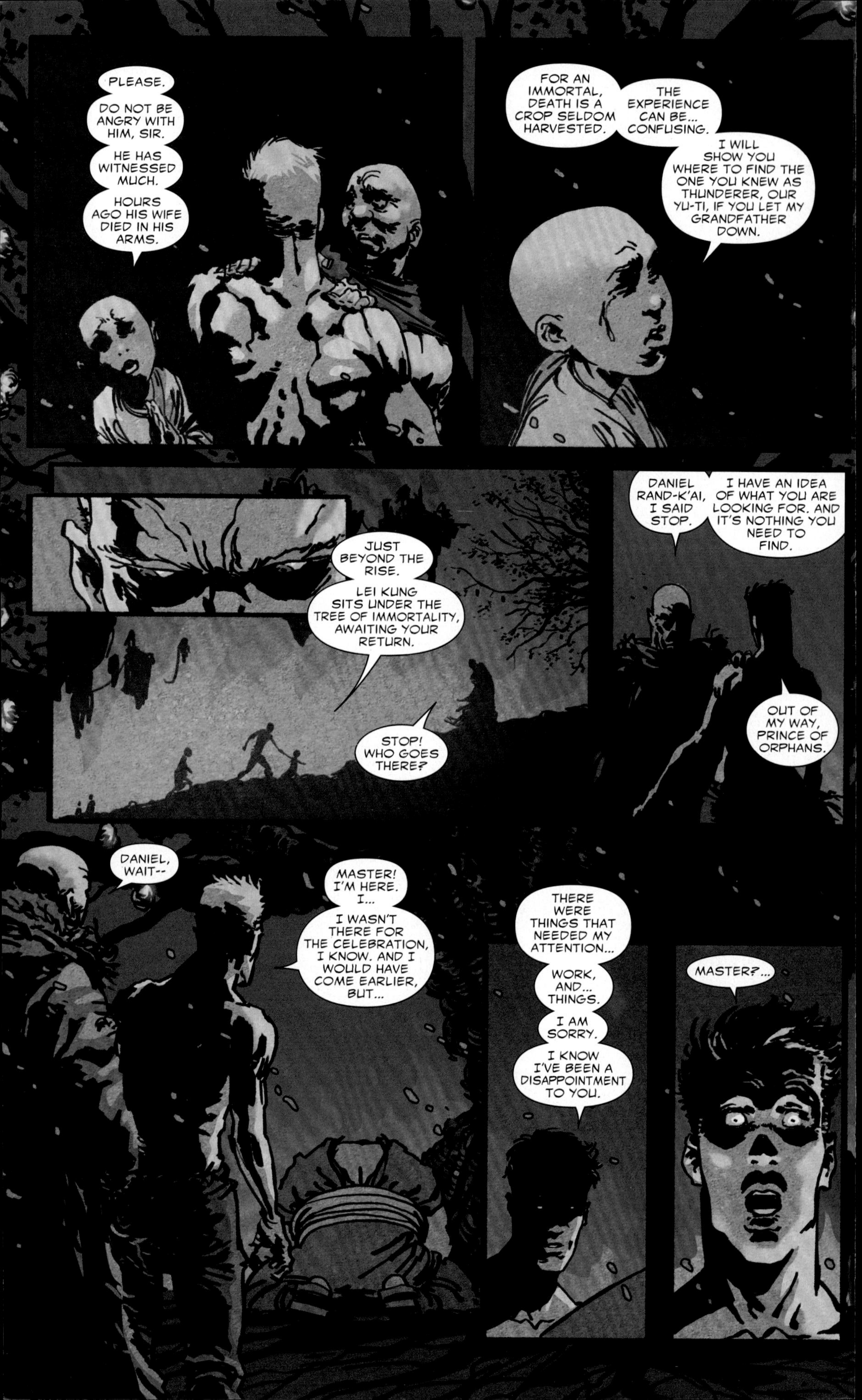
PLEASE.
DO NOT BE ANGRY WITH HIM, SIR.
HE HAS WITNESSED MUCH.
HOURS AGO HIS WIFE DIED IN HIS ARMS.
FOR AN IMMORTAL, DEATH IS A CROP SELDOM HARVESTED.
THE EXPERIENCE CAN BE... CONFUSING.
I WILL SHOW YOU WHERE TO FIND THE ONE YOU KNEW AS THUNDERER, OUR YU-TI, IF YOU LET MY GRANDFATHER DOWN.
JUST BEYOND THE RISE.
LEI KUNG SITS UNDER THE TREE OF IMMORTALITY, AWAITING YOUR RETURN.
STOP! WHO GOES THERE?
DANIEL RAND-K'AI, I SAID STOP.
I HAVE AN IDEA OF WHAT YOU ARE LOOKING FOR. AND IT'S NOTHING YOU NEED TO FIND.
OUT OF MY WAY, PRINCE OF ORPHANS.
DANIEL, WAIT--
MASTER! I'M HERE. I...
I WASN'T THERE FOR THE CELEBRATION, I KNOW. AND I WOULD HAVE COME EARLIER, BUT...
THERE WERE THINGS THAT NEEDED MY ATTENTION...
WORK, AND... THINGS.
I AM SORRY.
I KNOW I'VE BEEN A DISAPPOINTMENT TO YOU.
MASTER?...

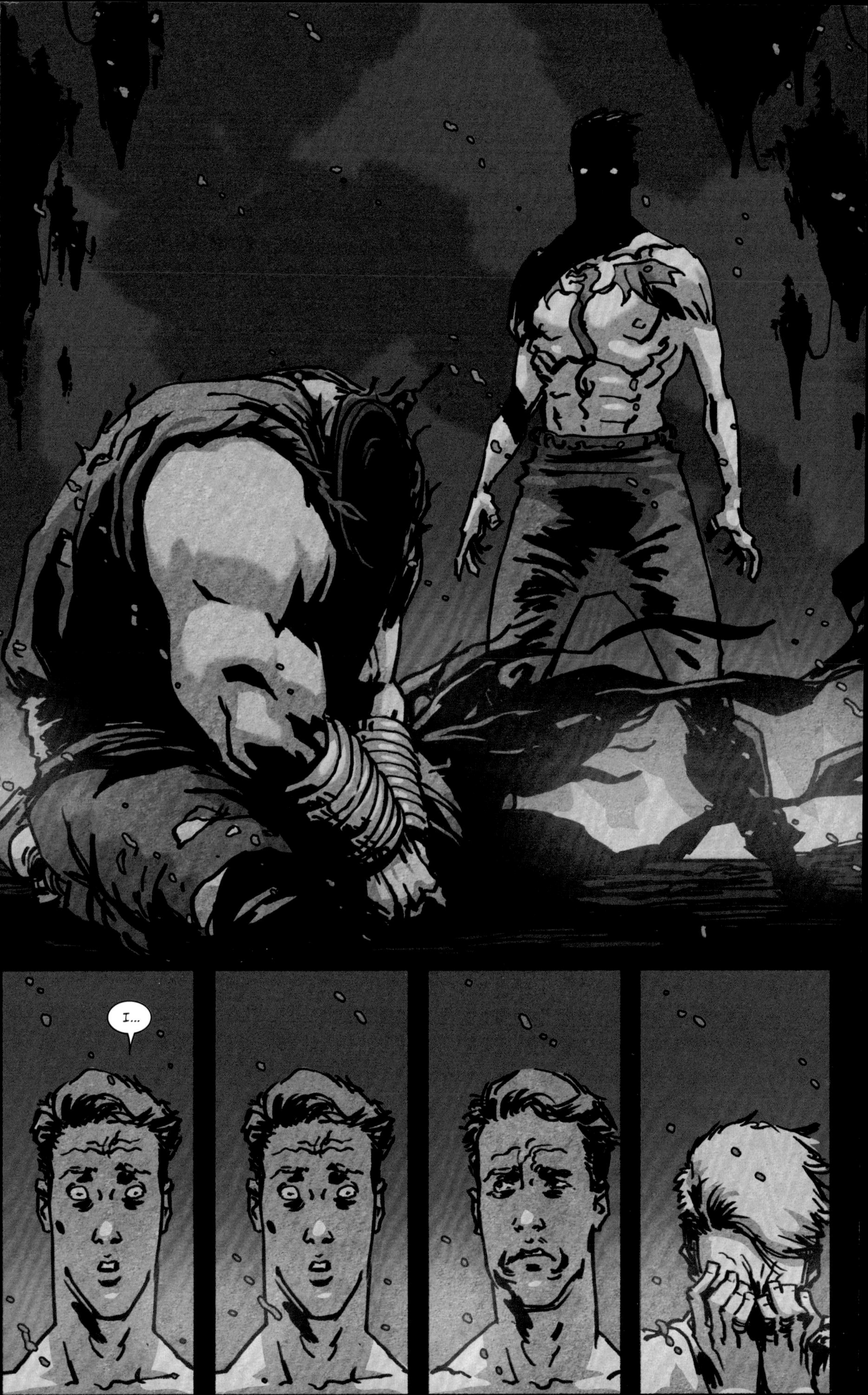
I...

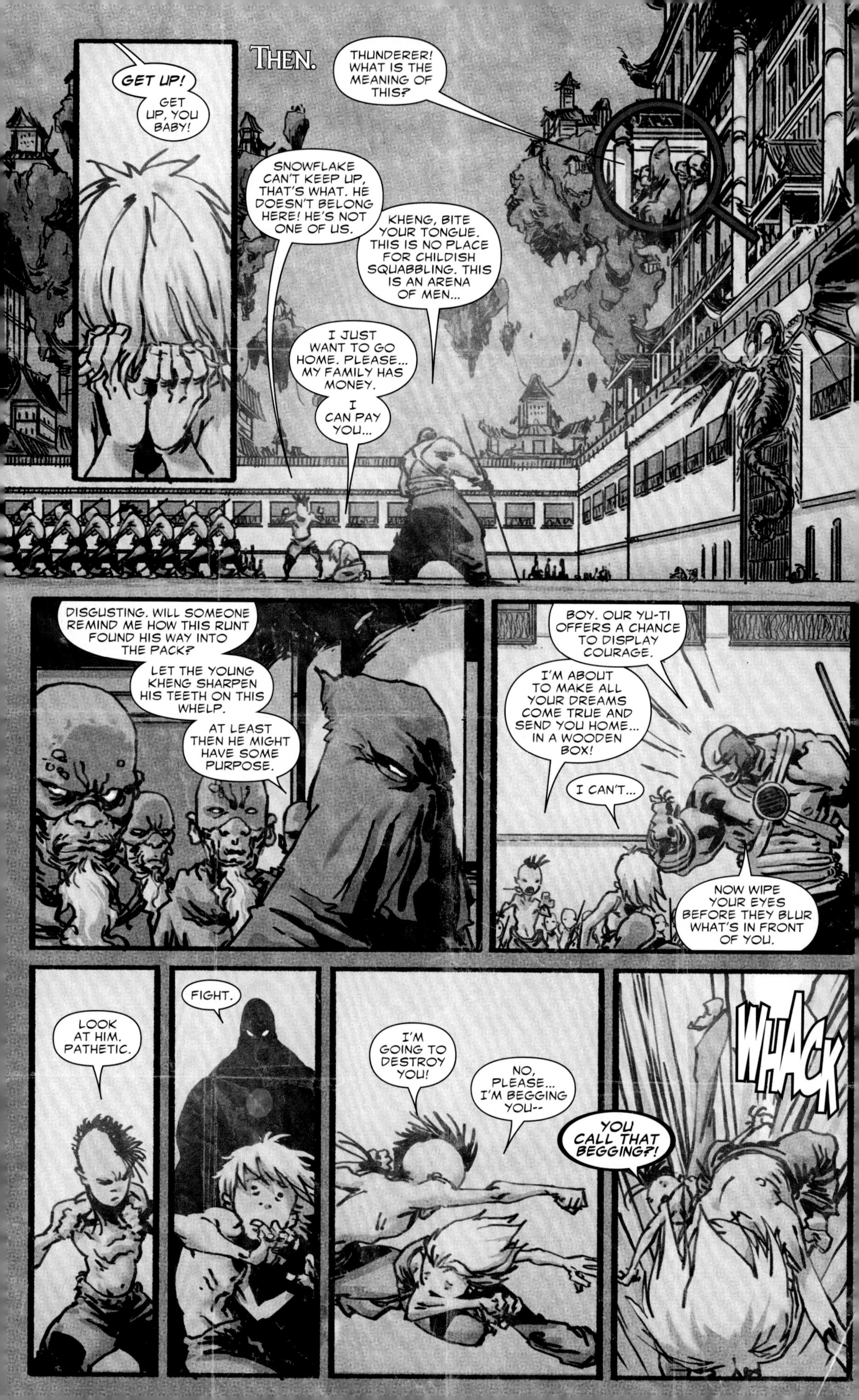
GET UP!
GET UP, YOU BABY!
THEN.
THUNDERER! WHAT IS THE MEANING OF THIS?
SNOWFLAKE CAN'T KEEP UP, THAT'S WHAT. HE DOESN'T BELONG HERE! HE'S NOT ONE OF US.
KHENG, BITE YOUR TONGUE. THIS IS NO PLACE FOR CHILDISH SQUABBLING. THIS IS AN ARENA OF MEN...
I JUST WANT TO GO HOME. PLEASE... MY FAMILY HAS MONEY.
I CAN PAY YOU...
DISGUSTING. WILL SOMEONE REMIND ME HOW THIS RUNT FOUND HIS WAY INTO THE PACK?
LET THE YOUNG KHENG SHARPEN HIS TEETH ON THIS WHELP.
AT LEAST THEN HE MIGHT HAVE SOME PURPOSE.
BOY. OUR YU-TI OFFERS A CHANCE TO DISPLAY COURAGE.
I'M ABOUT TO MAKE ALL YOUR DREAMS COME TRUE AND SEND YOU HOME... IN A WOODEN BOX!
I CAN'T...
NOW WIPE YOUR EYES BEFORE THEY BLUR WHAT'S IN FRONT OF YOU.
LOOK AT HIM. PATHETIC.
FIGHT.
I'M GOING TO DESTROY YOU!
NO, PLEASE... I'M BEGGING YOU--
WHACK
YOU CALL THAT BEGGING?!

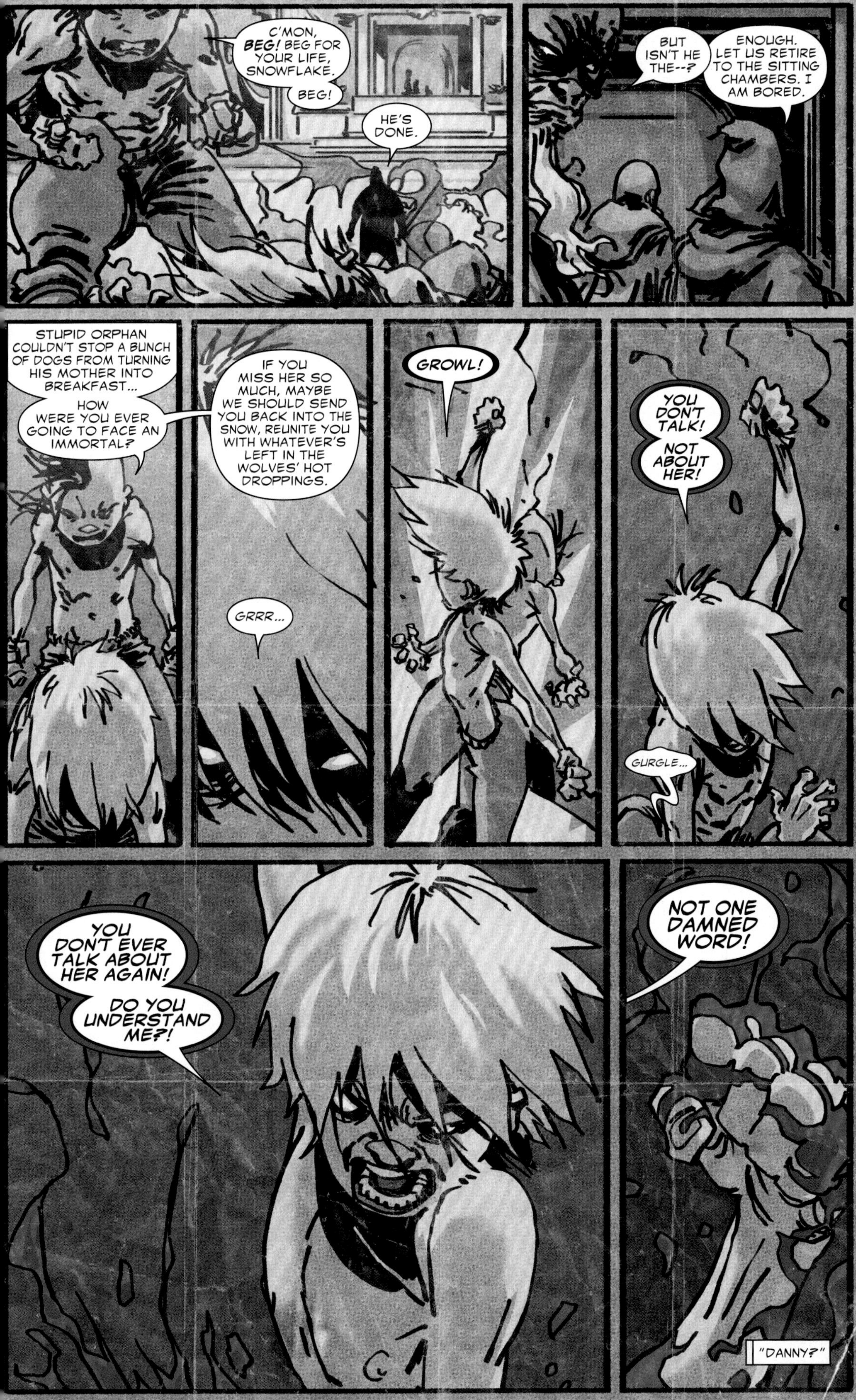

C'MON, BEG! BEG FOR YOUR LIFE, SNOWFLAKE.
BEG!
HE'S DONE.
BUT ISN'T HE THE--?
ENOUGH. LET US RETIRE TO THE SITTING CHAMBERS. I AM BORED.
STUPID ORPHAN COULDN'T STOP A BUNCH OF DOGS FROM TURNING HIS MOTHER INTO BREAKFAST...
HOW WERE YOU EVER GOING TO FACE AN IMMORTAL?
IF YOU MISS HER SO MUCH, MAYBE WE SHOULD SEND YOU BACK INTO THE SNOW, REUNITE YOU WITH WHATEVER'S LEFT IN THE WOLVES' HOT DROPPINGS.
GRRR...
GROWL!
YOU DON'T TALK!
NOT ABOUT HER!
GURGLE...
YOU DON'T EVER TALK ABOUT HER AGAIN!
DO YOU UNDERSTAND ME?!
NOT ONE DAMNED WORD!
"DANNY?"

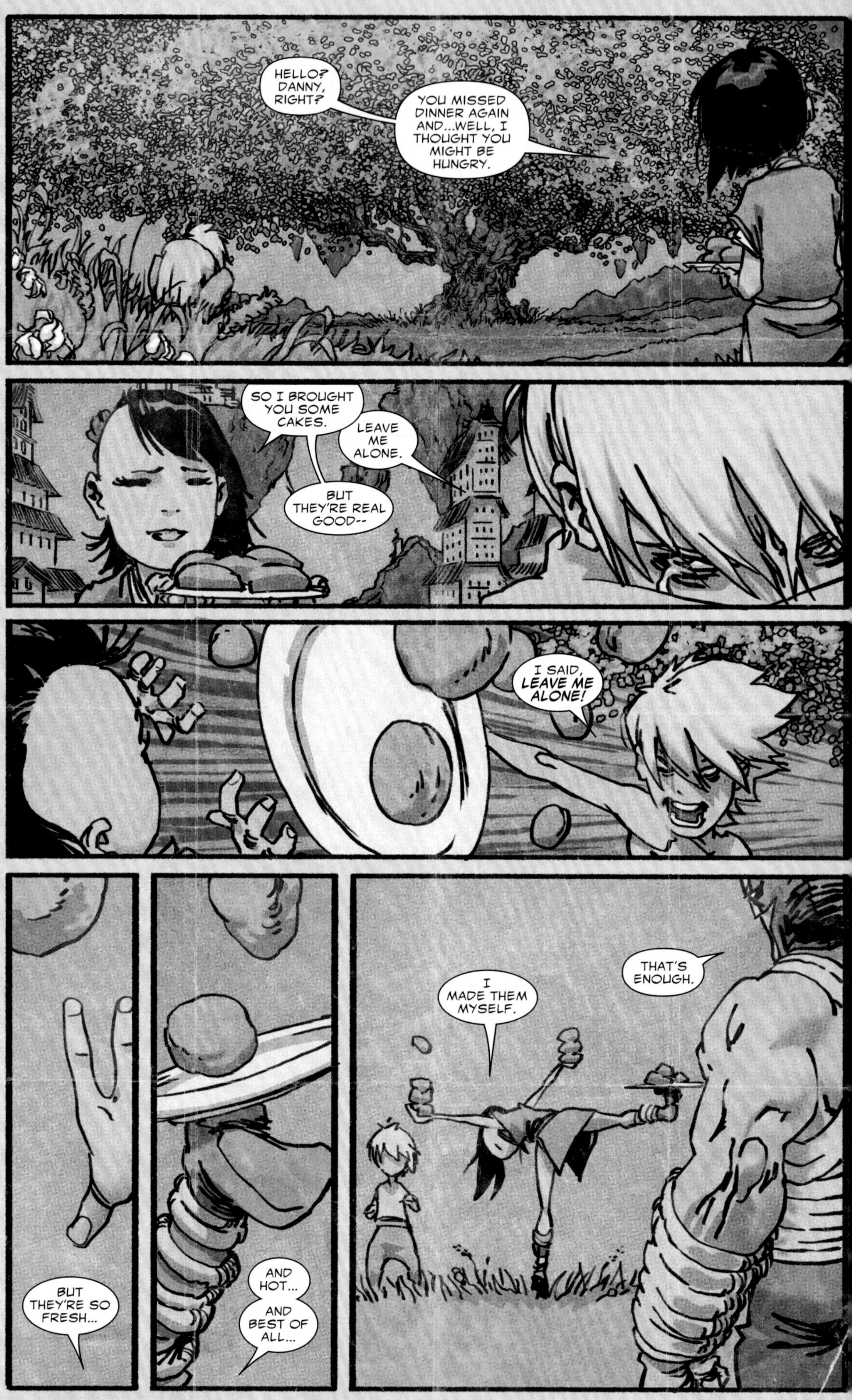
HELLO? DANNY, RIGHT?
YOU MISSED DINNER AGAIN AND...WELL, I THOUGHT YOU MIGHT BE HUNGRY.
SO I BROUGHT YOU SOME CAKES.
LEAVE ME ALONE.
BUT THEY'RE REAL GOOD--
I SAID, LEAVE ME ALONE!
BUT THEY'RE SO FRESH...
AND HOT...
AND BEST OF ALL...
I MADE THEM MYSELF.
THAT'S ENOUGH.

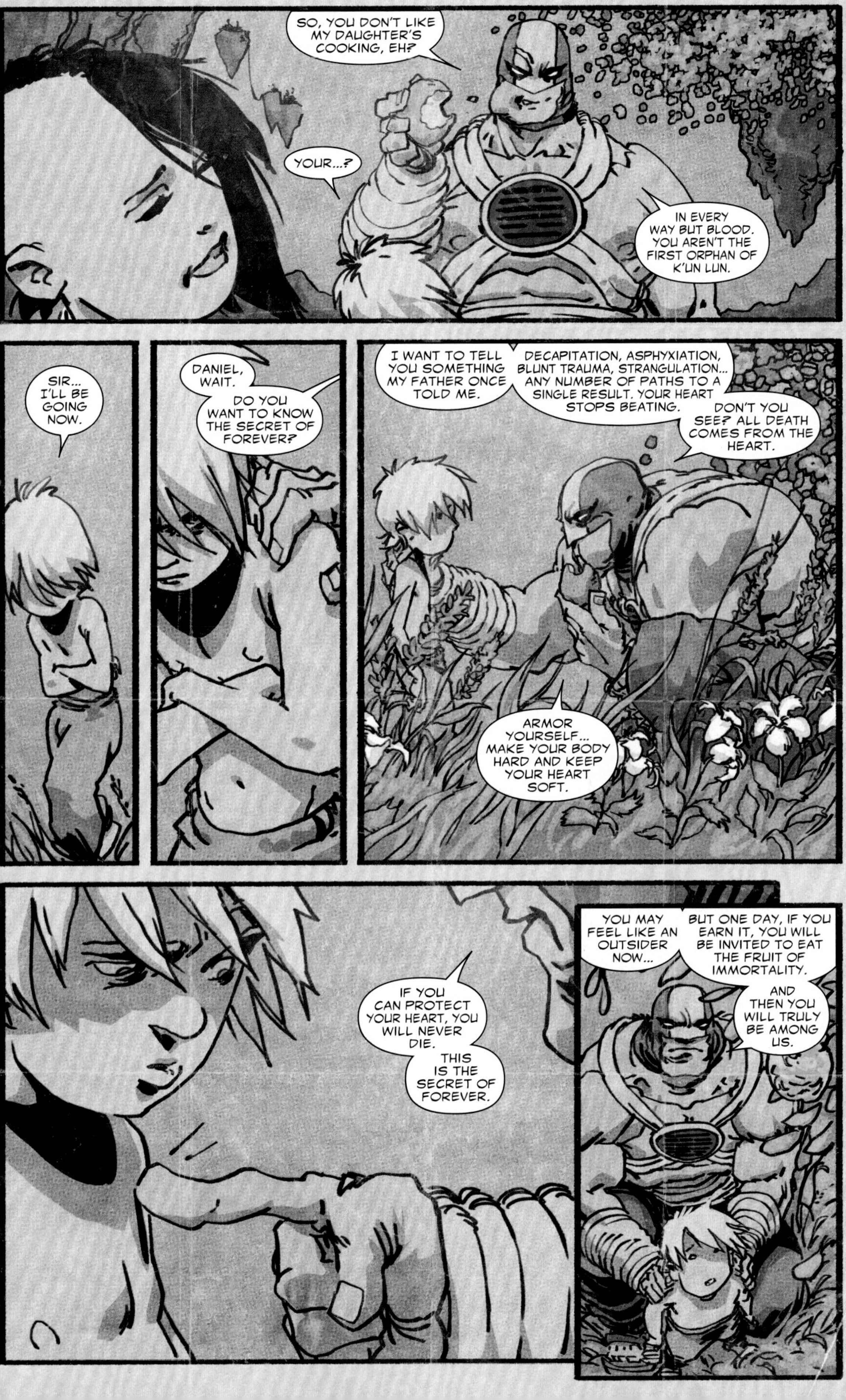
SO, YOU DON'T LIKE MY DAUGHTER'S COOKING, EH?
YOUR...?
IN EVERY WAY BUT BLOOD. YOU AREN'T THE FIRST ORPHAN OF K'UN LUN.
SIR... I'LL BE GOING NOW.
DANIEL, WAIT.
DO YOU WANT TO KNOW THE SECRET OF FOREVER?
I WANT TO TELL YOU SOMETHING MY FATHER ONCE TOLD ME.
DECAPITATION, ASPHYXIATION, BLUNT TRAUMA, STRANGULATION... ANY NUMBER OF PATHS TO A SINGLE RESULT. YOUR HEART STOPS BEATING.
DON'T YOU SEE? ALL DEATH COMES FROM THE HEART.
ARMOR YOURSELF... MAKE YOUR BODY HARD AND KEEP YOUR HEART SOFT.
IF YOU CAN PROTECT YOUR HEART, YOU WILL NEVER DIE.
THIS IS THE SECRET OF FOREVER.
YOU MAY FEEL LIKE AN OUTSIDER NOW...
BUT ONE DAY, IF YOU EARN IT, YOU WILL BE INVITED TO EAT THE FRUIT OF IMMORTALITY.
AND THEN YOU WILL TRULY BE AMONG US.

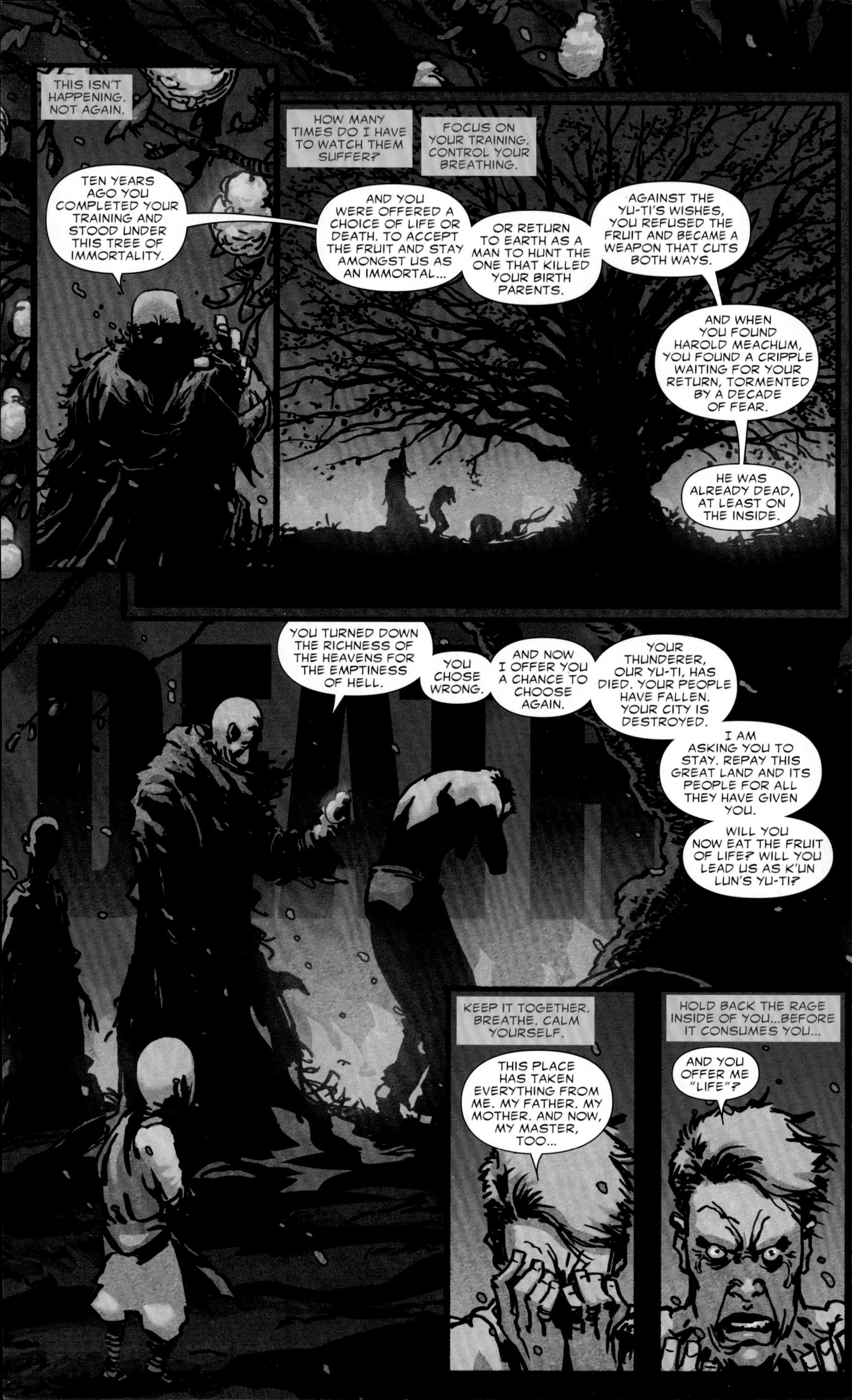
THIS ISN'T HAPPENING. NOT AGAIN.
HOW MANY TIMES DO I HAVE TO WATCH THEM SUFFER?
FOCUS ON YOUR TRAINING. CONTROL YOUR BREATHING.
TEN YEARS AGO YOU COMPLETED YOUR TRAINING AND STOOD UNDER THIS TREE OF IMMORTALITY.
AND YOU WERE OFFERED A CHOICE OF LIFE OR DEATH. TO ACCEPT THE FRUIT AND STAY AMONGST US AS AN IMMORTAL...
OR RETURN TO EARTH AS A MAN TO HUNT THE ONE THAT KILLED YOUR BIRTH PARENTS.
AGAINST THE YU-TI'S WISHES, YOU REFUSED THE FRUIT AND BECAME A WEAPON THAT CUTS BOTH WAYS.
AND WHEN YOU FOUND HAROLD MEACHUM, YOU FOUND A CRIPPLE WAITING FOR YOUR RETURN, TORMENTED BY A DECADE OF FEAR.
HE WAS ALREADY DEAD, AT LEAST ON THE INSIDE.
YOU TURNED DOWN THE RICHNESS OF THE HEAVENS FOR THE EMPTINESS OF HELL.
YOU CHOSE WRONG.
AND NOW I OFFER YOU A CHANCE TO CHOOSE AGAIN.
YOUR THUNDERER, OUR YU-TI, HAS DIED. YOUR PEOPLE HAVE FALLEN. YOUR CITY IS DESTROYED.
I AM ASKING YOU TO STAY. REPAY THIS GREAT LAND AND ITS PEOPLE FOR ALL THEY HAVE GIVEN YOU.
WILL YOU NOW EAT THE FRUIT OF LIFE? WILL YOU LEAD US AS K'UN LUN'S YU-TI?
KEEP IT TOGETHER. BREATHE. CALM YOURSELF.
THIS PLACE HAS TAKEN EVERYTHING FROM ME. MY FATHER. MY MOTHER. AND NOW, MY MASTER, TOO...
HOLD BACK THE RAGE INSIDE OF YOU...BEFORE IT CONSUMES YOU...
AND YOU OFFER ME "LIFE"?

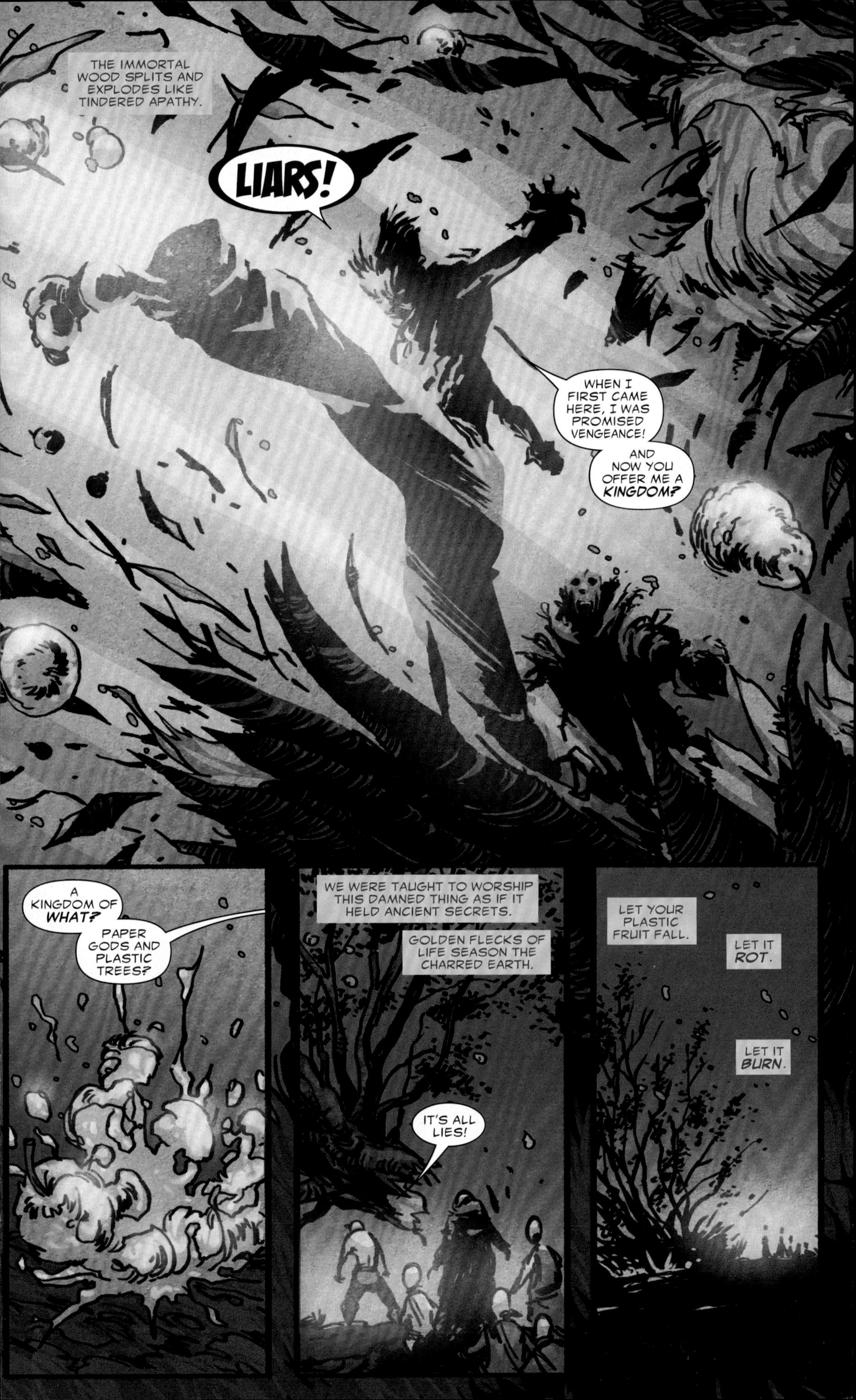
THE IMMORTAL WOOD SPLITS AND EXPLODES LIKE TINDERED APATHY.
LIARS!
WHEN I FIRST CAME HERE, I WAS PROMISED VENGEANCE!
AND NOW YOU OFFER ME A KINGDOM?
A KINGDOM OF WHAT?
PAPER GODS AND PLASTIC TREES?
WE WERE TAUGHT TO WORSHIP THIS DAMNED THING AS IF IT HELD ANCIENT SECRETS.
GOLDEN FLECKS OF LIFE SEASON THE CHARRED EARTH.
IT'S ALL LIES!
LET YOUR PLASTIC FRUIT FALL.
LET IT ROT.
LET IT BURN.

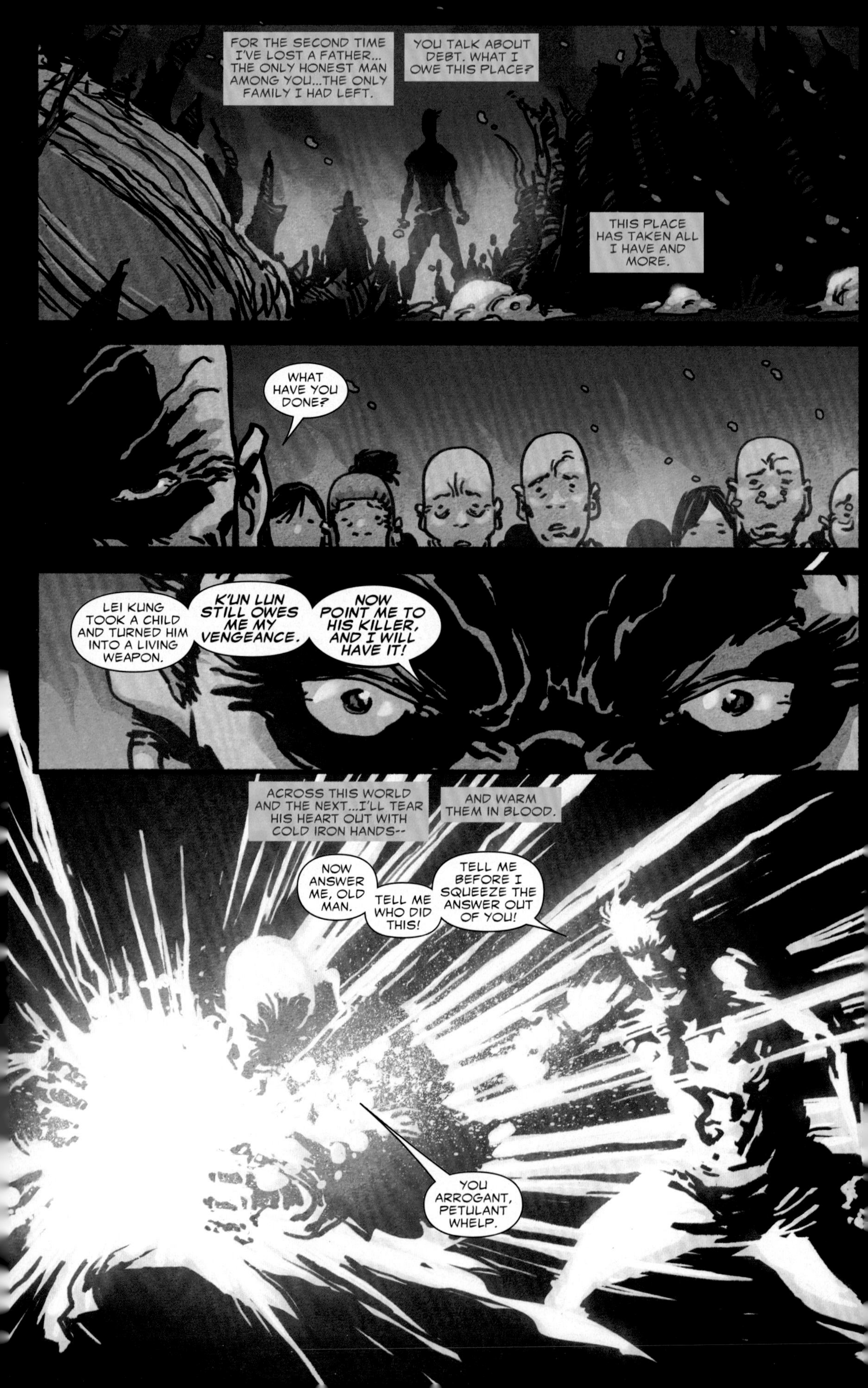
FOR THE SECOND TIME I'VE LOST A FATHER... THE ONLY HONEST MAN AMONG YOU...THE ONLY FAMILY I HAD LEFT.
YOU TALK ABOUT DEBT. WHAT I OWE THIS PLACE?
THIS PLACE HAS TAKEN ALL I HAVE AND MORE.
WHAT HAVE YOU DONE?
LEI KUNG TOOK A CHILD AND TURNED HIM INTO A LIVING WEAPON.
K'UN LUN STILL OWES ME MY VENGEANCE.
NOW POINT ME TO HIS KILLER, AND I WILL HAVE IT!
ACROSS THIS WORLD AND THE NEXT...I'LL TEAR HIS HEART OUT WITH COLD IRON HANDS--
AND WARM THEM IN BLOOD.
NOW ANSWER ME, OLD MAN.
TELL ME WHO DID THIS!
TELL ME BEFORE I SQUEEZE THE ANSWER OUT OF YOU!
YOU ARROGANT, PETULANT WHELP.

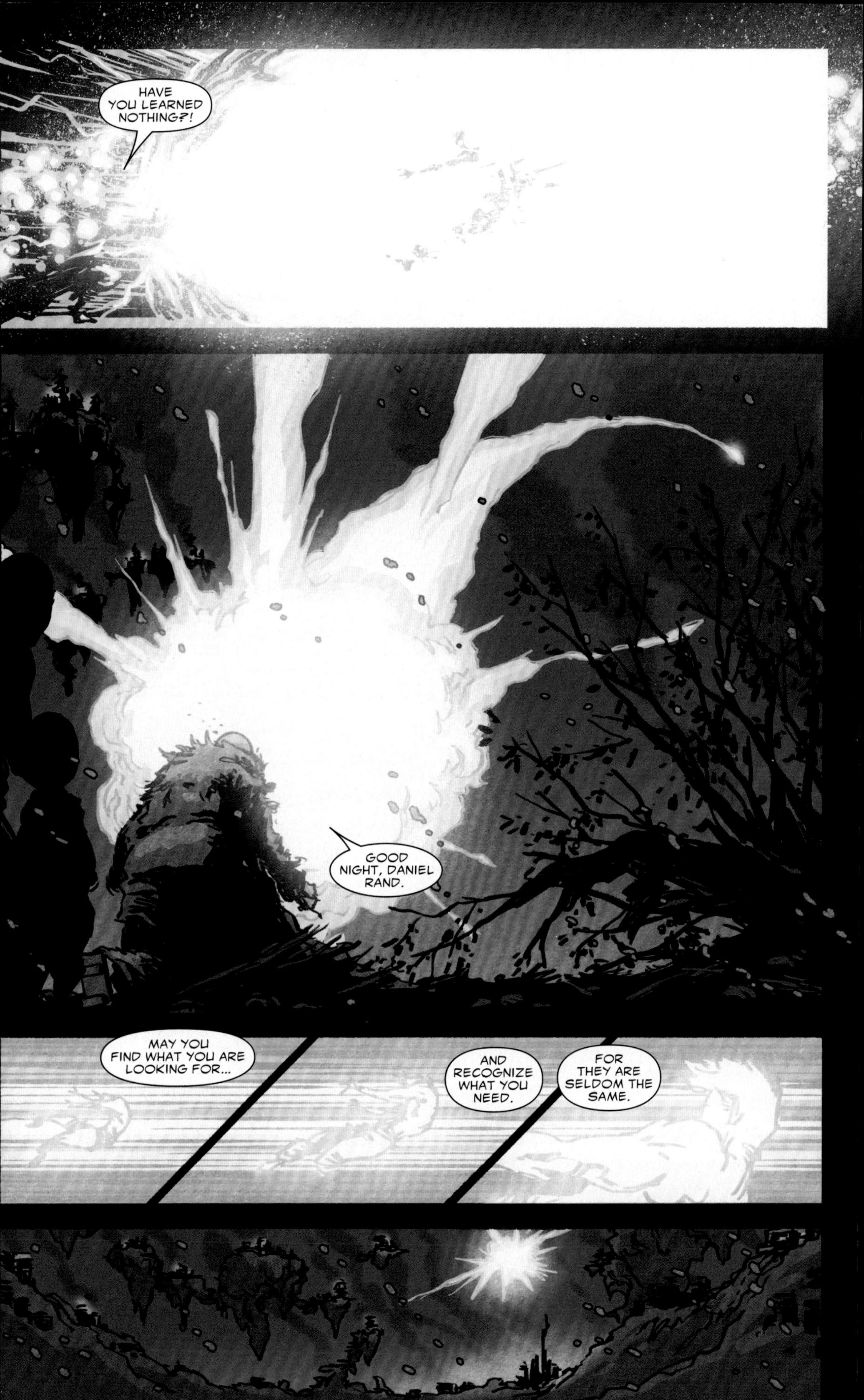
HAVE YOU LEARNED NOTHING?!
GOOD NIGHT, DANIEL RAND.
MAY YOU FIND WHAT YOU ARE LOOKING FOR...
AND RECOGNIZE WHAT YOU NEED.
FOR THEY ARE SELDOM THE SAME.

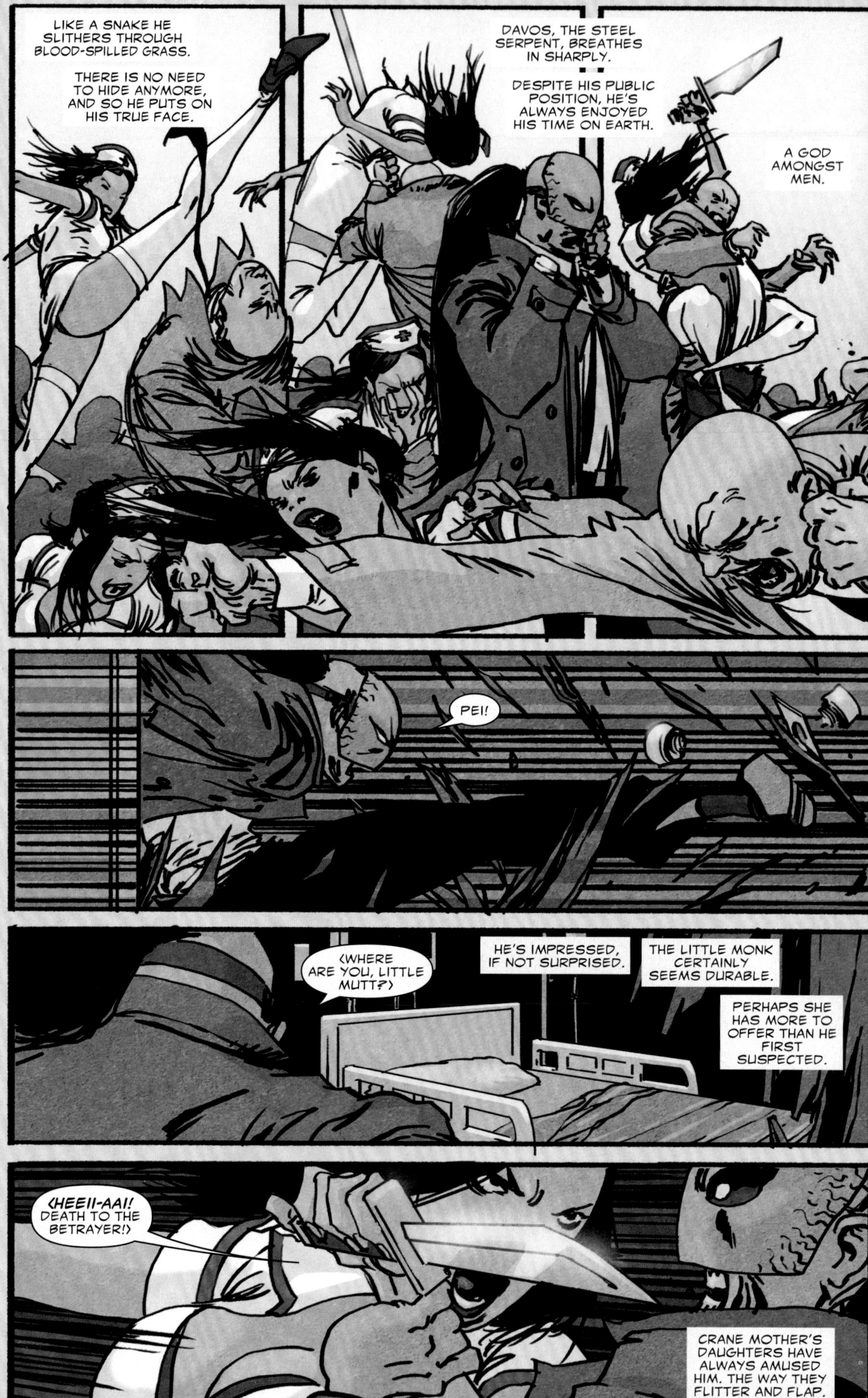
LIKE A SNAKE HE SLITHERS THROUGH BLOOD-SPILLED GRASS.
THERE IS NO NEED TO HIDE ANYMORE, AND SO HE PUTS ON HIS TRUE FACE.
DAVOS, THE STEEL SERPENT, BREATHES IN SHARPLY.
DESPITE HIS PUBLIC POSITION, HE'S ALWAYS ENJOYED HIS TIME ON EARTH.
A GOD AMONGST MEN.
PEI!
<WHERE ARE YOU, LITTLE MUTT?>
HE'S IMPRESSED, IF NOT SURPRISED.
THE LITTLE MONK CERTAINLY SEEMS DURABLE.
PERHAPS SHE HAS MORE TO OFFER THAN HE FIRST SUSPECTED.
<HEEII-AAI! DEATH TO THE BETRAYER!>
CRANE MOTHER'S DAUGHTERS HAVE ALWAYS AMUSED HIM. THE WAY THEY FLITTER AND FLAP.

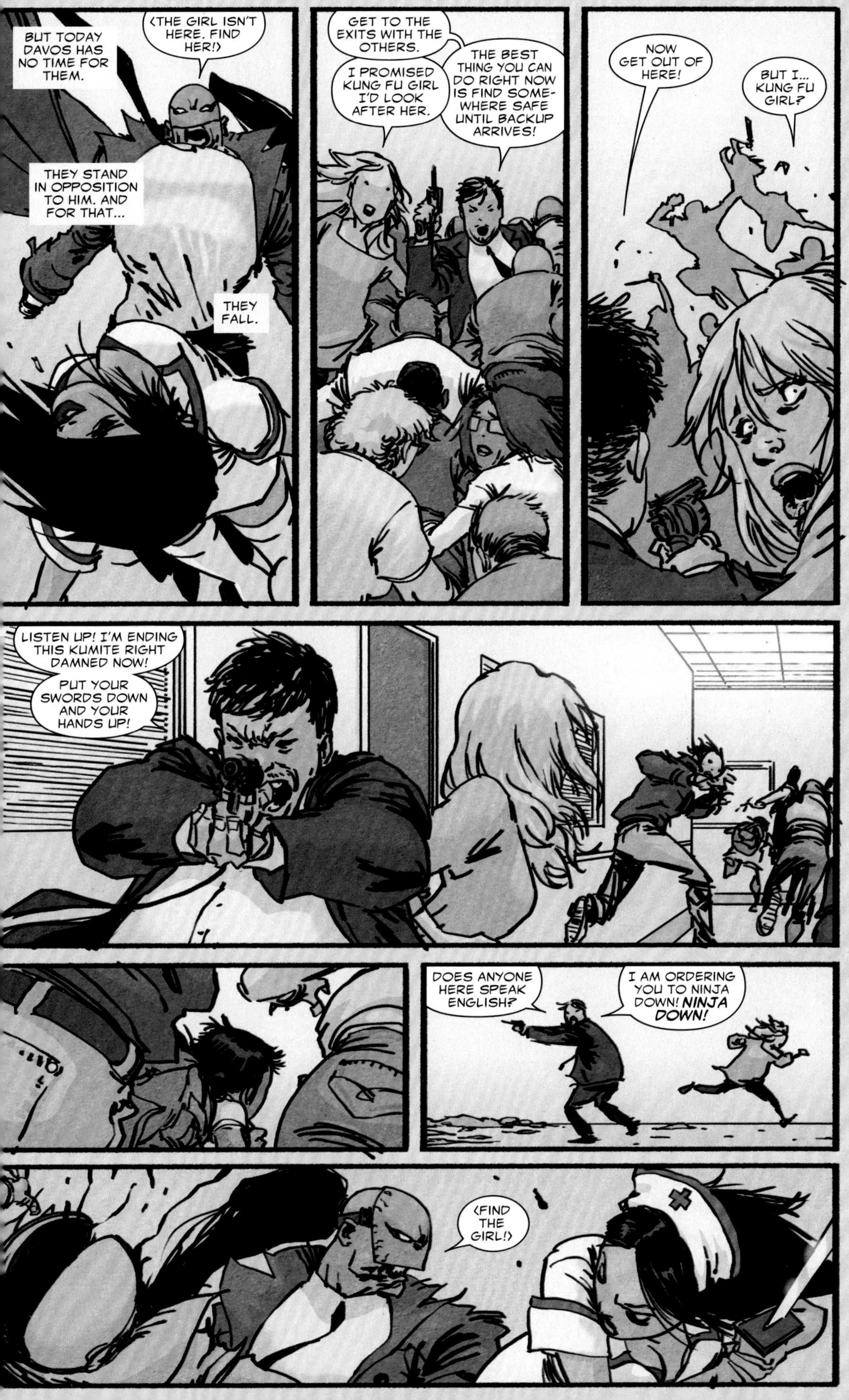
BUT TODAY DAVOS HAS NO TIME FOR THEM.
‹THE GIRL ISN'T HERE. FIND HER!›
THEY STAND IN OPPOSITION TO HIM. AND FOR THAT...
THEY FALL.
GET TO THE EXITS WITH THE OTHERS.
I PROMISED KUNG FU GIRL I'D LOOK AFTER HER.
THE BEST THING YOU CAN DO RIGHT NOW IS FIND SOME-WHERE SAFE UNTIL BACKUP ARRIVES!
NOW GET OUT OF HERE!
BUT I... KUNG FU GIRL?
LISTEN UP! I'M ENDING THIS KUMITE RIGHT DAMNED NOW!
PUT YOUR SWORDS DOWN AND YOUR HANDS UP!
DOES ANYONE HERE SPEAK ENGLISH?
I AM ORDERING YOU TO NINJA DOWN! NINJA DOWN!
‹FIND THE GIRL!›

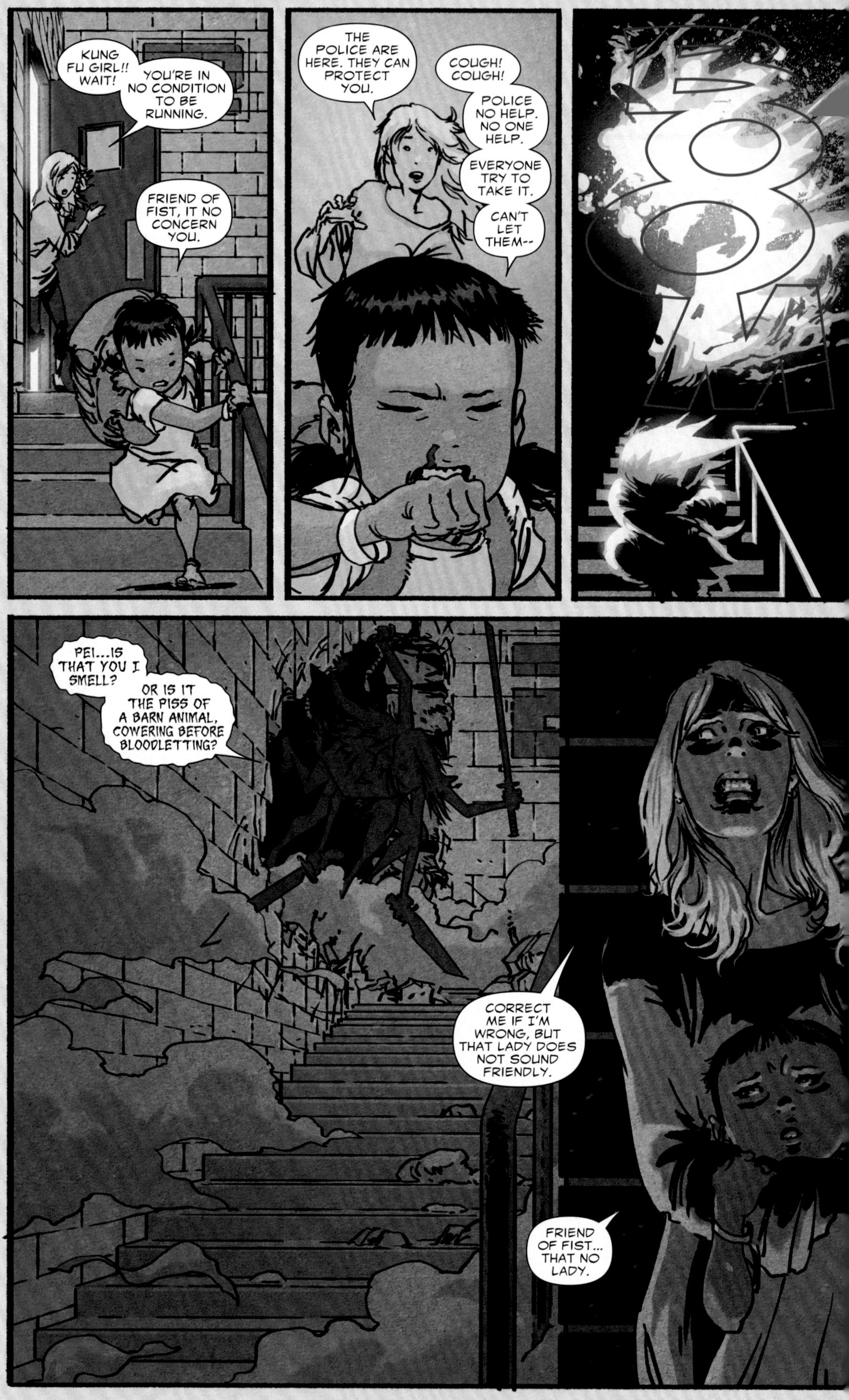

KUNG FU GIRL!! WAIT!
YOU'RE IN NO CONDITION TO BE RUNNING.
FRIEND OF FIST, IT NO CONCERN YOU.
THE POLICE ARE HERE. THEY CAN PROTECT YOU.
COUGH! COUGH!
POLICE NO HELP. NO ONE HELP.
EVERYONE TRY TO TAKE IT.
CAN'T LET THEM--
PEI...IS THAT YOU I SMELL?
OR IS IT THE PISS OF A BARN ANIMAL, COWERING BEFORE BLOODLETTING?
CORRECT ME IF I'M WRONG, BUT THAT LADY DOES NOT SOUND FRIENDLY.
FRIEND OF FIST... THAT NO LADY.

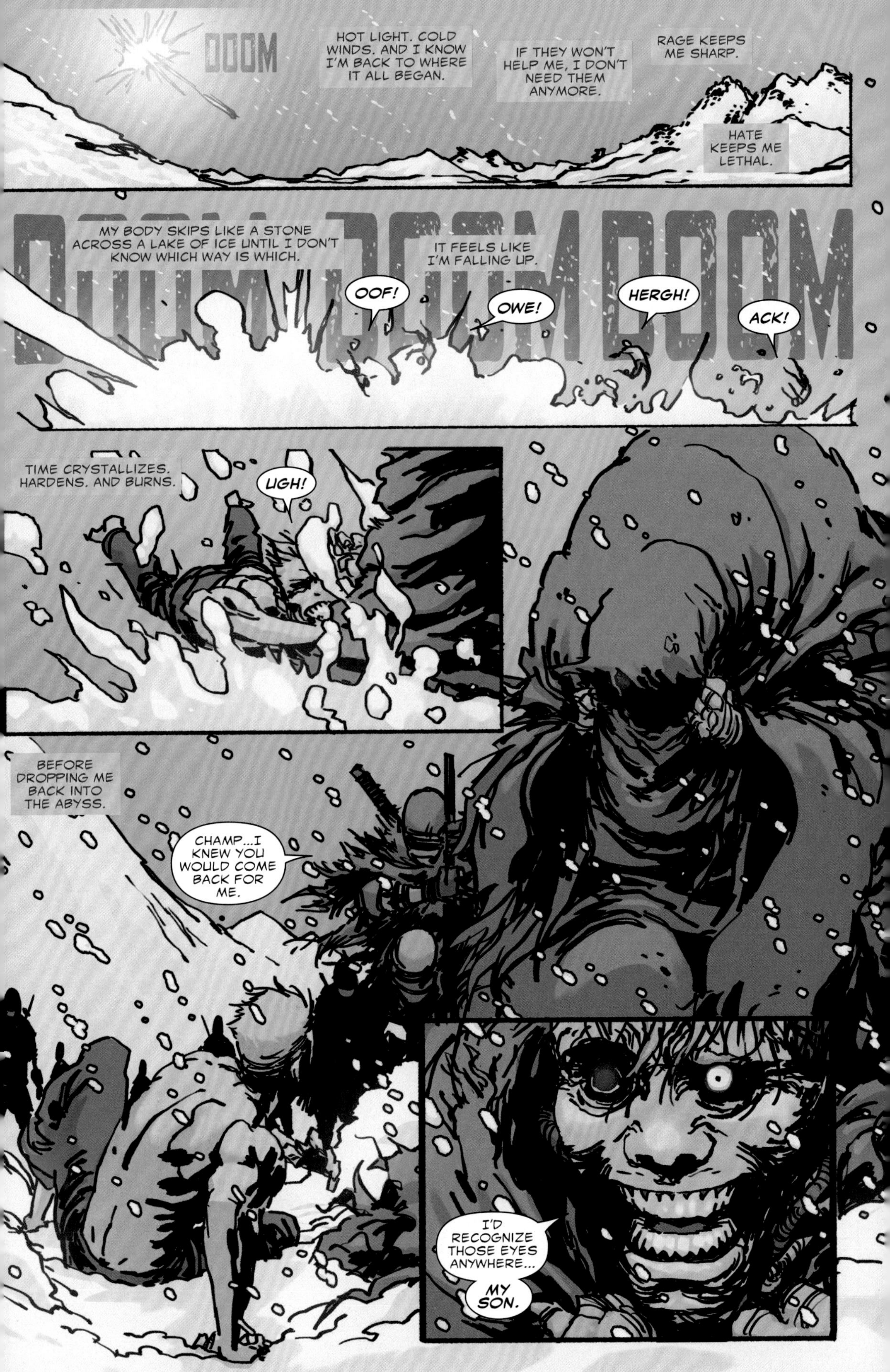
DOOM
HOT LIGHT. COLD WINDS. AND I KNOW I'M BACK TO WHERE IT ALL BEGAN.
IF THEY WON'T HELP ME, I DON'T NEED THEM ANYMORE.
RAGE KEEPS ME SHARP.
HATE KEEPS ME LETHAL.
MY BODY SKIPS LIKE A STONE ACROSS A LAKE OF ICE UNTIL I DON'T KNOW WHICH WAY IS WHICH.
IT FEELS LIKE I'M FALLING UP.
DOOM DOOM DOOM DOOM
OOF!
OWE!
HERGH!
ACK!
TIME CRYSTALLIZES. HARDENS. AND BURNS.
UGH!
BEFORE DROPPING ME BACK INTO THE ABYSS.
CHAMP...I KNEW YOU WOULD COME BACK FOR ME.
I'D RECOGNIZE THOSE EYES ANYWHERE...
MY SON.

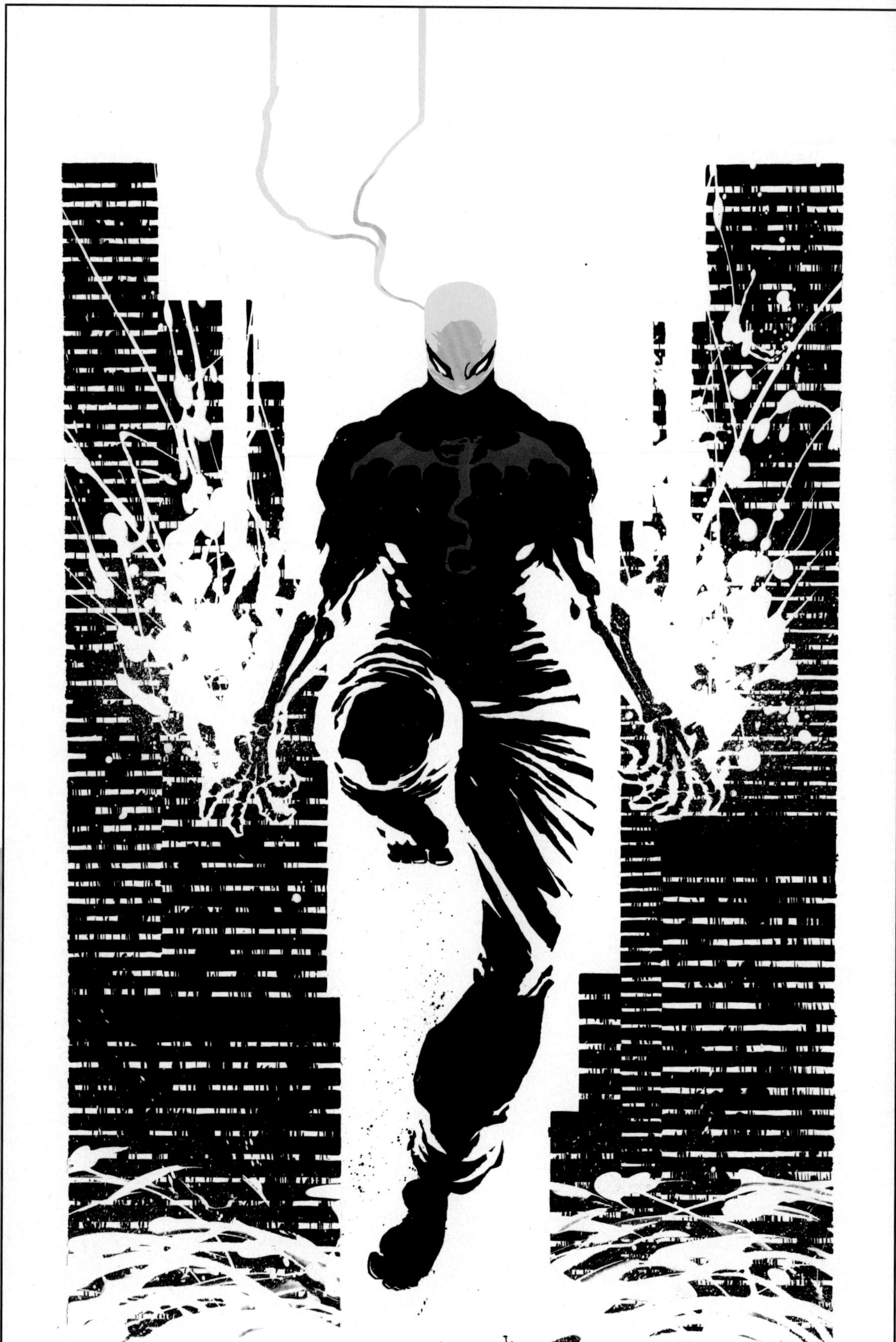

4

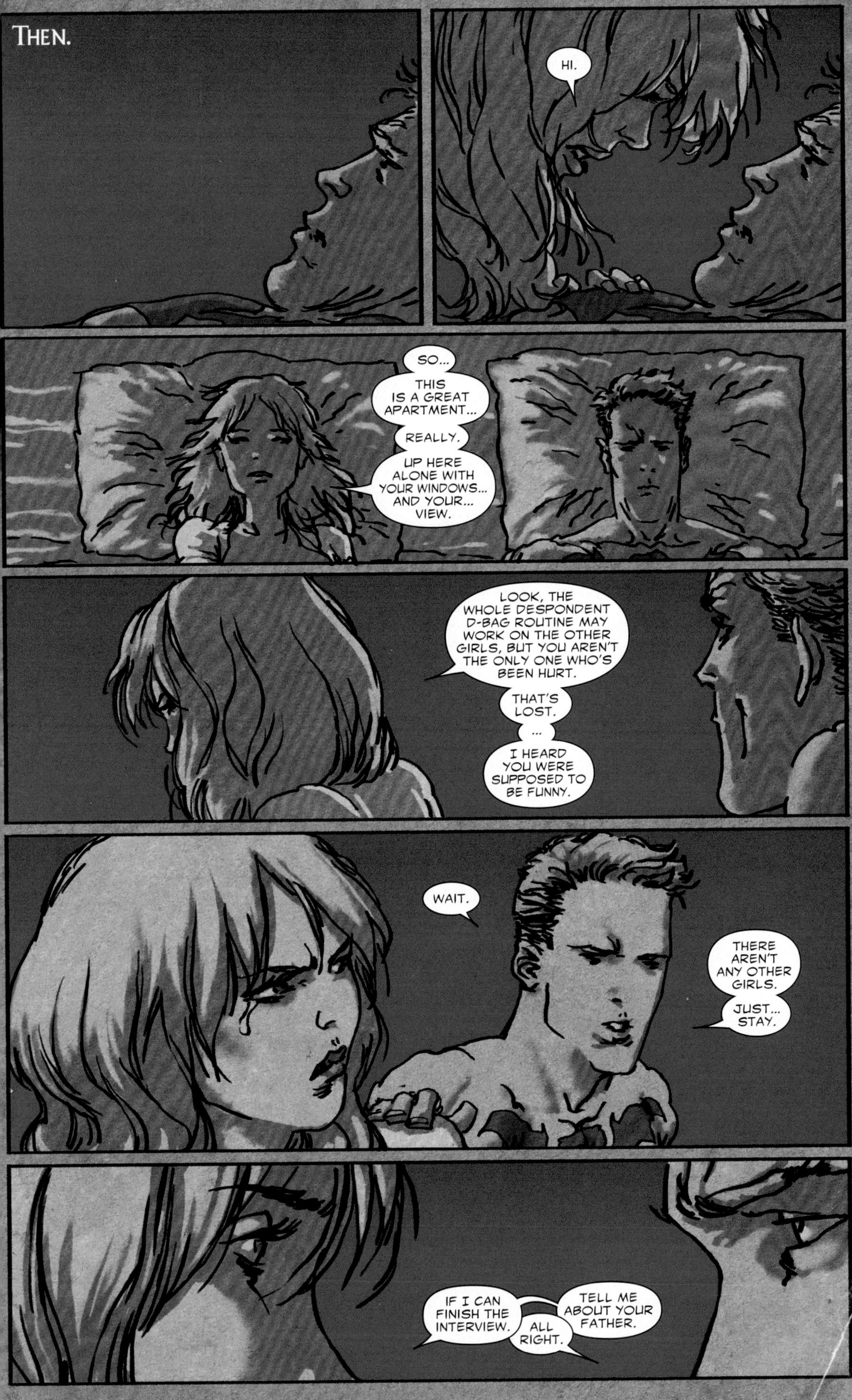
THEN.
HI.
SO...
THIS IS A GREAT APARTMENT...
REALLY.
UP HERE ALONE WITH YOUR WINDOWS... AND YOUR... VIEW.
LOOK, THE WHOLE DESPONDENT D-BAG ROUTINE MAY WORK ON THE OTHER GIRLS, BUT YOU AREN'T THE ONLY ONE WHO'S BEEN HURT.
THAT'S LOST.
...
I HEARD YOU WERE SUPPOSED TO BE FUNNY.
WAIT.
THERE AREN'T ANY OTHER GIRLS.
JUST... STAY.
TELL ME ABOUT YOUR FATHER.
IF I CAN FINISH THE INTERVIEW.
ALL RIGHT.

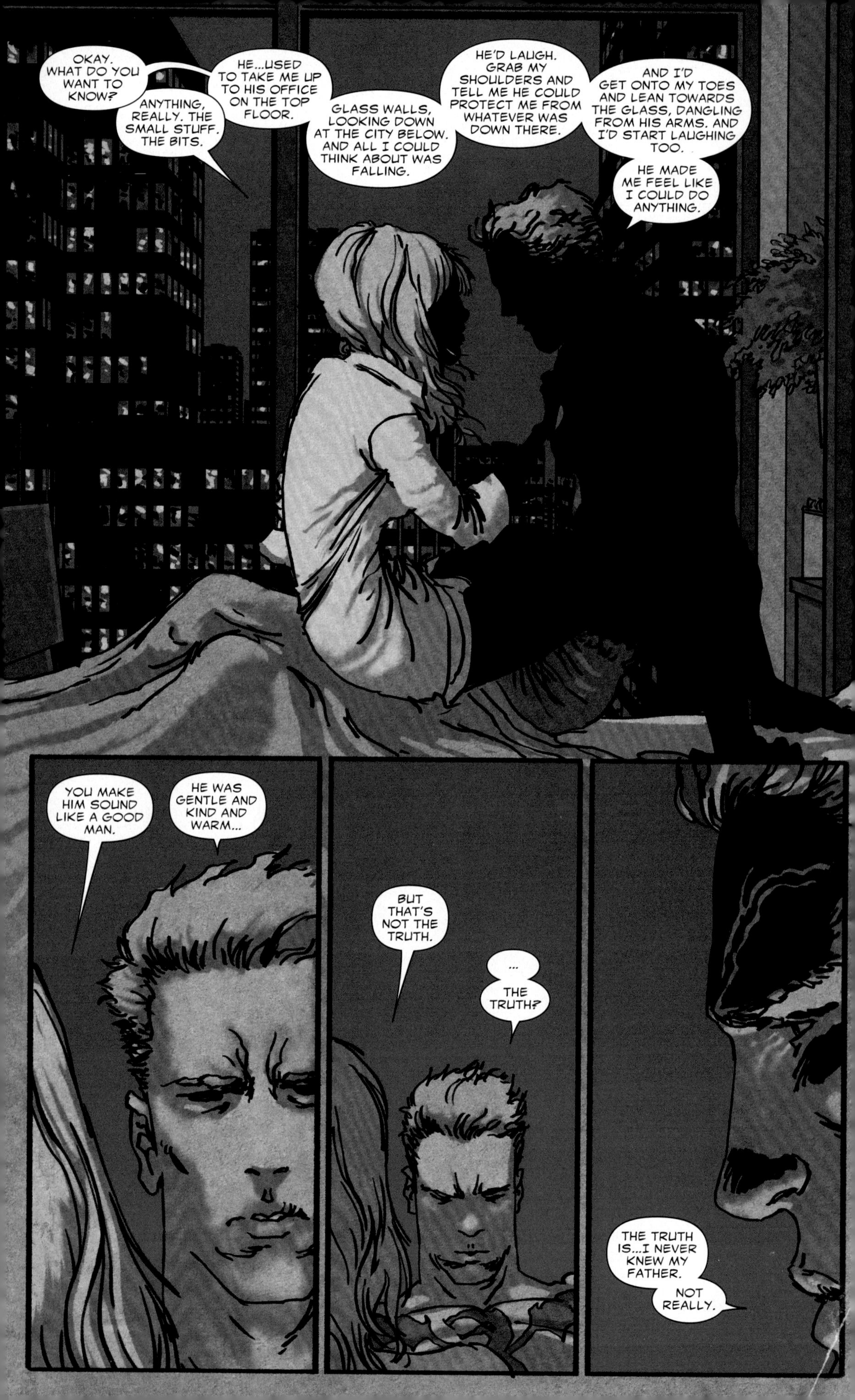
OKAY. WHAT DO YOU WANT TO KNOW?
ANYTHING, REALLY. THE SMALL STUFF. THE BITS.
HE...USED TO TAKE ME UP TO HIS OFFICE ON THE TOP FLOOR.
GLASS WALLS, LOOKING DOWN AT THE CITY BELOW. AND ALL I COULD THINK ABOUT WAS FALLING.
HE'D LAUGH. GRAB MY SHOULDERS AND TELL ME HE COULD PROTECT ME FROM WHATEVER WAS DOWN THERE.
AND I'D GET ONTO MY TOES AND LEAN TOWARDS THE GLASS, DANGLING FROM HIS ARMS. AND I'D START LAUGHING TOO.
HE MADE ME FEEL LIKE I COULD DO ANYTHING.
YOU MAKE HIM SOUND LIKE A GOOD MAN.
HE WAS GENTLE AND KIND AND WARM...
BUT THAT'S NOT THE TRUTH.
...
THE TRUTH?
THE TRUTH IS...I NEVER KNEW MY FATHER.
NOT REALLY.

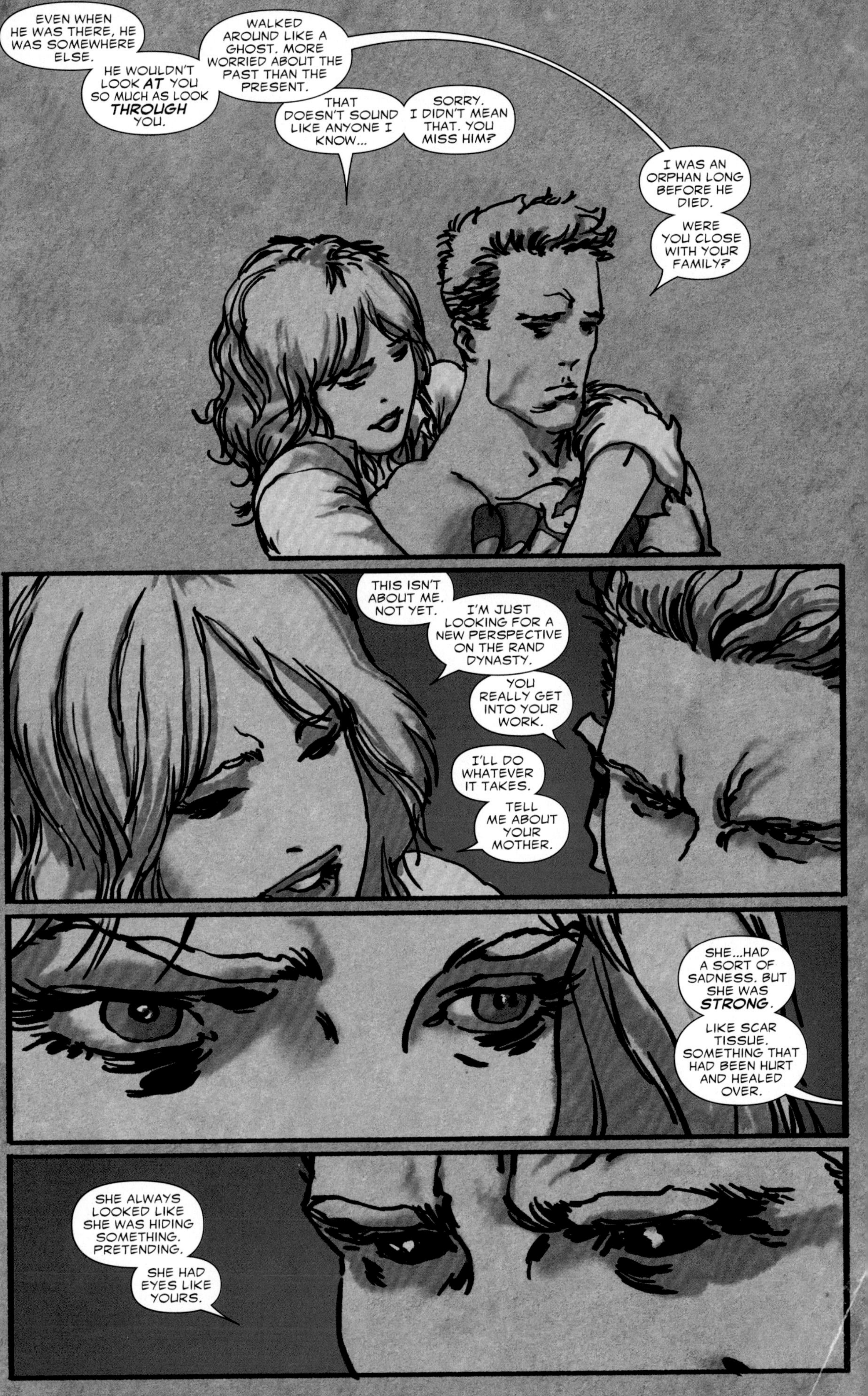
EVEN WHEN HE WAS THERE, HE WAS SOMEWHERE ELSE.
HE WOULDN'T LOOK AT YOU SO MUCH AS LOOK THROUGH YOU.
WALKED AROUND LIKE A GHOST. MORE WORRIED ABOUT THE PAST THAN THE PRESENT.
THAT DOESN'T SOUND LIKE ANYONE I KNOW...
SORRY. I DIDN'T MEAN THAT. YOU MISS HIM?
I WAS AN ORPHAN LONG BEFORE HE DIED.
WERE YOU CLOSE WITH YOUR FAMILY?
THIS ISN'T ABOUT ME. NOT YET.
I'M JUST LOOKING FOR A NEW PERSPECTIVE ON THE RAND DYNASTY.
YOU REALLY GET INTO YOUR WORK.
I'LL DO WHATEVER IT TAKES.
TELL ME ABOUT YOUR MOTHER.
SHE...HAD A SORT OF SADNESS. BUT SHE WAS STRONG.
LIKE SCAR TISSUE. SOMETHING THAT HAD BEEN HURT AND HEALED OVER.
SHE ALWAYS LOOKED LIKE SHE WAS HIDING SOMETHING. PRETENDING.
SHE HAD EYES LIKE YOURS.

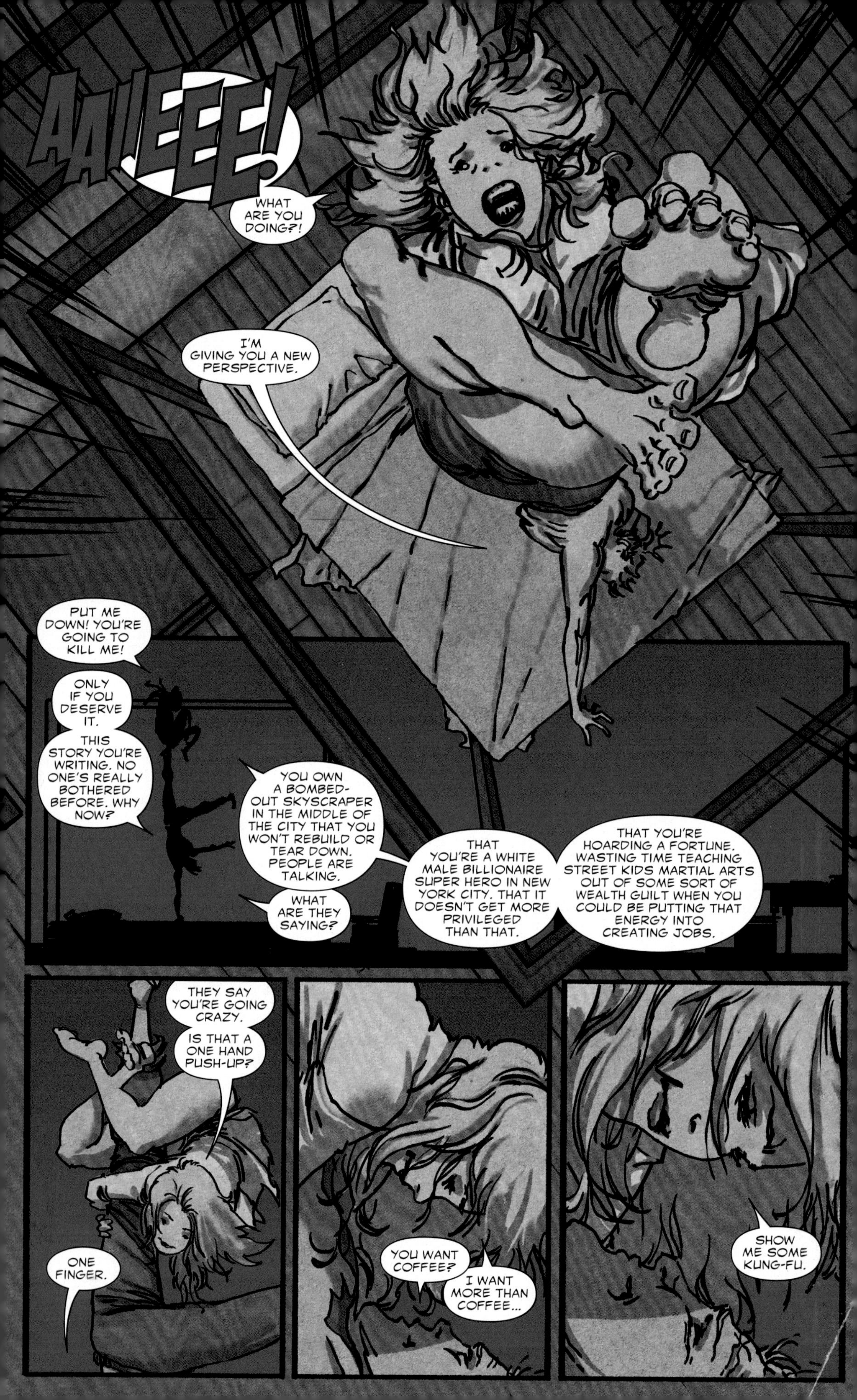
AAIIEEE!
WHAT ARE YOU DOING?!
I'M GIVING YOU A NEW PERSPECTIVE.
PUT ME DOWN! YOU'RE GOING TO KILL ME!
ONLY IF YOU DESERVE IT.
THIS STORY YOU'RE WRITING. NO ONE'S REALLY BOTHERED BEFORE. WHY NOW?
YOU OWN A BOMBED-OUT SKYSCRAPER IN THE MIDDLE OF THE CITY THAT YOU WON'T REBUILD OR TEAR DOWN. PEOPLE ARE TALKING.
WHAT ARE THEY SAYING?
THAT YOU'RE A WHITE MALE BILLIONAIRE SUPER HERO IN NEW YORK CITY. THAT IT DOESN'T GET MORE PRIVILEGED THAN THAT.
THAT YOU'RE HOARDING A FORTUNE. WASTING TIME TEACHING STREET KIDS MARTIAL ARTS OUT OF SOME SORT OF WEALTH GUILT WHEN YOU COULD BE PUTTING THAT ENERGY INTO CREATING JOBS.
THEY SAY YOU'RE GOING CRAZY.
IS THAT A ONE HAND PUSH-UP?
ONE FINGER.
YOU WANT COFFEE?
I WANT MORE THAN COFFEE...
SHOW ME SOME KUNG-FU.

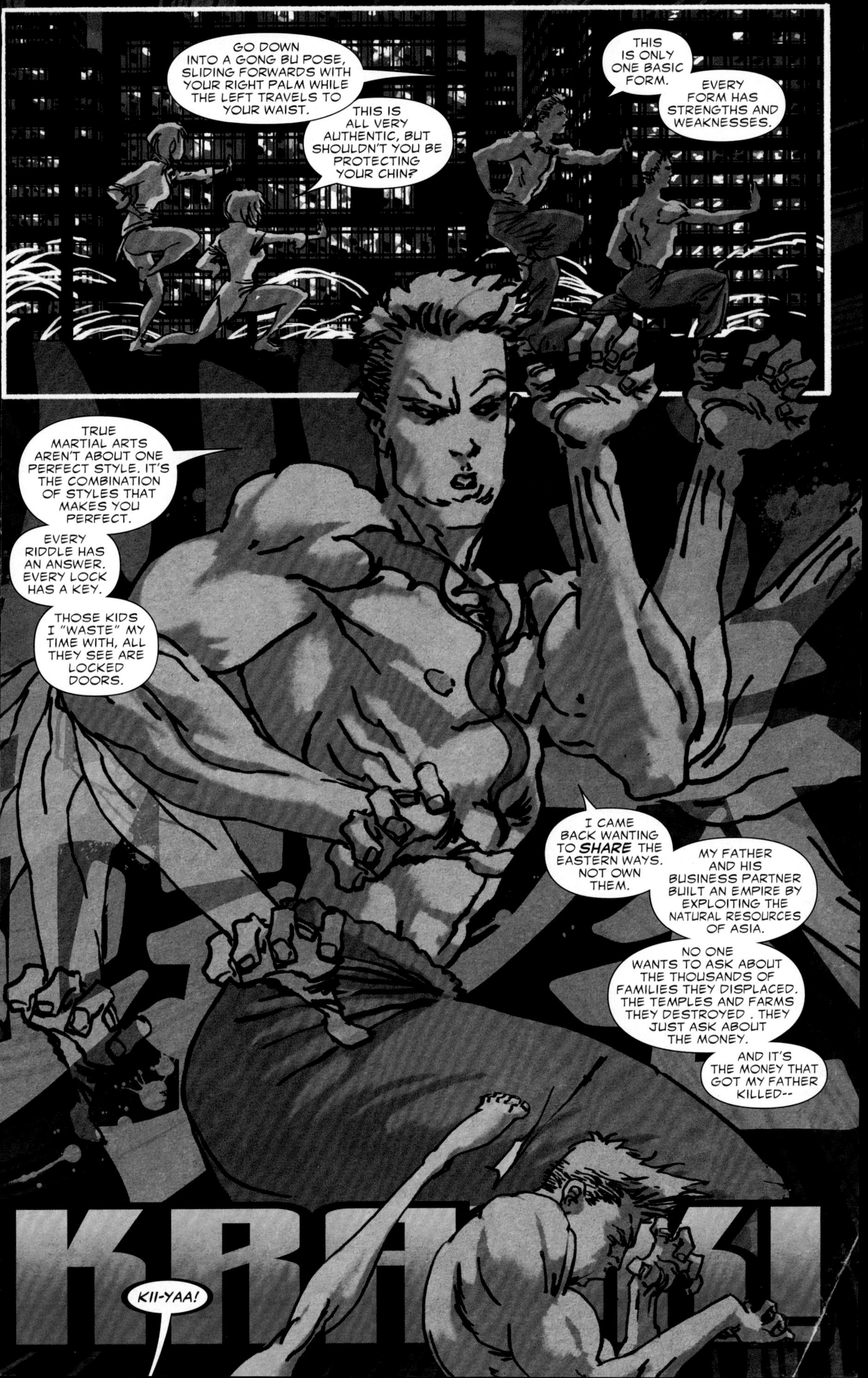
GO DOWN INTO A GONG BU POSE, SLIDING FORWARDS WITH YOUR RIGHT PALM WHILE THE LEFT TRAVELS TO YOUR WAIST.
THIS IS ALL VERY AUTHENTIC, BUT SHOULDN'T YOU BE PROTECTING YOUR CHIN?
THIS IS ONLY ONE BASIC FORM.
EVERY FORM HAS STRENGTHS AND WEAKNESSES.
TRUE MARTIAL ARTS AREN'T ABOUT ONE PERFECT STYLE. IT'S THE COMBINATION OF STYLES THAT MAKES YOU PERFECT.
EVERY RIDDLE HAS AN ANSWER. EVERY LOCK HAS A KEY.
THOSE KIDS I "WASTE" MY TIME WITH, ALL THEY SEE ARE LOCKED DOORS.
I CAME BACK WANTING TO SHARE THE EASTERN WAYS. NOT OWN THEM.
MY FATHER AND HIS BUSINESS PARTNER BUILT AN EMPIRE BY EXPLOITING THE NATURAL RESOURCES OF ASIA.
NO ONE WANTS TO ASK ABOUT THE THOUSANDS OF FAMILIES THEY DISPLACED. THE TEMPLES AND FARMS THEY DESTROYED . THEY JUST ASK ABOUT THE MONEY.
AND IT'S THE MONEY THAT GOT MY FATHER KILLED--
KII-YAA!

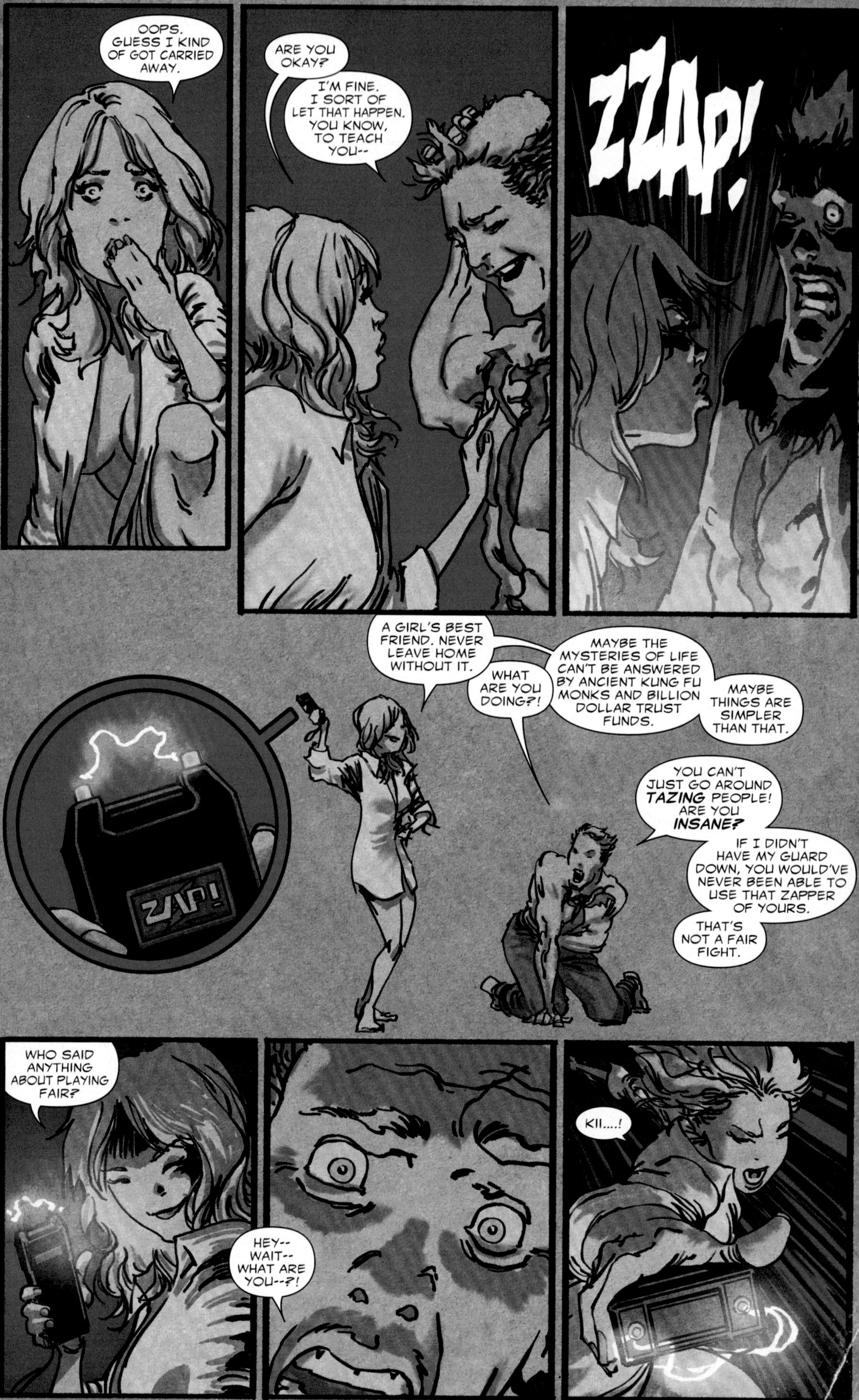

OOPS. GUESS I KIND OF GOT CARRIED AWAY.
ARE YOU OKAY?
I'M FINE. I SORT OF LET THAT HAPPEN. YOU KNOW, TO TEACH YOU--
ZZAP!
A GIRL'S BEST FRIEND. NEVER LEAVE HOME WITHOUT IT.
ZAP!
WHAT ARE YOU DOING?!
MAYBE THE MYSTERIES OF LIFE CAN'T BE ANSWERED BY ANCIENT KUNG FU MONKS AND BILLION DOLLAR TRUST FUNDS.
MAYBE THINGS ARE SIMPLER THAN THAT.
YOU CAN'T JUST GO AROUND TAZING PEOPLE! ARE YOU INSANE?
IF I DIDN'T HAVE MY GUARD DOWN, YOU WOULD'VE NEVER BEEN ABLE TO USE THAT ZAPPER OF YOURS.
THAT'S NOT A FAIR FIGHT.
WHO SAID ANYTHING ABOUT PLAYING FAIR?
HEY-- WAIT-- WHAT ARE YOU--?!
KII....!

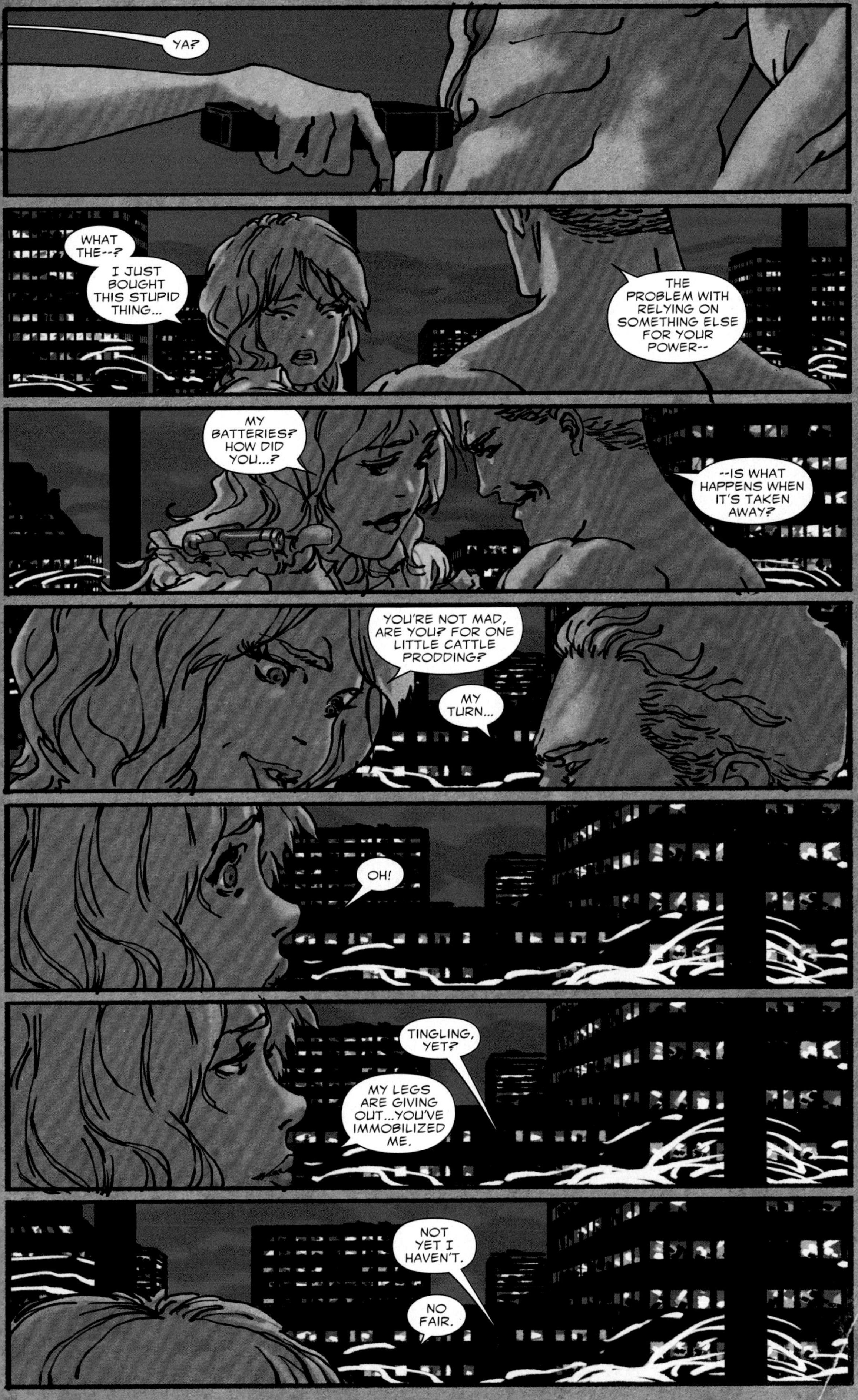
YA?
WHAT THE--? I JUST BOUGHT THIS STUPID THING...
THE PROBLEM WITH RELYING ON SOMETHING ELSE FOR YOUR POWER--
MY BATTERIES? HOW DID YOU...?
--IS WHAT HAPPENS WHEN IT'S TAKEN AWAY?
YOU'RE NOT MAD, ARE YOU? FOR ONE LITTLE CATTLE PRODDING?
MY TURN...
OH!
TINGLING, YET?
MY LEGS ARE GIVING OUT...YOU'VE IMMOBILIZED ME.
NOT YET I HAVEN'T.
NO FAIR.

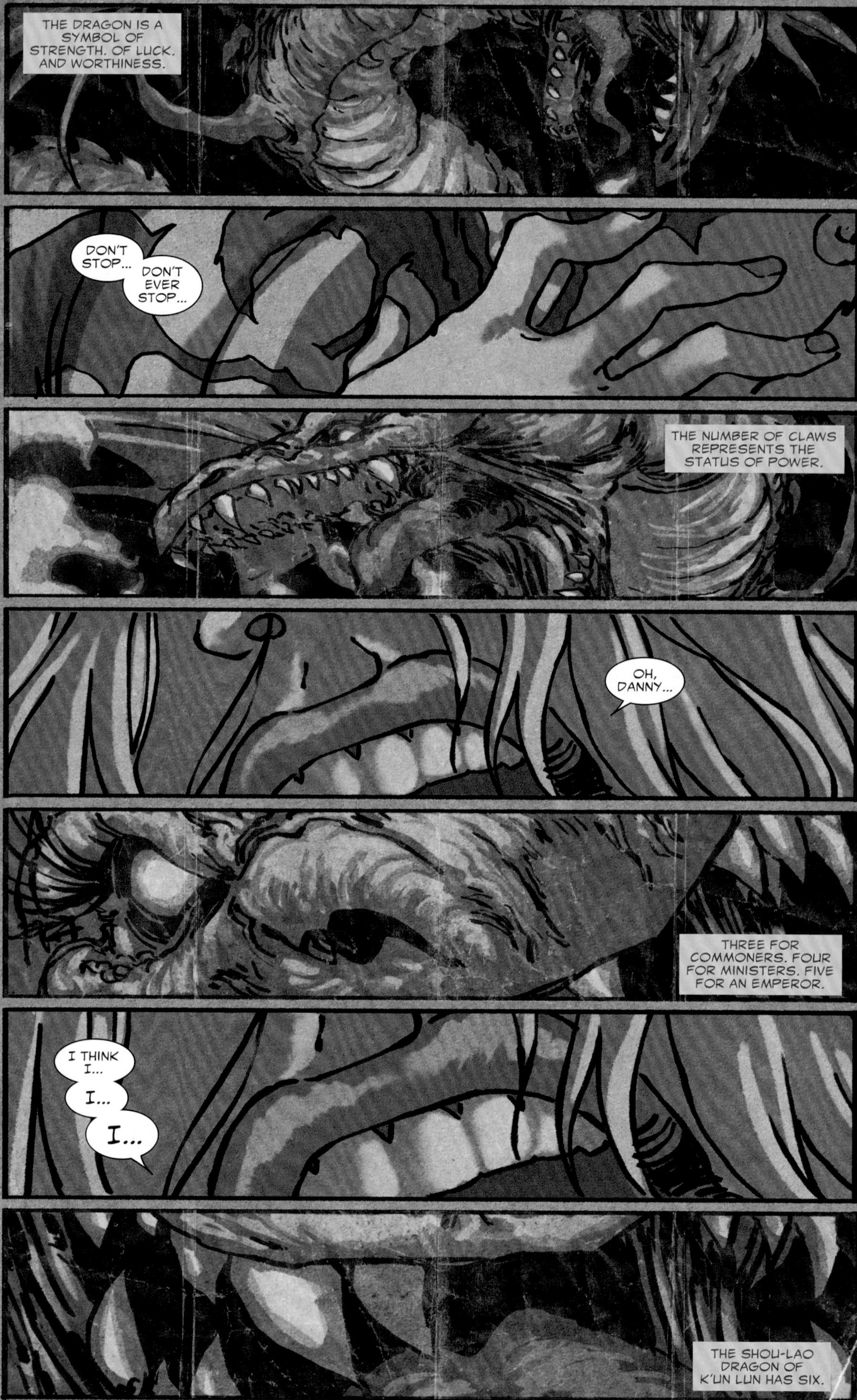
THE DRAGON IS A SYMBOL OF STRENGTH. OF LUCK. AND WORTHINESS.
DON'T STOP...
DON'T EVER STOP...
THE NUMBER OF CLAWS REPRESENTS THE STATUS OF POWER.
OH, DANNY...
THREE FOR COMMONERS. FOUR FOR MINISTERS. FIVE FOR AN EMPEROR.
I THINK I...
I...
I...
THE SHOU-LAO DRAGON OF K'UN LUN HAS SIX.

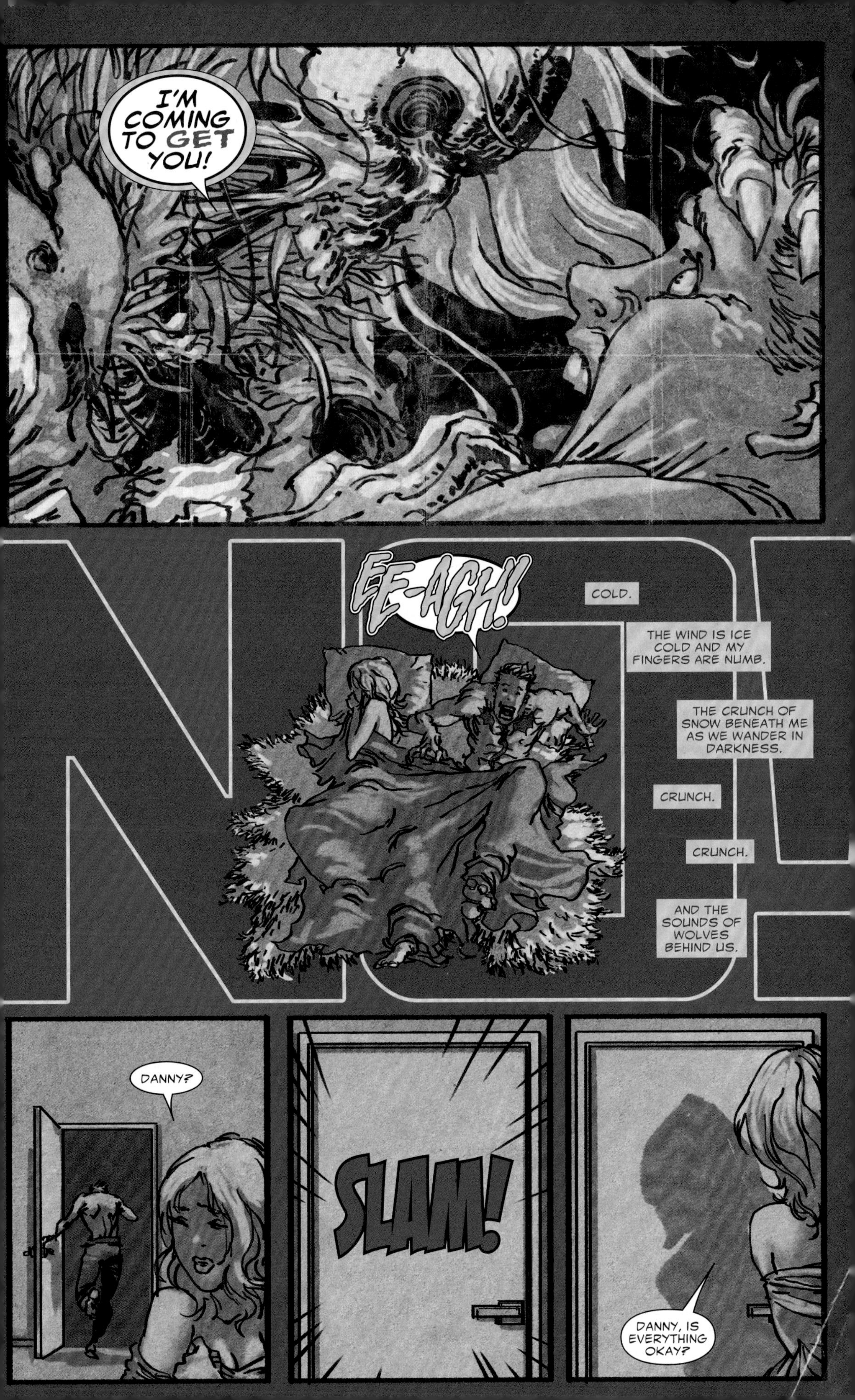
I'M COMING TO GET YOU!
NO!
EE-AGH!
COLD.
THE WIND IS ICE COLD AND MY FINGERS ARE NUMB.
THE CRUNCH OF SNOW BENEATH ME AS WE WANDER IN DARKNESS.
CRUNCH.
CRUNCH.
AND THE SOUNDS OF WOLVES BEHIND US.
DANNY?
SLAM!
DANNY, IS EVERYTHING OKAY?

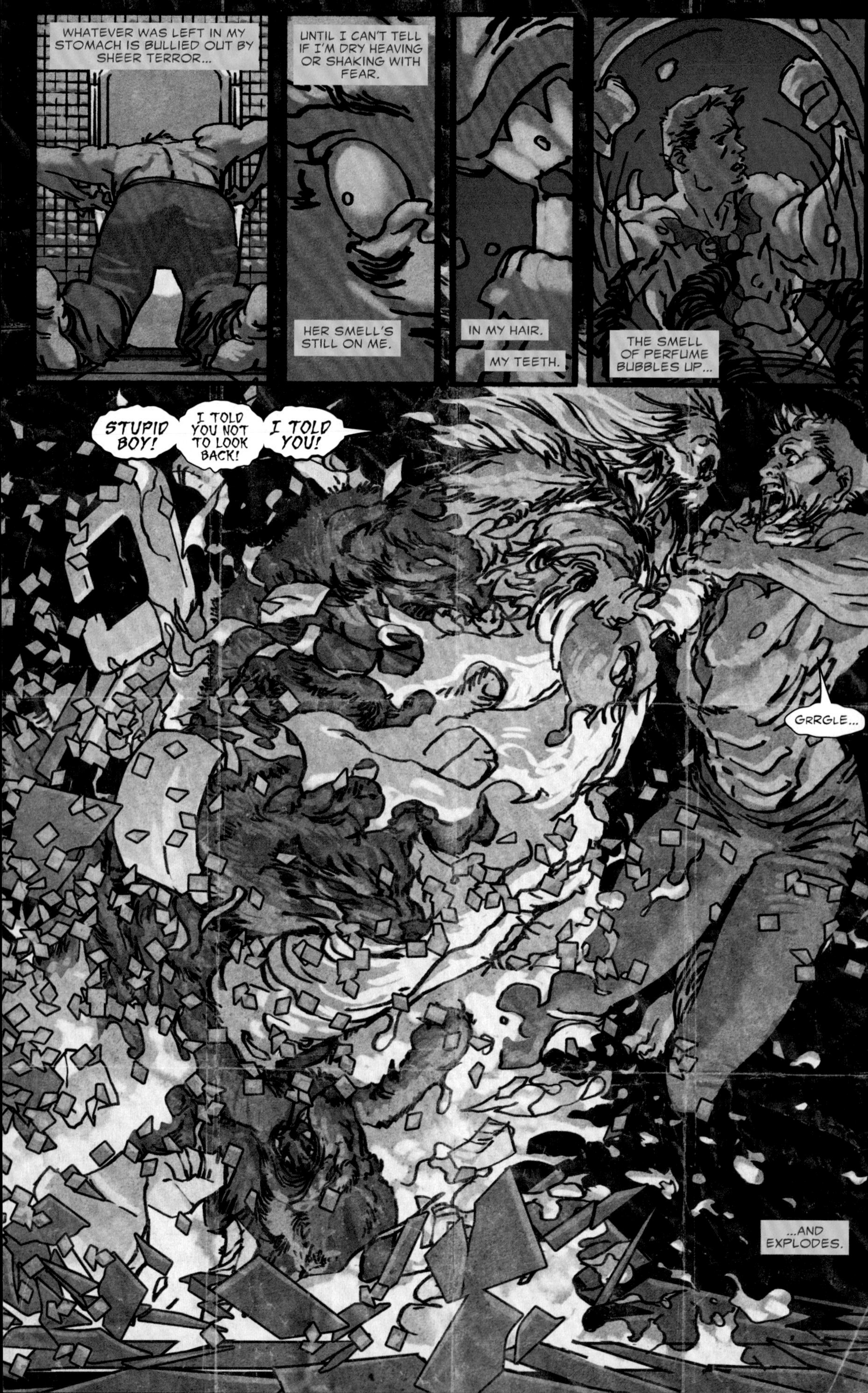
WHATEVER WAS LEFT IN MY STOMACH IS BULLIED OUT BY SHEER TERROR...
UNTIL I CAN'T TELL IF I'M DRY HEAVING OR SHAKING WITH FEAR.
HER SMELL'S STILL ON ME.
IN MY HAIR.
MY TEETH.
THE SMELL OF PERFUME BUBBLES UP...
STUPID BOY!
I TOLD YOU NOT TO LOOK BACK!
I TOLD YOU!
GRRGLE...
...AND EXPLODES.

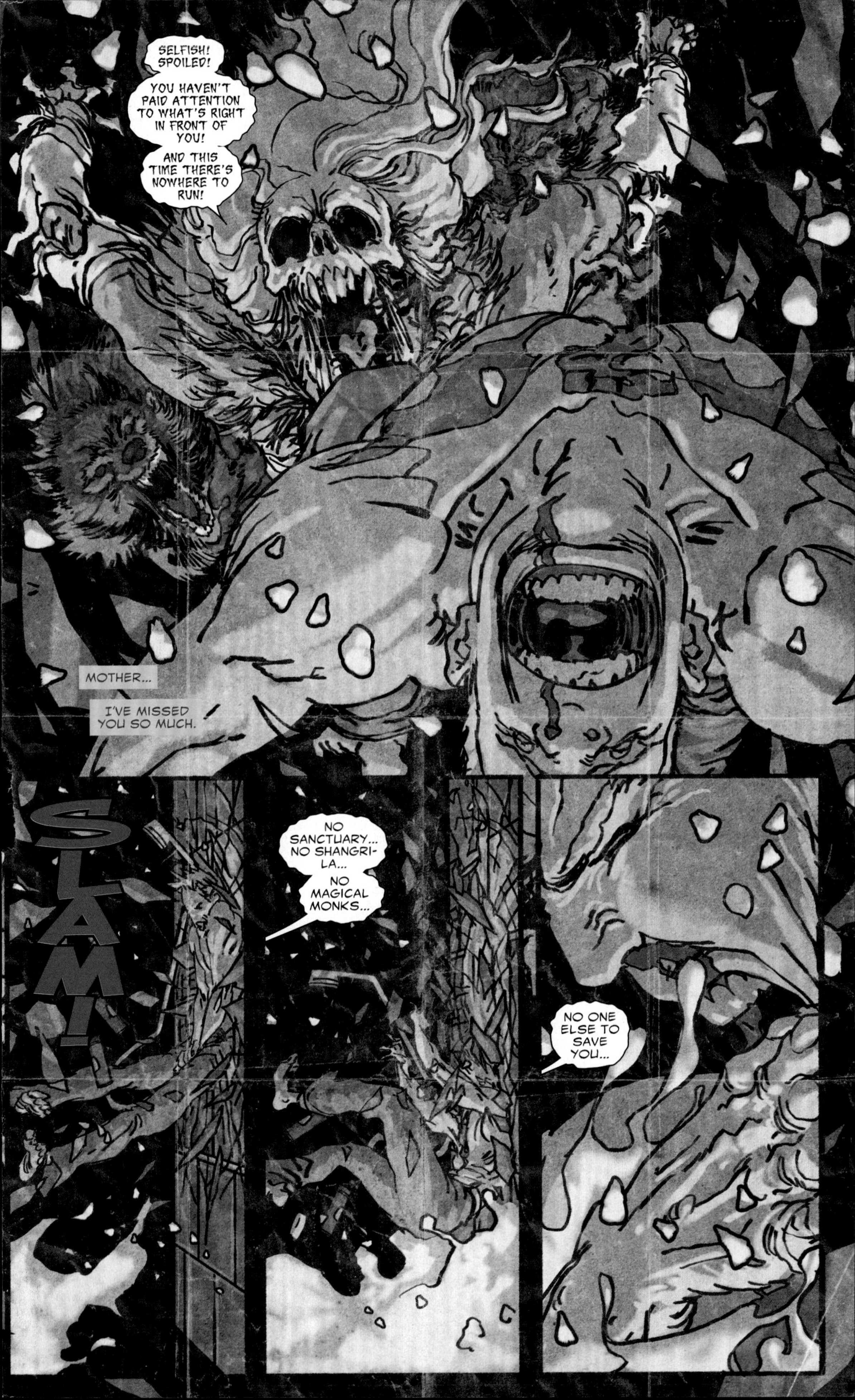
SELFISH! SPOILED!
YOU HAVEN'T PAID ATTENTION TO WHAT'S RIGHT IN FRONT OF YOU!
AND THIS TIME THERE'S NOWHERE TO RUN!
MOTHER...
I'VE MISSED YOU SO MUCH.
SLAM!
NO SANCTUARY... NO SHANGRI-LA...
NO MAGICAL MONKS...
NO ONE ELSE TO SAVE YOU...

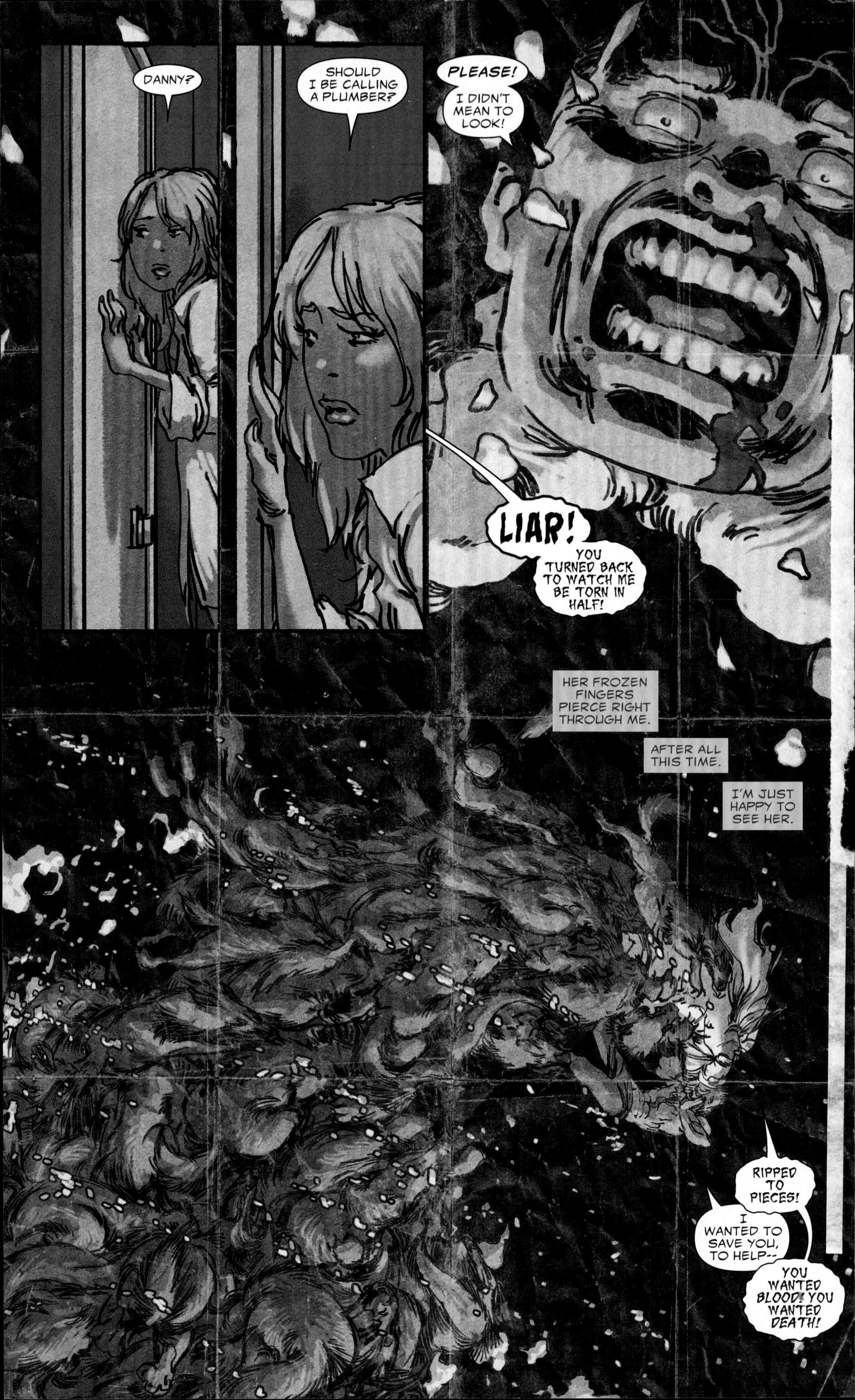

DANNY?
SHOULD I BE CALLING A PLUMBER?
PLEASE! I DIDN'T MEAN TO LOOK!
LIAR! YOU TURNED BACK TO WATCH ME BE TORN IN HALF!
HER FROZEN FINGERS PIERCE RIGHT THROUGH ME.
AFTER ALL THIS TIME.
I'M JUST HAPPY TO SEE HER.
RIPPED TO PIECES!
I WANTED TO SAVE YOU, TO HELP--
YOU WANTED BLOOD! YOU WANTED DEATH!

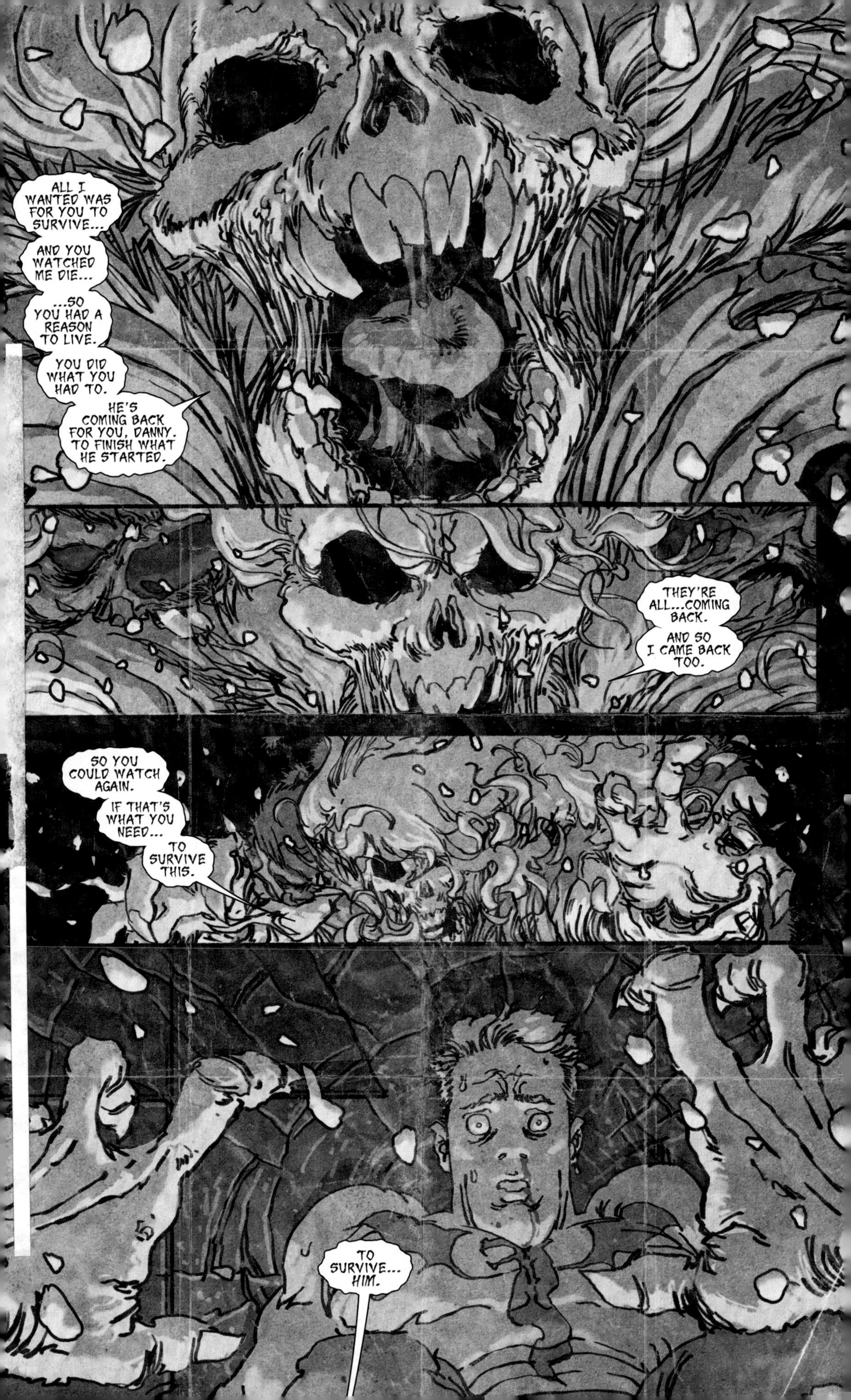
ALL I WANTED WAS FOR YOU TO SURVIVE...
AND YOU WATCHED ME DIE...
...SO YOU HAD A REASON TO LIVE.
YOU DID WHAT YOU HAD TO.
HE'S COMING BACK FOR YOU, DANNY. TO FINISH WHAT HE STARTED.
THEY'RE ALL...COMING BACK.
AND SO I CAME BACK TOO.
SO YOU COULD WATCH AGAIN.
IF THAT'S WHAT YOU NEED...
TO SURVIVE THIS.
TO SURVIVE... HIM.

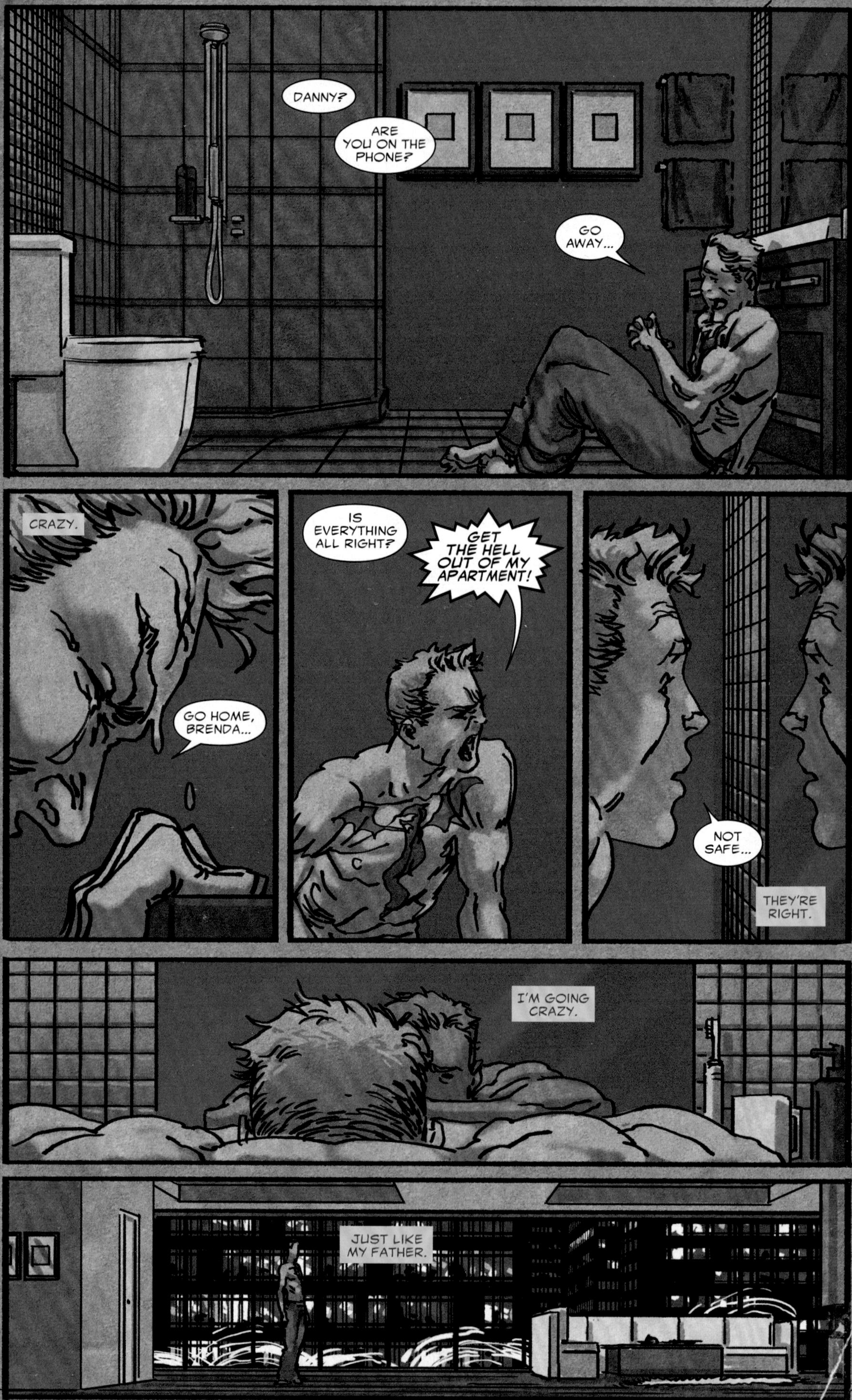
DANNY?
ARE YOU ON THE PHONE?
GO AWAY...
CRAZY.
GO HOME, BRENDA...
IS EVERYTHING ALL RIGHT?
GET THE HELL OUT OF MY APARTMENT!
NOT SAFE...
THEY'RE RIGHT.
I'M GOING CRAZY.
JUST LIKE MY FATHER.

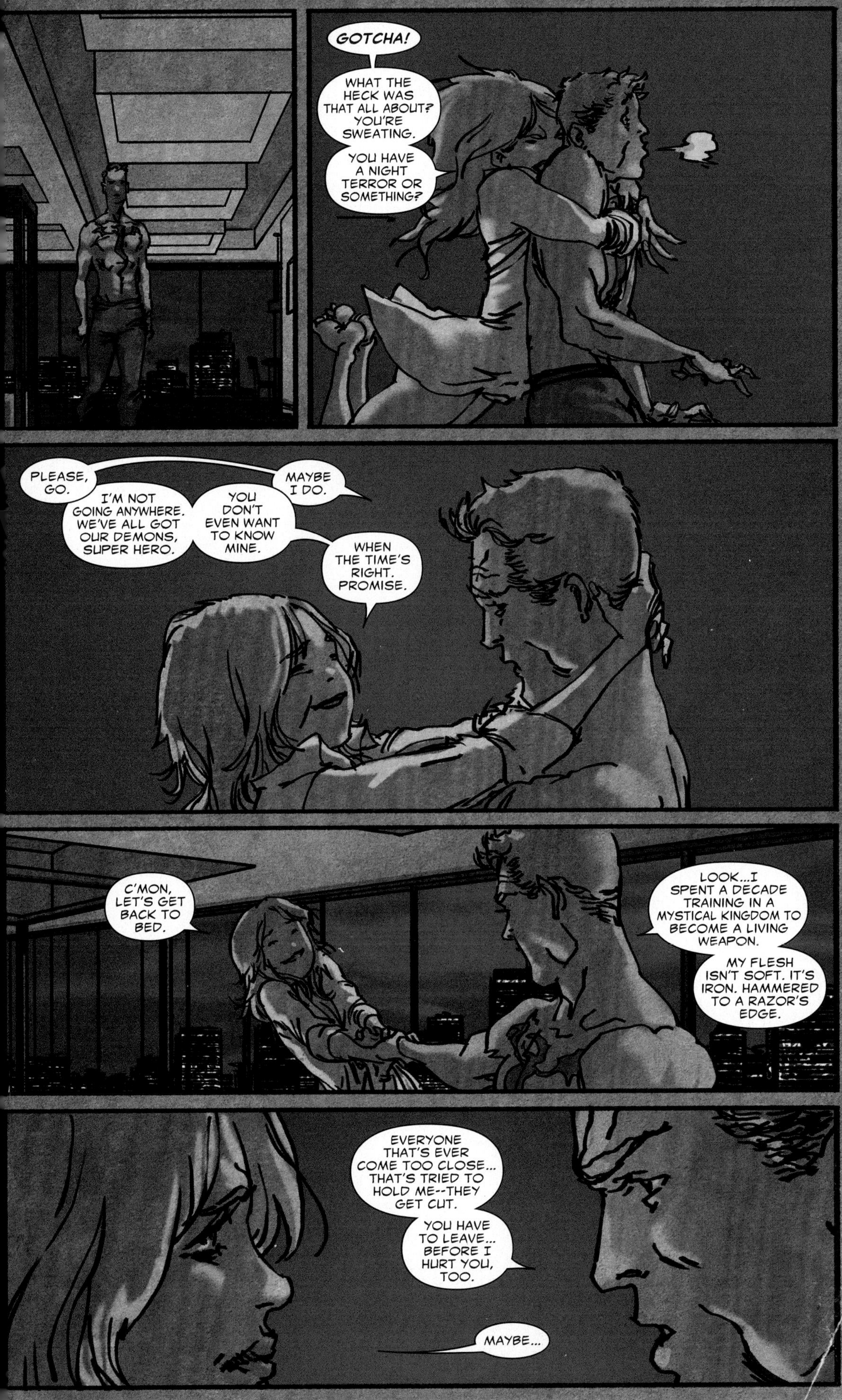
GOTCHA!
WHAT THE HECK WAS THAT ALL ABOUT? YOU'RE SWEATING.
YOU HAVE A NIGHT TERROR OR SOMETHING?
PLEASE, GO.
I'M NOT GOING ANYWHERE. WE'VE ALL GOT OUR DEMONS, SUPER HERO.
YOU DON'T EVEN WANT TO KNOW MINE.
MAYBE I DO.
WHEN THE TIME'S RIGHT. PROMISE.
C'MON, LET'S GET BACK TO BED.
LOOK...I SPENT A DECADE TRAINING IN A MYSTICAL KINGDOM TO BECOME A LIVING WEAPON.
MY FLESH ISN'T SOFT. IT'S IRON. HAMMERED TO A RAZOR'S EDGE.
EVERYONE THAT'S EVER COME TOO CLOSE... THAT'S TRIED TO HOLD ME--THEY GET CUT.
YOU HAVE TO LEAVE... BEFORE I HURT YOU, TOO.
MAYBE...

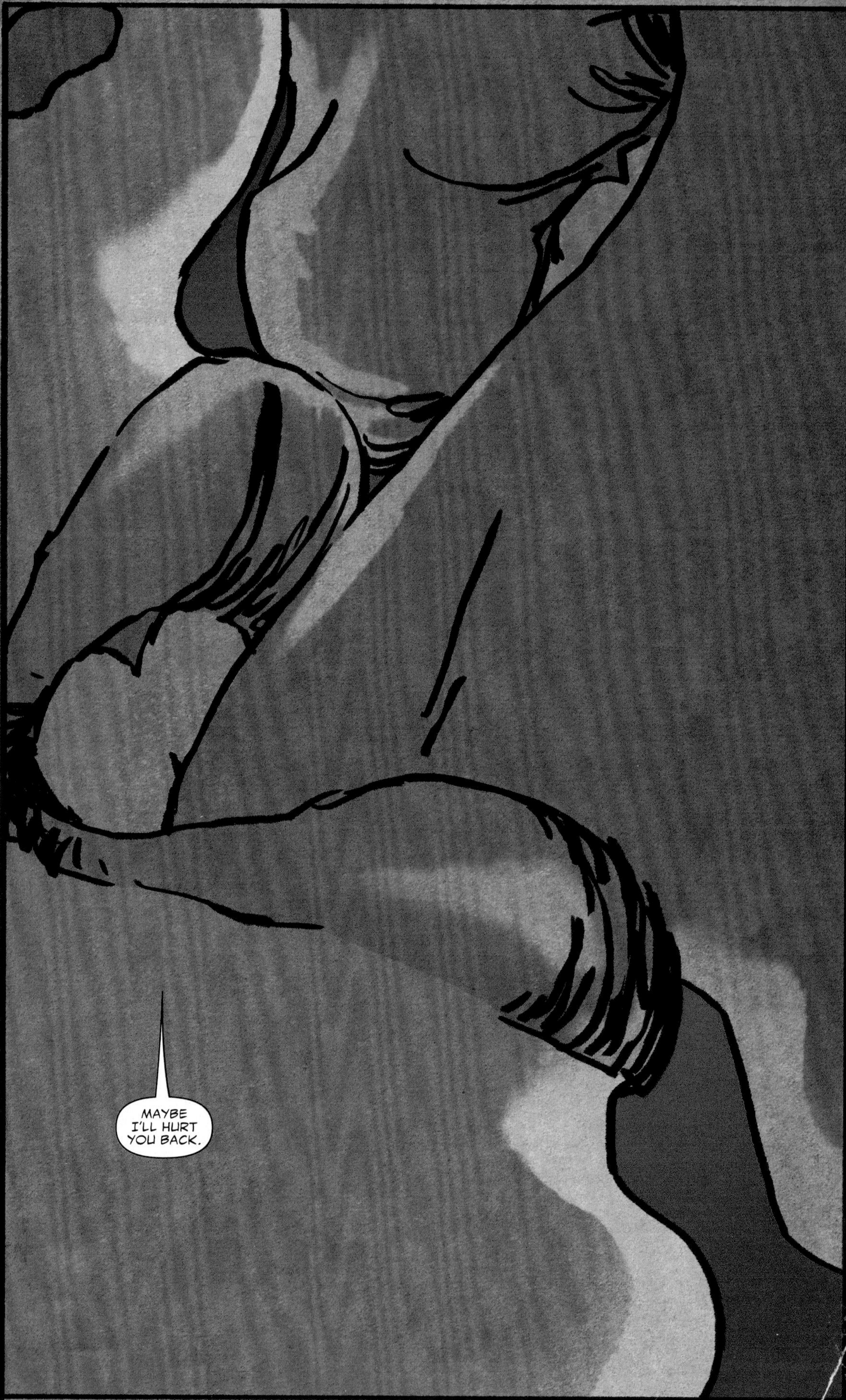
MAYBE I'LL HURT YOU BACK.

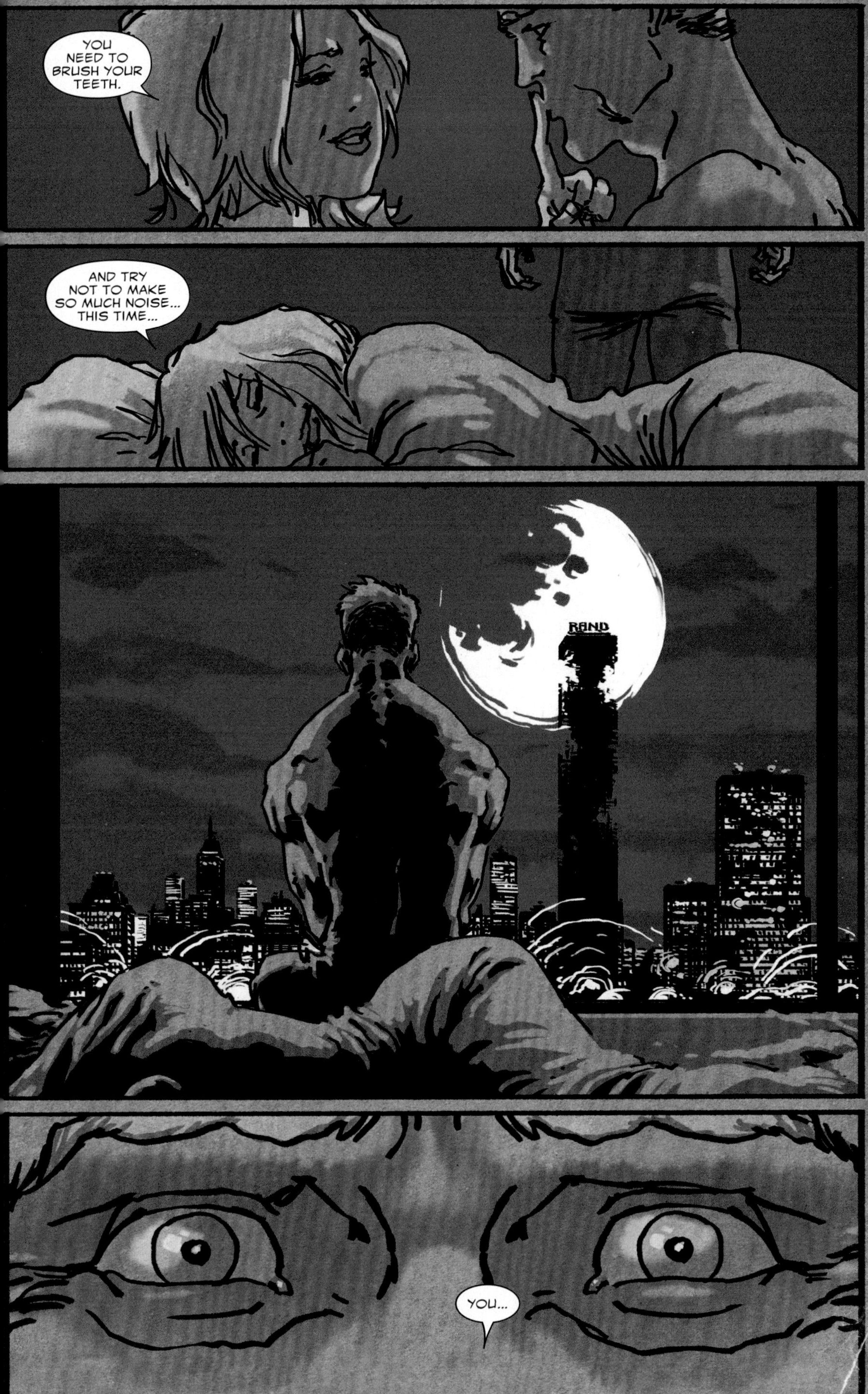
YOU NEED TO BRUSH YOUR TEETH.
AND TRY NOT TO MAKE SO MUCH NOISE... THIS TIME...
RAND
YOU...

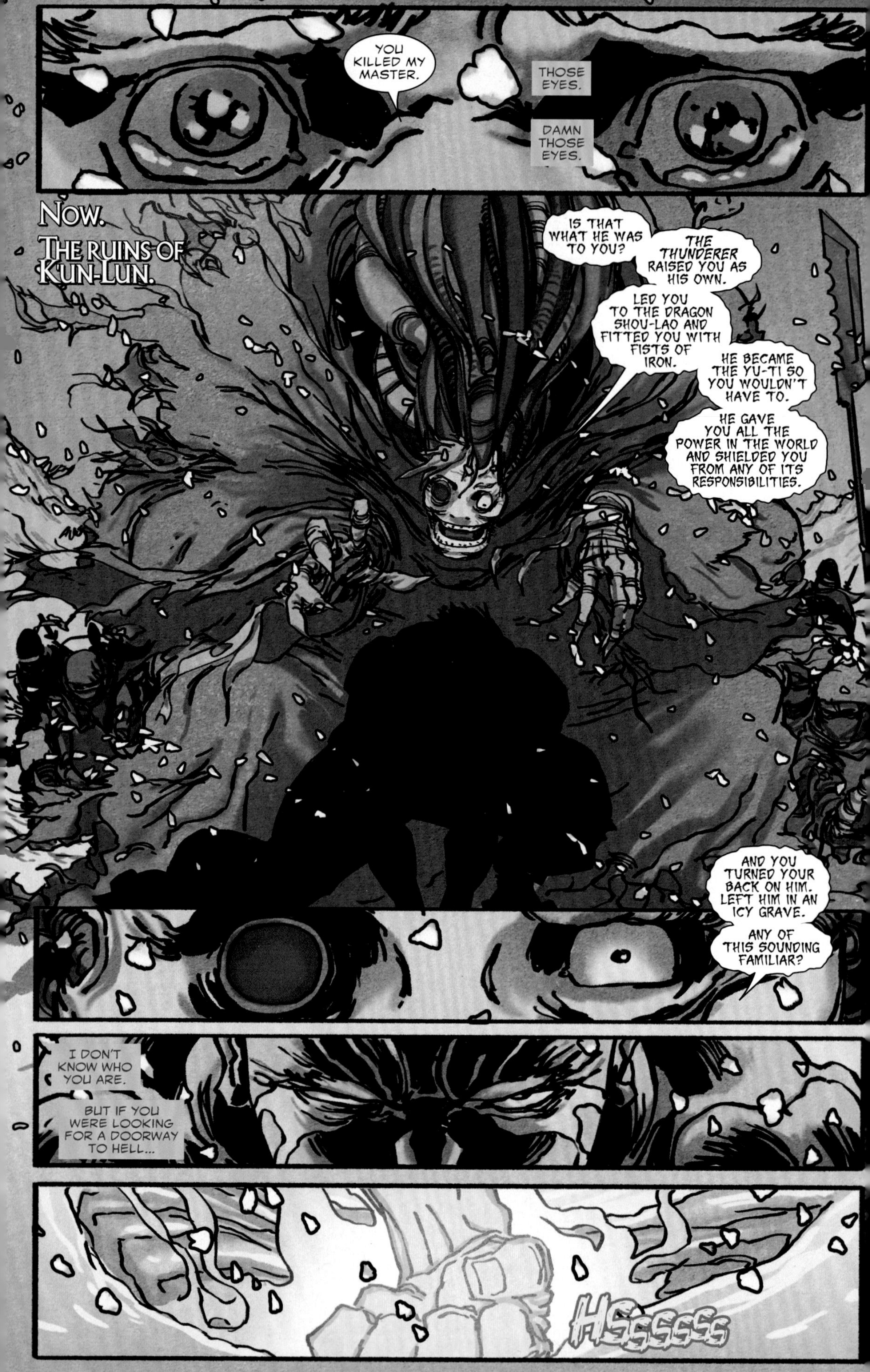
YOU KILLED MY MASTER.
THOSE EYES.
DAMN THOSE EYES.
NOW.
THE RUINS OF K'UN-LUN.
IS THAT WHAT HE WAS TO YOU?
THE THUNDERER RAISED YOU AS HIS OWN.
LED YOU TO THE DRAGON SHOU-LAO AND FITTED YOU WITH FISTS OF IRON.
HE BECAME THE YU-TI SO YOU WOULDN'T HAVE TO.
HE GAVE YOU ALL THE POWER IN THE WORLD AND SHIELDED YOU FROM ANY OF ITS RESPONSIBILITIES.
AND YOU TURNED YOUR BACK ON HIM. LEFT HIM IN AN ICY GRAVE.
ANY OF THIS SOUNDING FAMILIAR?
I DON'T KNOW WHO YOU ARE.
BUT IF YOU WERE LOOKING FOR A DOORWAY TO HELL...
HSSSSSS

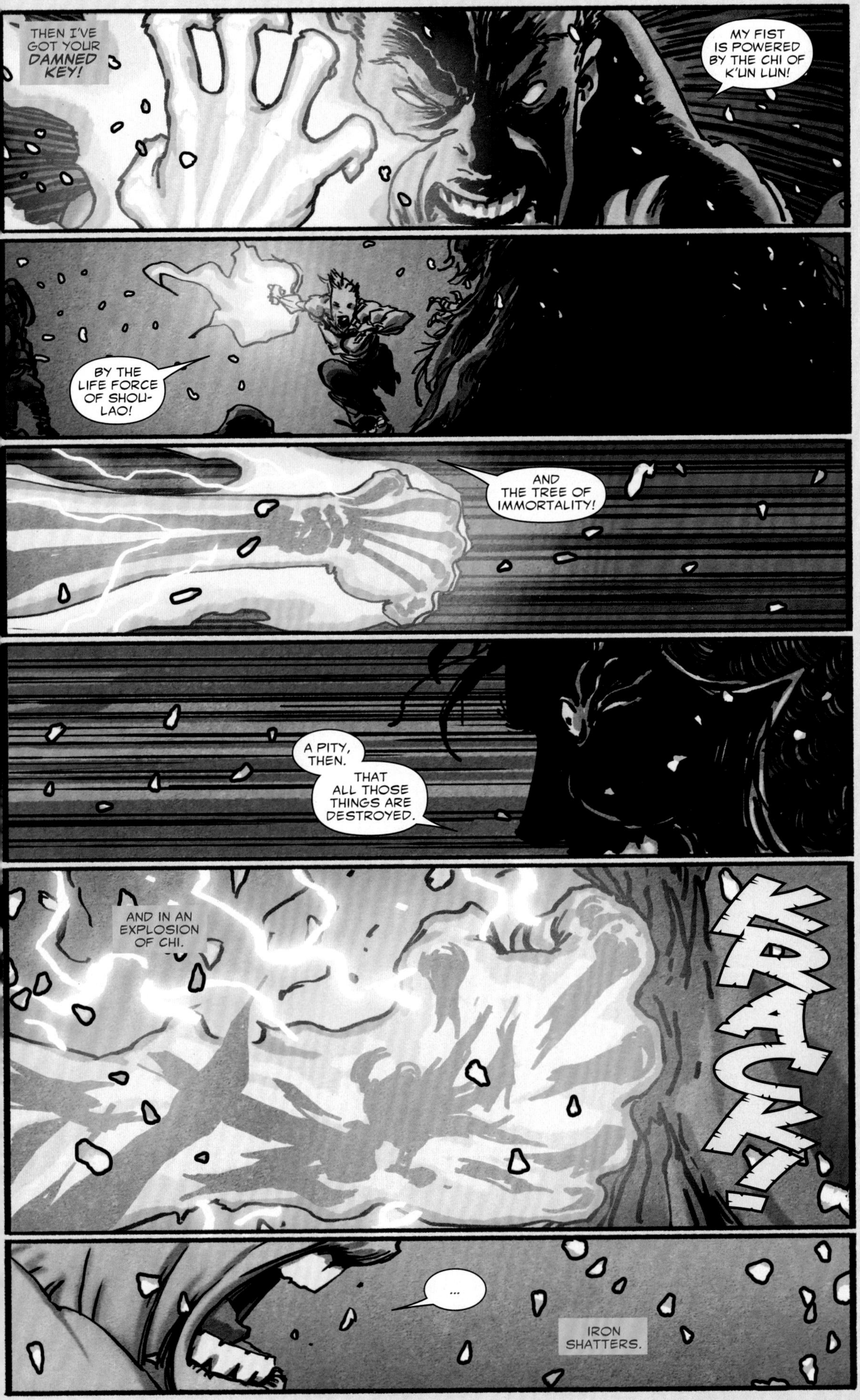

THEN I'VE GOT YOUR *DAMNED* KEY!
MY FIST IS POWERED BY THE CHI OF K'UN LUN!
BY THE LIFE FORCE OF SHOU-LAO!
AND THE TREE OF IMMORTALITY!
A PITY, THEN.
THAT ALL THOSE THINGS ARE DESTROYED.
AND IN AN EXPLOSION OF CHI.
KRACK!!
...
IRON SHATTERS.

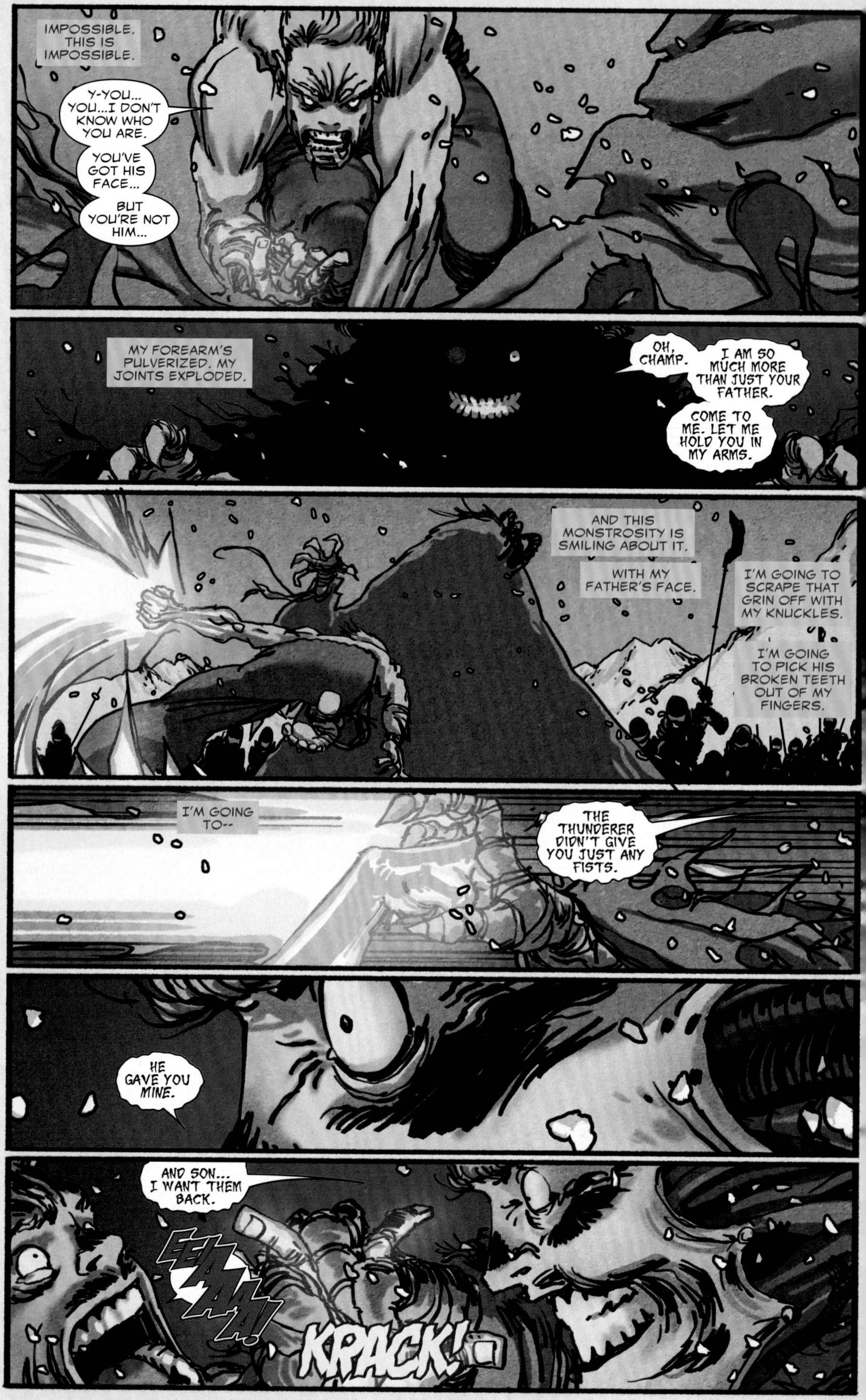

IMPOSSIBLE. THIS IS IMPOSSIBLE.
Y-YOU... YOU...I DON'T KNOW WHO YOU ARE.
YOU'VE GOT HIS FACE...
BUT YOU'RE NOT HIM...
MY FOREARM'S PULVERIZED. MY JOINTS EXPLODED.
OH, CHAMP.
I AM SO MUCH MORE THAN JUST YOUR FATHER.
COME TO ME. LET ME HOLD YOU IN MY ARMS.
AND THIS MONSTROSITY IS SMILING ABOUT IT.
WITH MY FATHER'S FACE.
I'M GOING TO SCRAPE THAT GRIN OFF WITH MY KNUCKLES.
I'M GOING TO PICK HIS BROKEN TEETH OUT OF MY FINGERS.
I'M GOING TO--
THE THUNDERER DIDN'T GIVE YOU JUST ANY FISTS.
HE GAVE YOU MINE.
AND SON... I WANT THEM BACK.
EEAAAA!
KRACK!

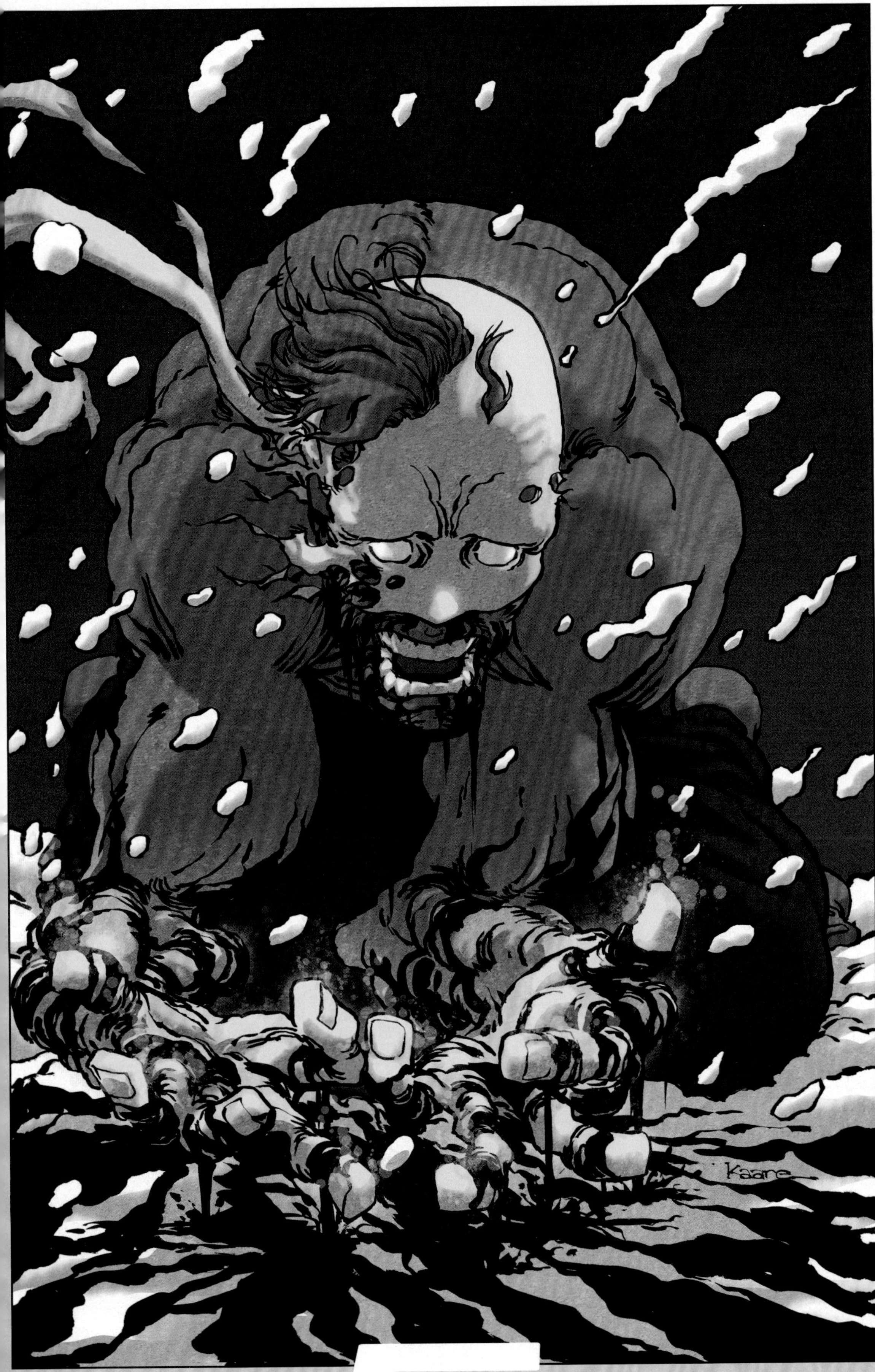
Kaare

5

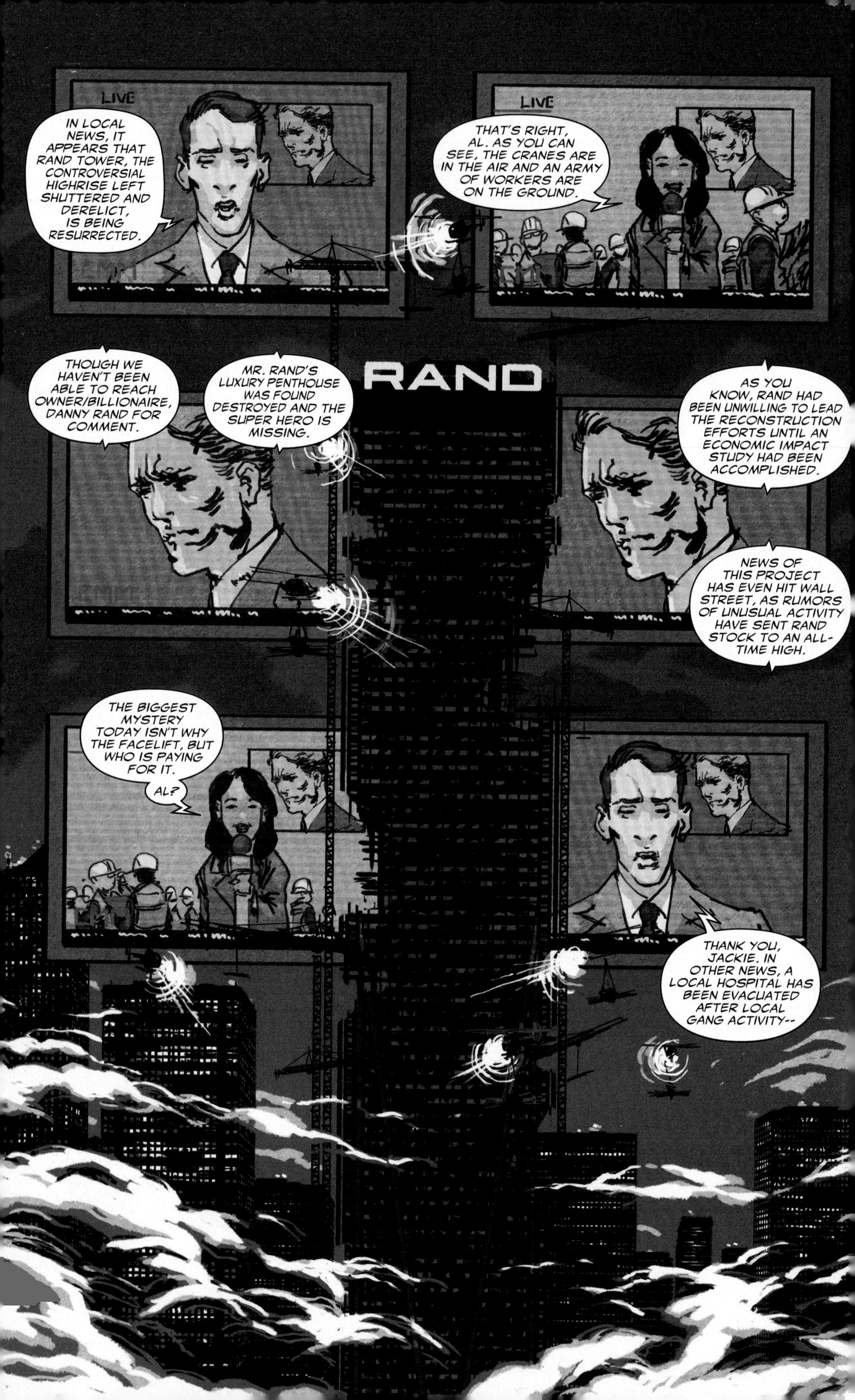
LIVE
IN LOCAL NEWS, IT APPEARS THAT RAND TOWER, THE CONTROVERSIAL HIGHRISE LEFT SHUTTERED AND DERELICT, IS BEING RESURRECTED.
LIVE
THAT'S RIGHT, AL. AS YOU CAN SEE, THE CRANES ARE IN THE AIR AND AN ARMY OF WORKERS ARE ON THE GROUND.
RAND
THOUGH WE HAVEN'T BEEN ABLE TO REACH OWNER/BILLIONAIRE, DANNY RAND FOR COMMENT.
MR. RAND'S LUXURY PENTHOUSE WAS FOUND DESTROYED AND THE SUPER HERO IS MISSING.
AS YOU KNOW, RAND HAD BEEN UNWILLING TO LEAD THE RECONSTRUCTION EFFORTS UNTIL AN ECONOMIC IMPACT STUDY HAD BEEN ACCOMPLISHED.
NEWS OF THIS PROJECT HAS EVEN HIT WALL STREET, AS RUMORS OF UNUSUAL ACTIVITY HAVE SENT RAND STOCK TO AN ALL-TIME HIGH.
THE BIGGEST MYSTERY TODAY ISN'T WHY THE FACELIFT, BUT WHO IS PAYING FOR IT.
AL?
THANK YOU, JACKIE. IN OTHER NEWS, A LOCAL HOSPITAL HAS BEEN EVACUATED AFTER LOCAL GANG ACTIVITY--

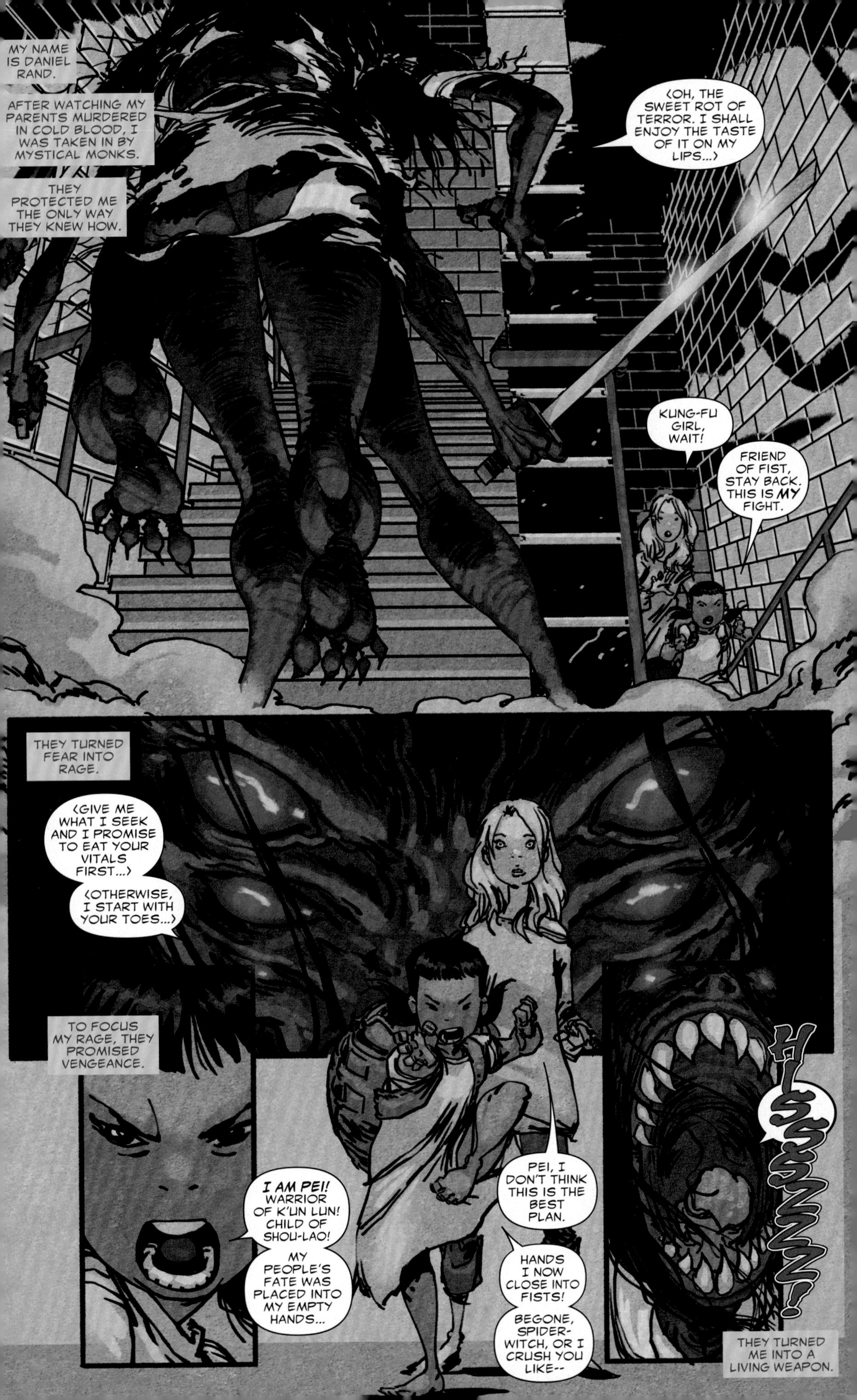

MY NAME IS DANIEL RAND.
AFTER WATCHING MY PARENTS MURDERED IN COLD BLOOD, I WAS TAKEN IN BY MYSTICAL MONKS.
THEY PROTECTED ME THE ONLY WAY THEY KNEW HOW.
‹OH, THE SWEET ROT OF TERROR. I SHALL ENJOY THE TASTE OF IT ON MY LIPS...›
KUNG-FU GIRL, WAIT!
FRIEND OF FIST, STAY BACK. THIS IS *MY* FIGHT.
THEY TURNED FEAR INTO RAGE.
‹GIVE ME WHAT I SEEK AND I PROMISE TO EAT YOUR VITALS FIRST...›
‹OTHERWISE, I START WITH YOUR TOES...›
TO FOCUS MY RAGE, THEY PROMISED VENGEANCE.
I AM PEI! WARRIOR OF K'UN LUN! CHILD OF SHOU-LAO!
MY PEOPLE'S FATE WAS PLACED INTO MY EMPTY HANDS...
PEI, I DON'T THINK THIS IS THE BEST PLAN.
HANDS I NOW CLOSE INTO FISTS!
BEGONE, SPIDER-WITCH, OR I CRUSH YOU LIKE--
HISSSZZZZ!
THEY TURNED ME INTO A LIVING WEAPON.

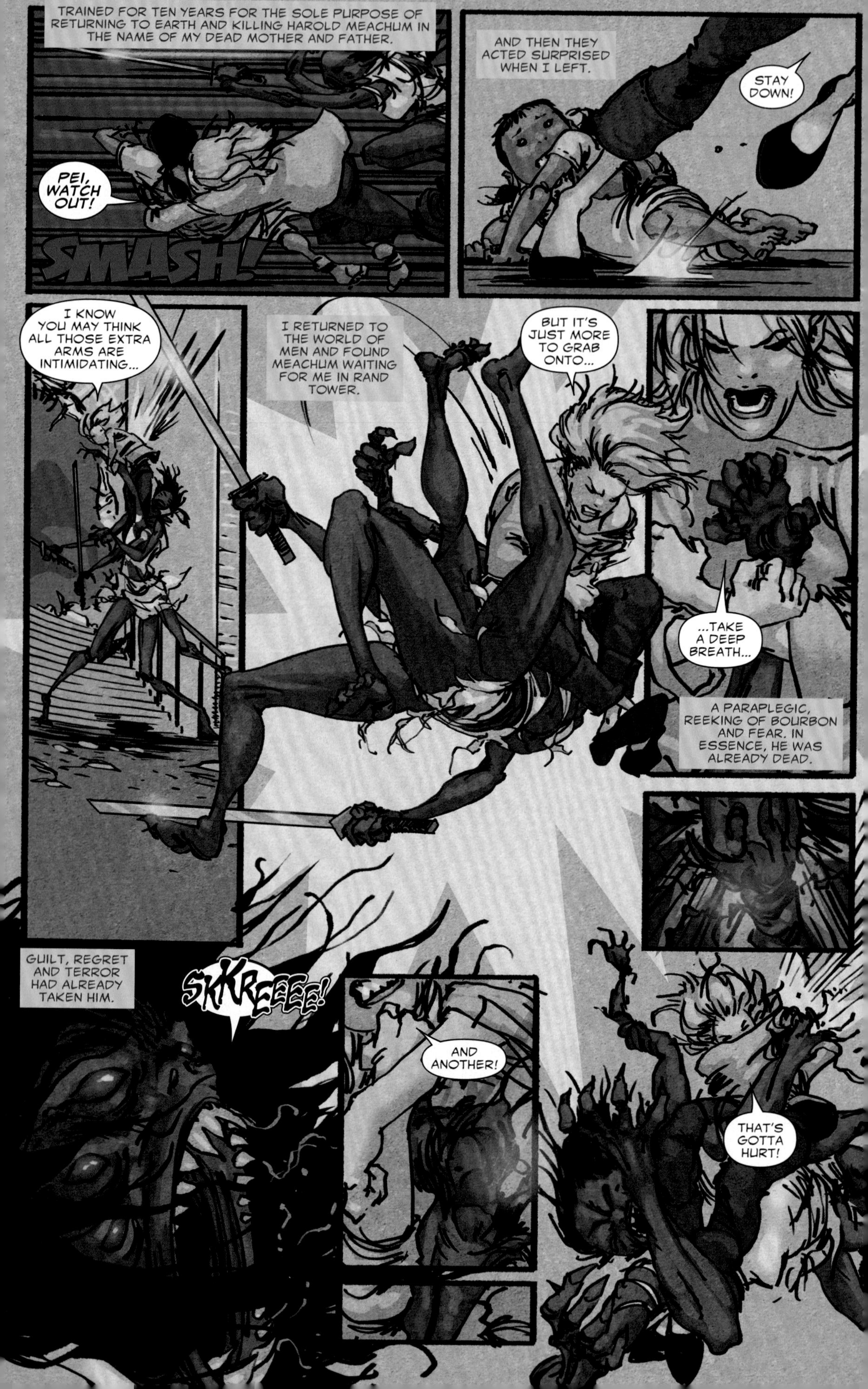
TRAINED FOR TEN YEARS FOR THE SOLE PURPOSE OF RETURNING TO EARTH AND KILLING HAROLD MEACHUM IN THE NAME OF MY DEAD MOTHER AND FATHER.
PEI, WATCH OUT!
SMASH!
AND THEN THEY ACTED SURPRISED WHEN I LEFT.
STAY DOWN!
I KNOW YOU MAY THINK ALL THOSE EXTRA ARMS ARE INTIMIDATING...
I RETURNED TO THE WORLD OF MEN AND FOUND MEACHUM WAITING FOR ME IN RAND TOWER.
BUT IT'S JUST MORE TO GRAB ONTO...
...TAKE A DEEP BREATH...
A PARAPLEGIC, REEKING OF BOURBON AND FEAR. IN ESSENCE, HE WAS ALREADY DEAD.
GUILT, REGRET AND TERROR HAD ALREADY TAKEN HIM.
SKKREEEEE!
AND ANOTHER!
THAT'S GOTTA HURT!

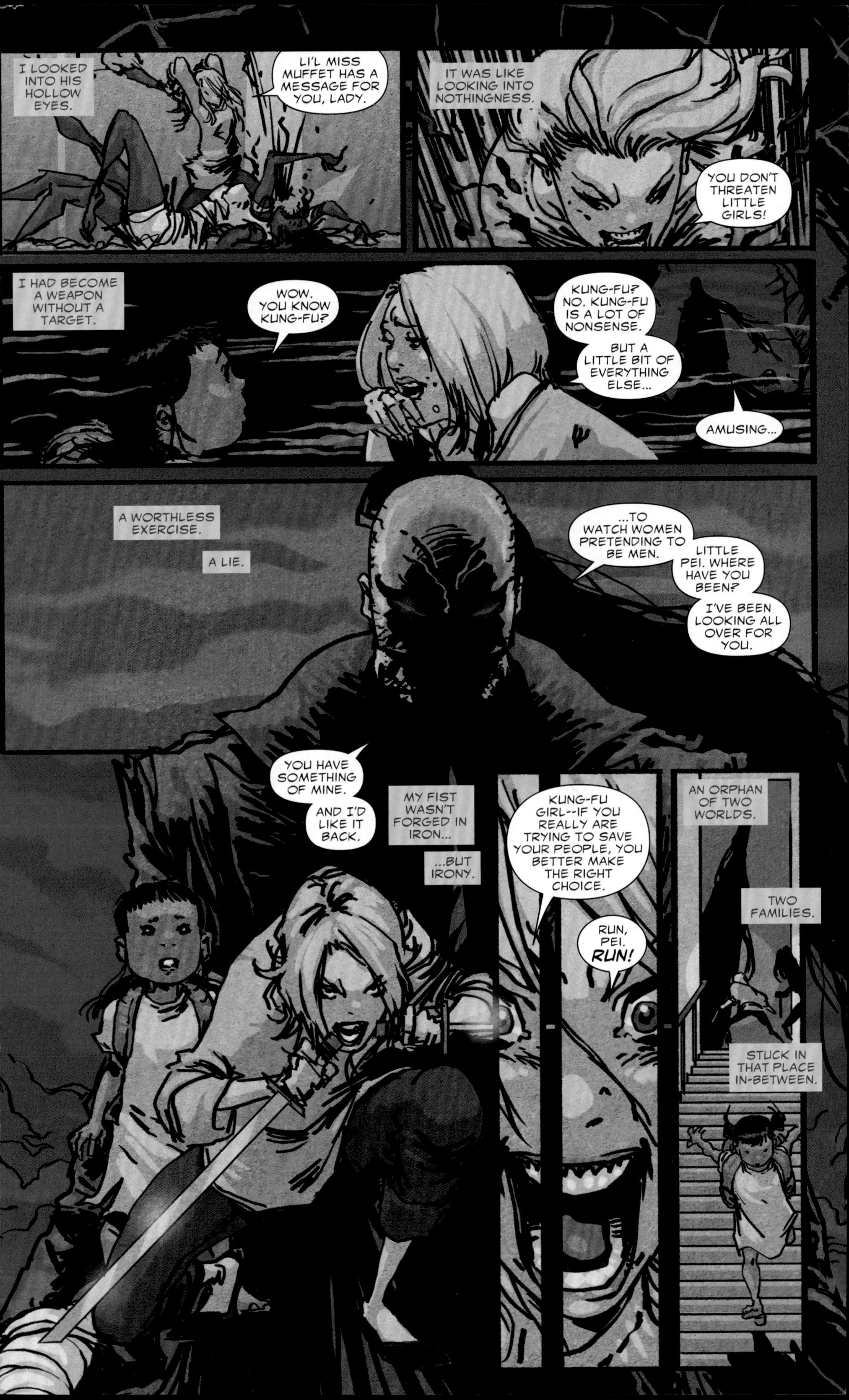

I LOOKED INTO HIS HOLLOW EYES.
LI'L MISS MUFFET HAS A MESSAGE FOR YOU, LADY.
IT WAS LIKE LOOKING INTO NOTHINGNESS.
YOU DON'T THREATEN LITTLE GIRLS!
I HAD BECOME A WEAPON WITHOUT A TARGET.
WOW. YOU KNOW KUNG-FU?
KUNG-FU? NO. KUNG-FU IS A LOT OF NONSENSE.
BUT A LITTLE BIT OF EVERYTHING ELSE...
AMUSING...
A WORTHLESS EXERCISE.
A LIE.
...TO WATCH WOMEN PRETENDING TO BE MEN.
LITTLE PEI. WHERE HAVE YOU BEEN?
I'VE BEEN LOOKING ALL OVER FOR YOU.
YOU HAVE SOMETHING OF MINE.
AND I'D LIKE IT BACK.
MY FIST WASN'T FORGED IN IRON...
...BUT IRONY.
KUNG-FU GIRL--IF YOU REALLY ARE TRYING TO SAVE YOUR PEOPLE, YOU BETTER MAKE THE RIGHT CHOICE.
RUN, PEI. RUN!
AN ORPHAN OF TWO WORLDS.
TWO FAMILIES.
STUCK IN THAT PLACE IN-BETWEEN.

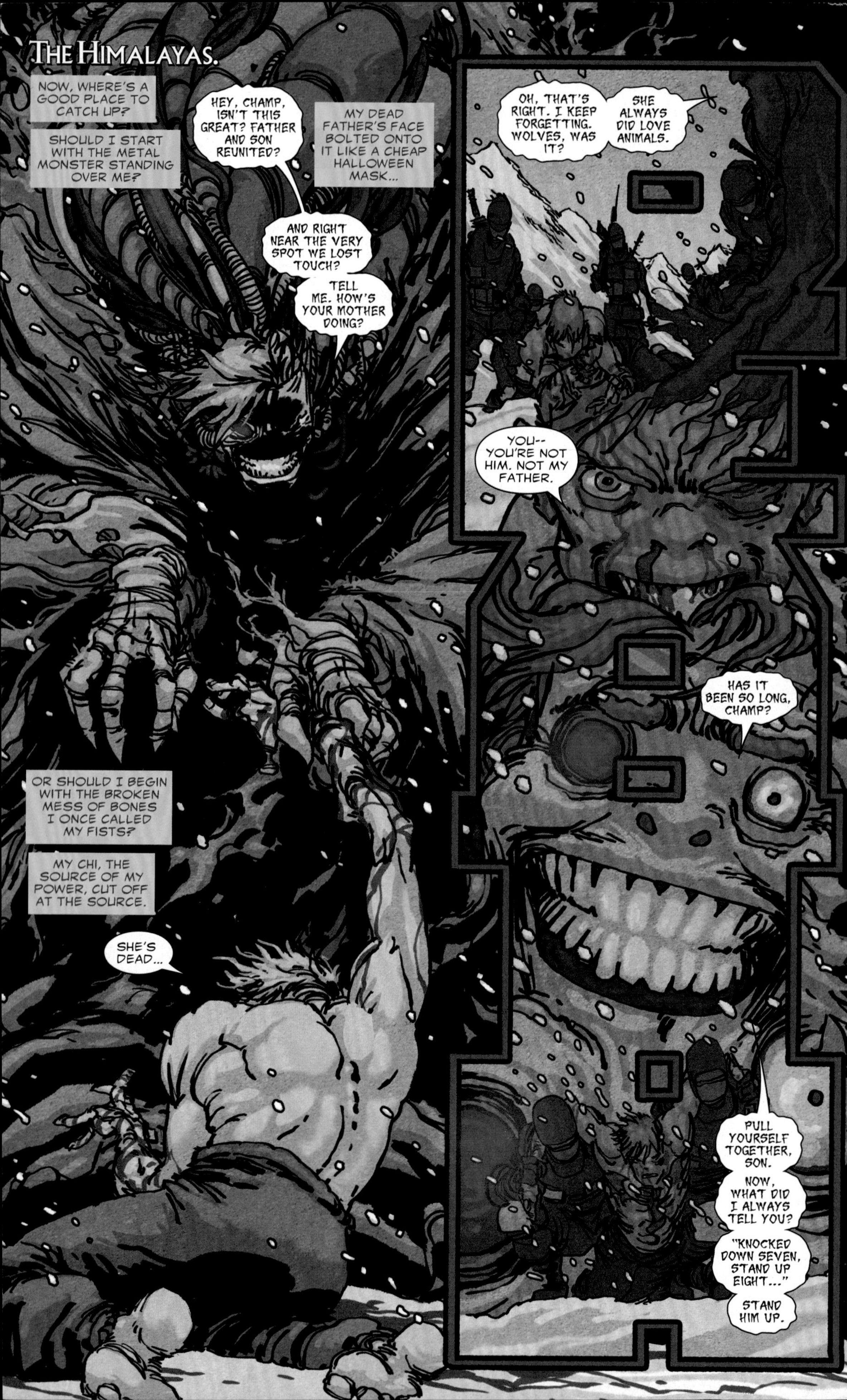
THE HIMALAYAS.
NOW, WHERE'S A GOOD PLACE TO CATCH UP?
SHOULD I START WITH THE METAL MONSTER STANDING OVER ME?
HEY, CHAMP, ISN'T THIS GREAT? FATHER AND SON REUNITED?
MY DEAD FATHER'S FACE BOLTED ONTO IT LIKE A CHEAP HALLOWEEN MASK...
AND RIGHT NEAR THE VERY SPOT WE LOST TOUCH?
TELL ME. HOW'S YOUR MOTHER DOING?
OR SHOULD I BEGIN WITH THE BROKEN MESS OF BONES I ONCE CALLED MY FISTS?
MY CHI, THE SOURCE OF MY POWER, CUT OFF AT THE SOURCE.
SHE'S DEAD...
OH, THAT'S RIGHT. I KEEP FORGETTING. WOLVES, WAS IT?
SHE ALWAYS DID LOVE ANIMALS.
YOU-- YOU'RE NOT HIM. NOT MY FATHER.
HAS IT BEEN SO LONG, CHAMP?
PULL YOURSELF TOGETHER, SON.
NOW, WHAT DID I ALWAYS TELL YOU?
"KNOCKED DOWN SEVEN, STAND UP EIGHT..."
STAND HIM UP.

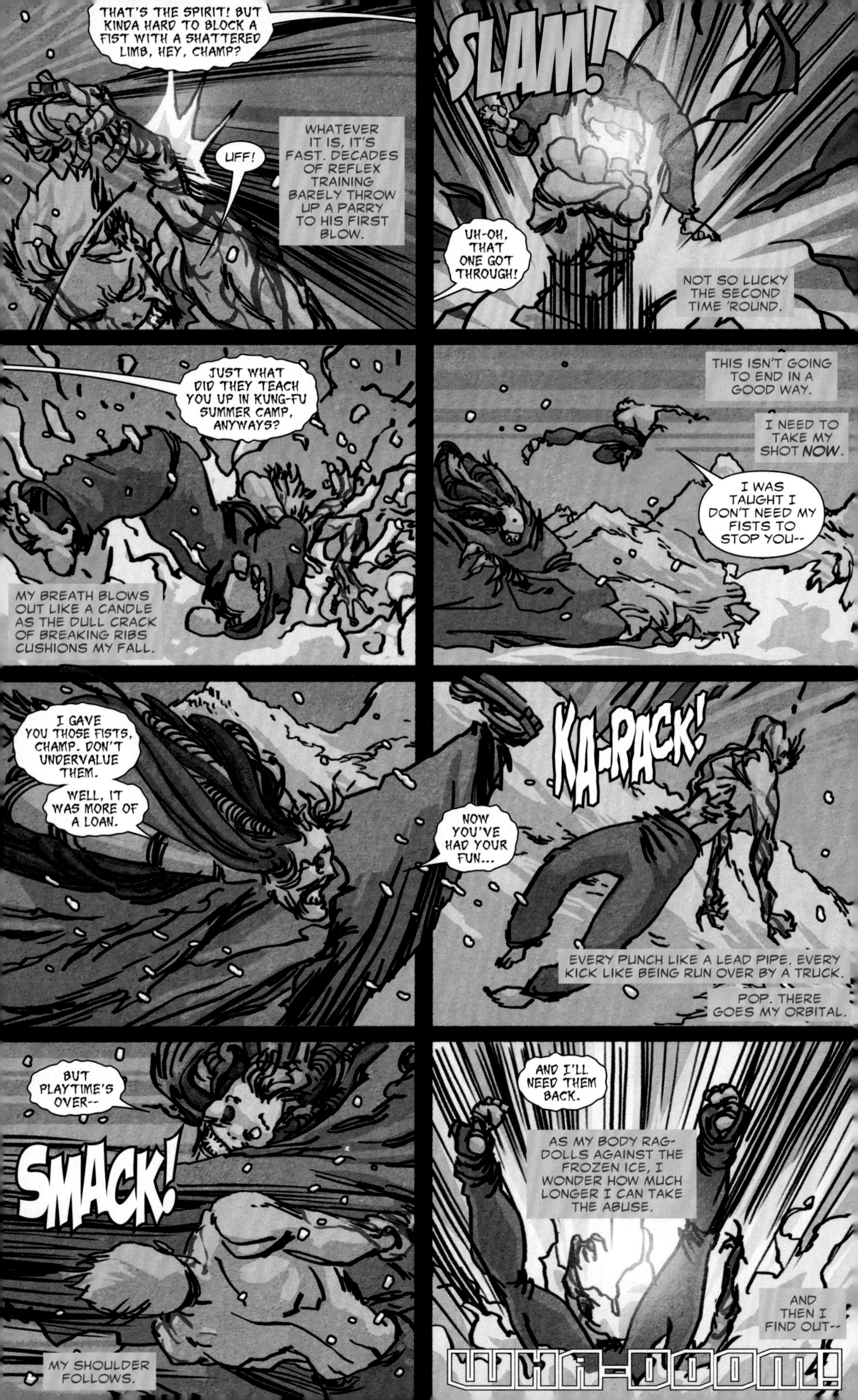
THAT'S THE SPIRIT! BUT KINDA HARD TO BLOCK A FIST WITH A SHATTERED LIMB, HEY, CHAMP?
UFF!
WHATEVER IT IS, IT'S FAST. DECADES OF REFLEX TRAINING BARELY THROW UP A PARRY TO HIS FIRST BLOW.
SLAM!
UH-OH, THAT ONE GOT THROUGH!
NOT SO LUCKY THE SECOND TIME 'ROUND.
JUST WHAT DID THEY TEACH YOU UP IN KUNG-FU SUMMER CAMP, ANYWAYS?
MY BREATH BLOWS OUT LIKE A CANDLE AS THE DULL CRACK OF BREAKING RIBS CUSHIONS MY FALL.
THIS ISN'T GOING TO END IN A GOOD WAY.
I NEED TO TAKE MY SHOT NOW.
I WAS TAUGHT I DON'T NEED MY FISTS TO STOP YOU--
I GAVE YOU THOSE FISTS, CHAMP. DON'T UNDERVALUE THEM.
WELL, IT WAS MORE OF A LOAN.
NOW YOU'VE HAD YOUR FUN...
KA-RACK!
EVERY PUNCH LIKE A LEAD PIPE. EVERY KICK LIKE BEING RUN OVER BY A TRUCK.
POP. THERE GOES MY ORBITAL.
BUT PLAYTIME'S OVER--
SMACK!
MY SHOULDER FOLLOWS.
AND I'LL NEED THEM BACK.
AS MY BODY RAG-DOLLS AGAINST THE FROZEN ICE, I WONDER HOW MUCH LONGER I CAN TAKE THE ABUSE.
AND THEN I FIND OUT--
WHA-DOOOM!

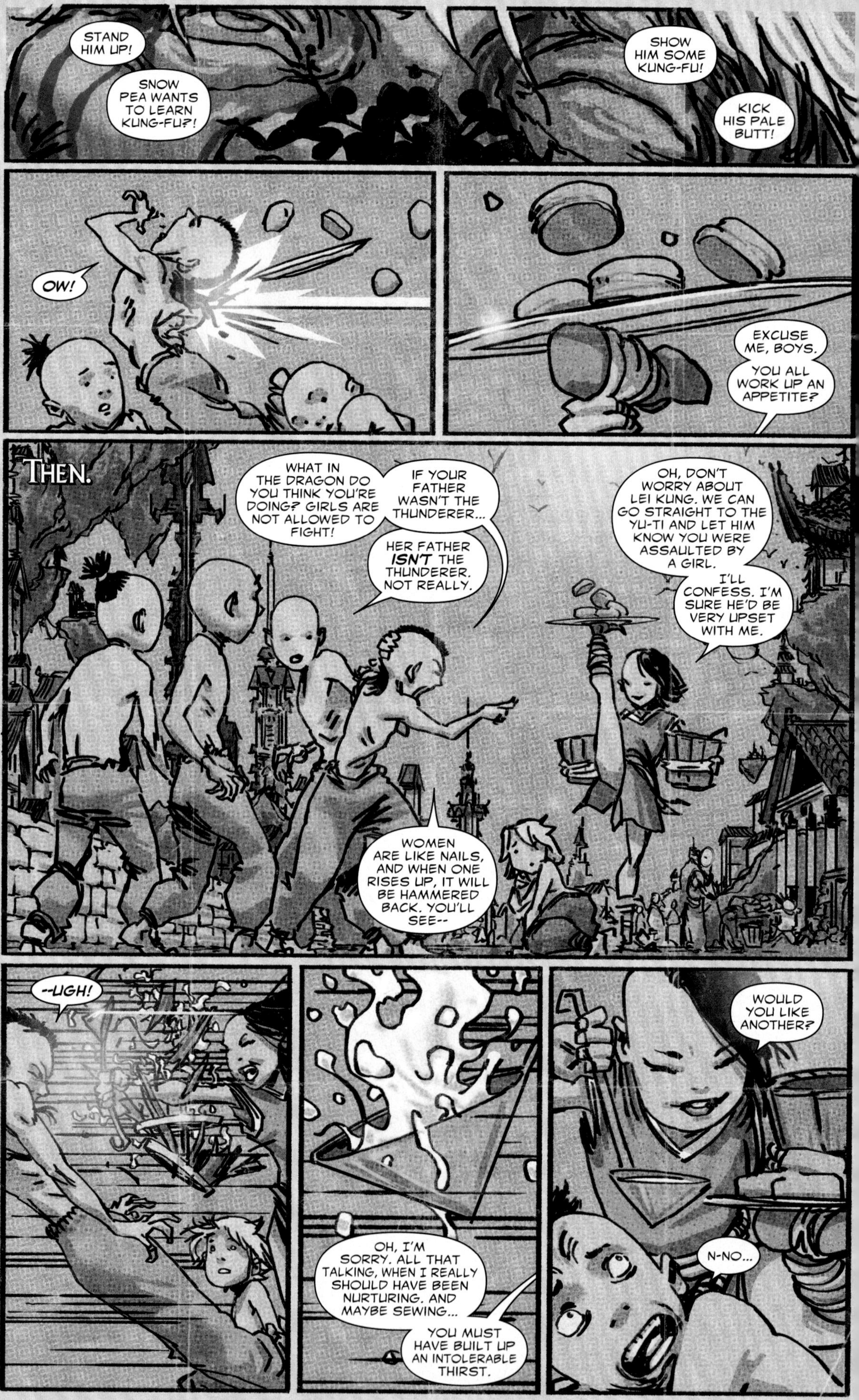
STAND HIM UP!
SNOW PEA WANTS TO LEARN KUNG-FU?!
SHOW HIM SOME KUNG-FU!
KICK HIS PALE BUTT!
OW!
EXCUSE ME, BOYS.
YOU ALL WORK UP AN APPETITE?
THEN.
WHAT IN THE DRAGON DO YOU THINK YOU'RE DOING? GIRLS ARE NOT ALLOWED TO FIGHT!
IF YOUR FATHER WASN'T THE THUNDERER...
HER FATHER ISN'T THE THUNDERER. NOT REALLY.
OH, DON'T WORRY ABOUT LEI KUNG. WE CAN GO STRAIGHT TO THE YU-TI AND LET HIM KNOW YOU WERE ASSAULTED BY A GIRL.
I'LL CONFESS. I'M SURE HE'D BE VERY UPSET WITH ME.
WOMEN ARE LIKE NAILS, AND WHEN ONE RISES UP, IT WILL BE HAMMERED BACK. YOU'LL SEE--
--UGH!
OH, I'M SORRY. ALL THAT TALKING, WHEN I REALLY SHOULD HAVE BEEN NURTURING. AND MAYBE SEWING...
YOU MUST HAVE BUILT UP AN INTOLERABLE THIRST.
WOULD YOU LIKE ANOTHER?
N-NO...

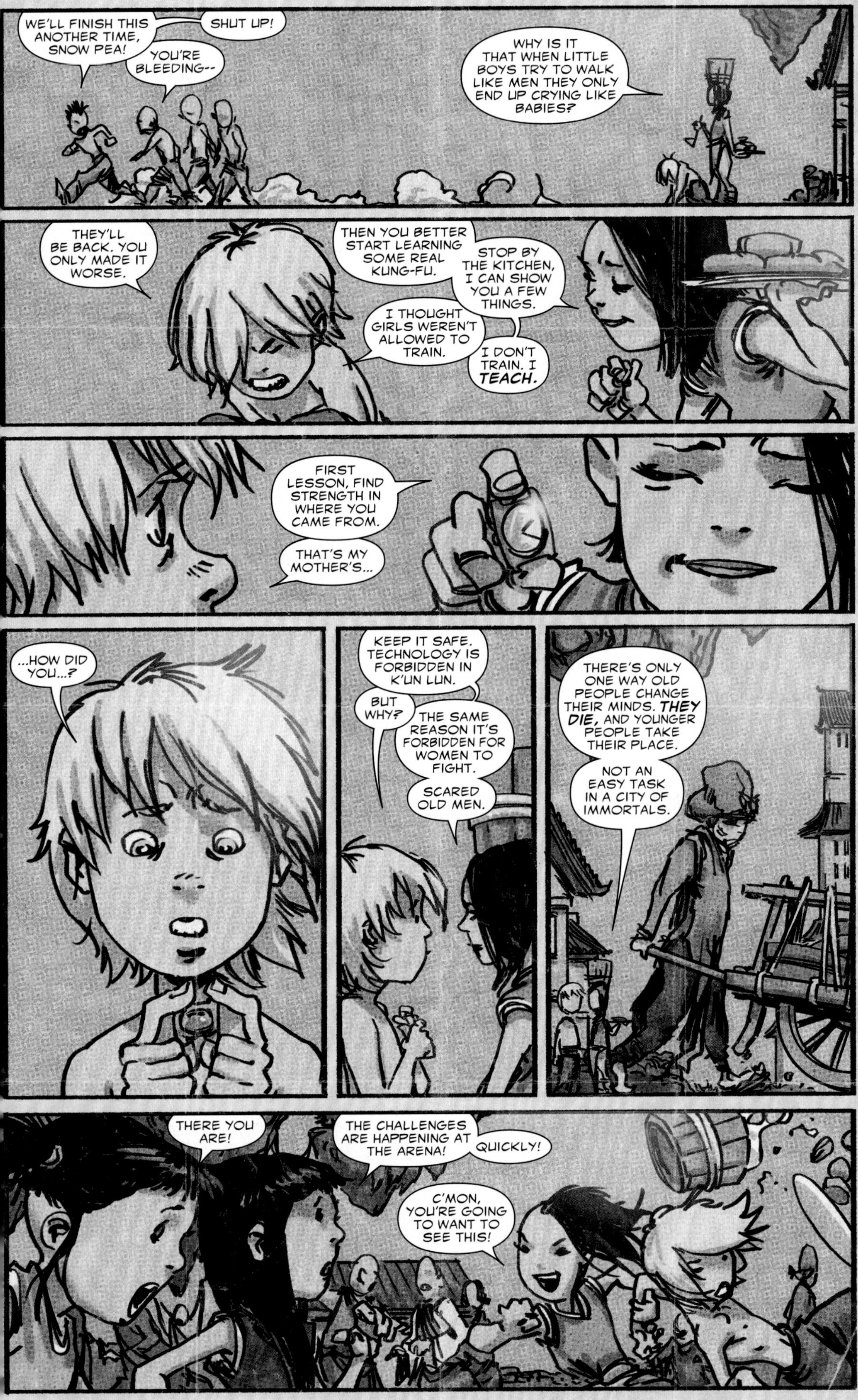
WE'LL FINISH THIS ANOTHER TIME, SNOW PEA!
SHUT UP!
YOU'RE BLEEDING--
WHY IS IT THAT WHEN LITTLE BOYS TRY TO WALK LIKE MEN THEY ONLY END UP CRYING LIKE BABIES?
THEY'LL BE BACK. YOU ONLY MADE IT WORSE.
THEN YOU BETTER START LEARNING SOME REAL KUNG-FU.
STOP BY THE KITCHEN, I CAN SHOW YOU A FEW THINGS.
I THOUGHT GIRLS WEREN'T ALLOWED TO TRAIN.
I DON'T TRAIN. I *TEACH.*
FIRST LESSON, FIND STRENGTH IN WHERE YOU CAME FROM.
THAT'S MY MOTHER'S...
...HOW DID YOU...?
KEEP IT SAFE. TECHNOLOGY IS FORBIDDEN IN K'UN LUN.
BUT WHY?
THE SAME REASON IT'S FORBIDDEN FOR WOMEN TO FIGHT.
SCARED OLD MEN.
THERE'S ONLY ONE WAY OLD PEOPLE CHANGE THEIR MINDS. *THEY DIE,* AND YOUNGER PEOPLE TAKE THEIR PLACE.
NOT AN EASY TASK IN A CITY OF IMMORTALS.
THERE YOU ARE!
THE CHALLENGES ARE HAPPENING AT THE ARENA!
QUICKLY!
C'MON, YOU'RE GOING TO WANT TO SEE THIS!

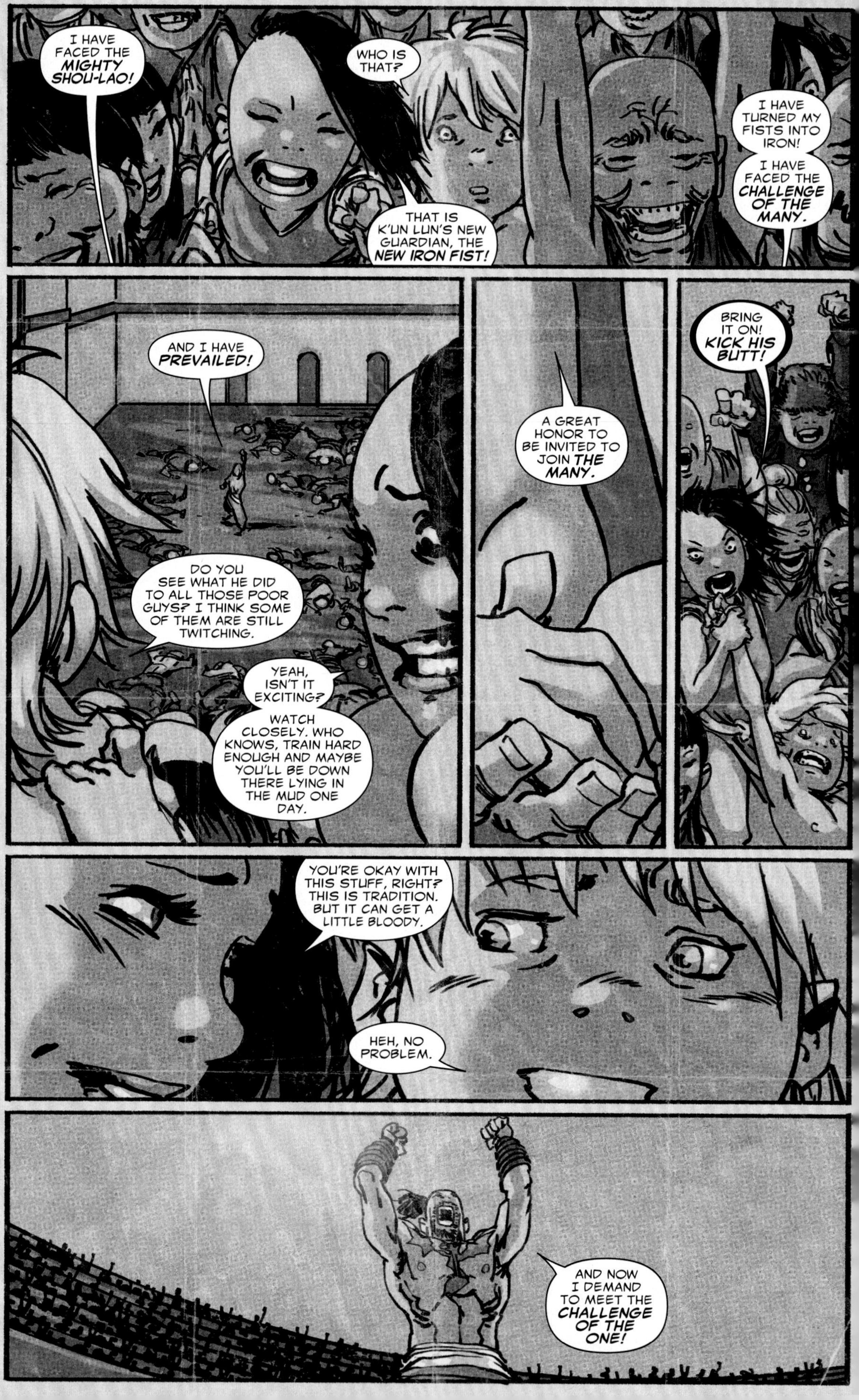
I HAVE FACED THE MIGHTY SHOU-LAO!
WHO IS THAT?
THAT IS K'UN LUN'S NEW GUARDIAN, THE NEW IRON FIST!
I HAVE TURNED MY FISTS INTO IRON!
I HAVE FACED THE CHALLENGE OF THE MANY.
AND I HAVE PREVAILED!
DO YOU SEE WHAT HE DID TO ALL THOSE POOR GUYS? I THINK SOME OF THEM ARE STILL TWITCHING.
YEAH, ISN'T IT EXCITING?
WATCH CLOSELY. WHO KNOWS, TRAIN HARD ENOUGH AND MAYBE YOU'LL BE DOWN THERE LYING IN THE MUD ONE DAY.
A GREAT HONOR TO BE INVITED TO JOIN THE MANY.
BRING IT ON! KICK HIS BUTT!
YOU'RE OKAY WITH THIS STUFF, RIGHT? THIS IS TRADITION. BUT IT CAN GET A LITTLE BLOODY.
HEH, NO PROBLEM.
AND NOW I DEMAND TO MEET THE CHALLENGE OF THE ONE!

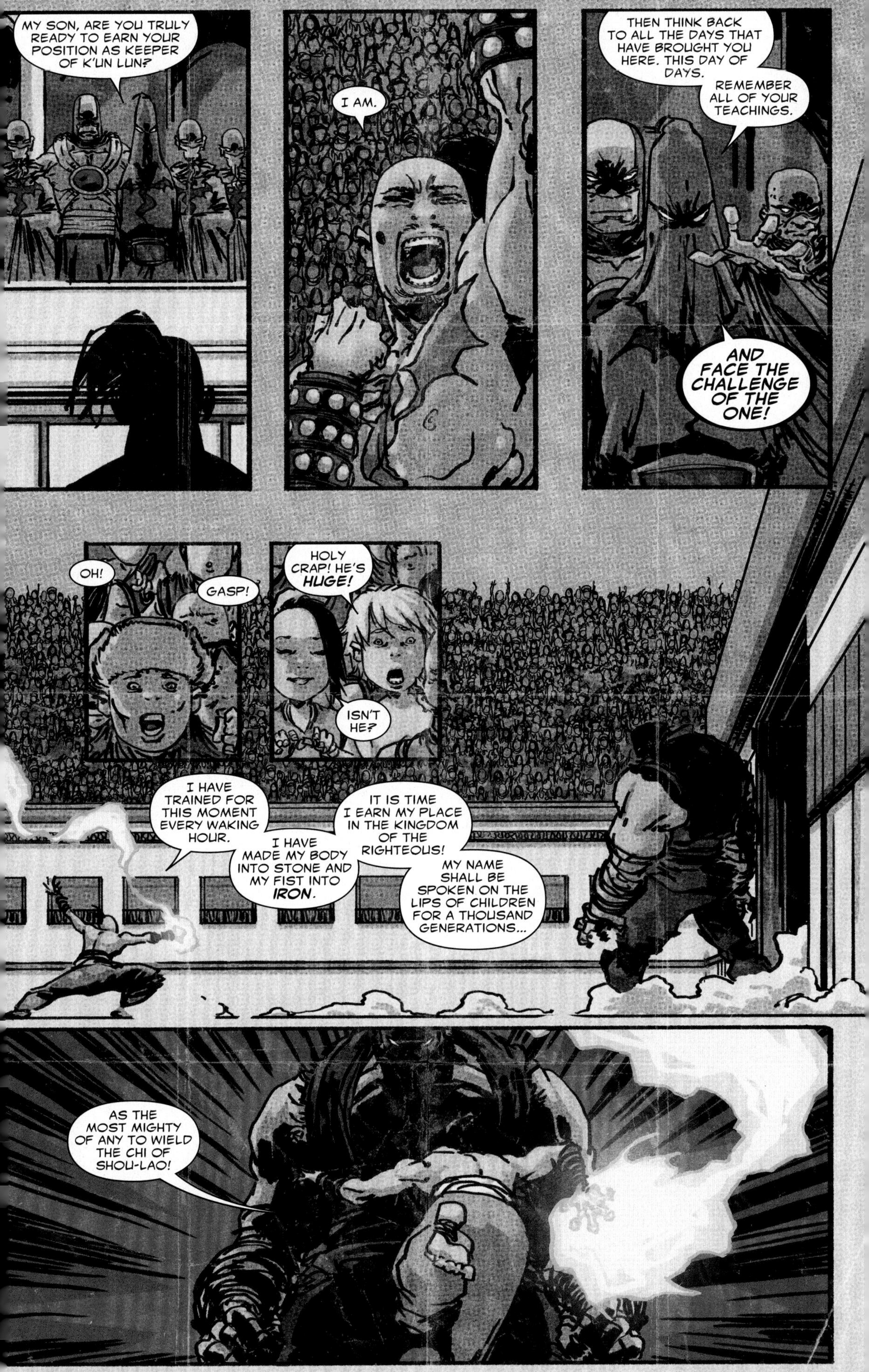
MY SON, ARE YOU TRULY READY TO EARN YOUR POSITION AS KEEPER OF K'UN LUN?
I AM.
THEN THINK BACK TO ALL THE DAYS THAT HAVE BROUGHT YOU HERE. THIS DAY OF DAYS.
REMEMBER ALL OF YOUR TEACHINGS.
AND FACE THE CHALLENGE OF THE ONE!
OH!
GASP!
HOLY CRAP! HE'S HUGE!
ISN'T HE?
I HAVE TRAINED FOR THIS MOMENT EVERY WAKING HOUR.
I HAVE MADE MY BODY INTO STONE AND MY FIST INTO IRON.
IT IS TIME I EARN MY PLACE IN THE KINGDOM OF THE RIGHTEOUS!
MY NAME SHALL BE SPOKEN ON THE LIPS OF CHILDREN FOR A THOUSAND GENERATIONS...
AS THE MOST MIGHTY OF ANY TO WIELD THE CHI OF SHOU-LAO!

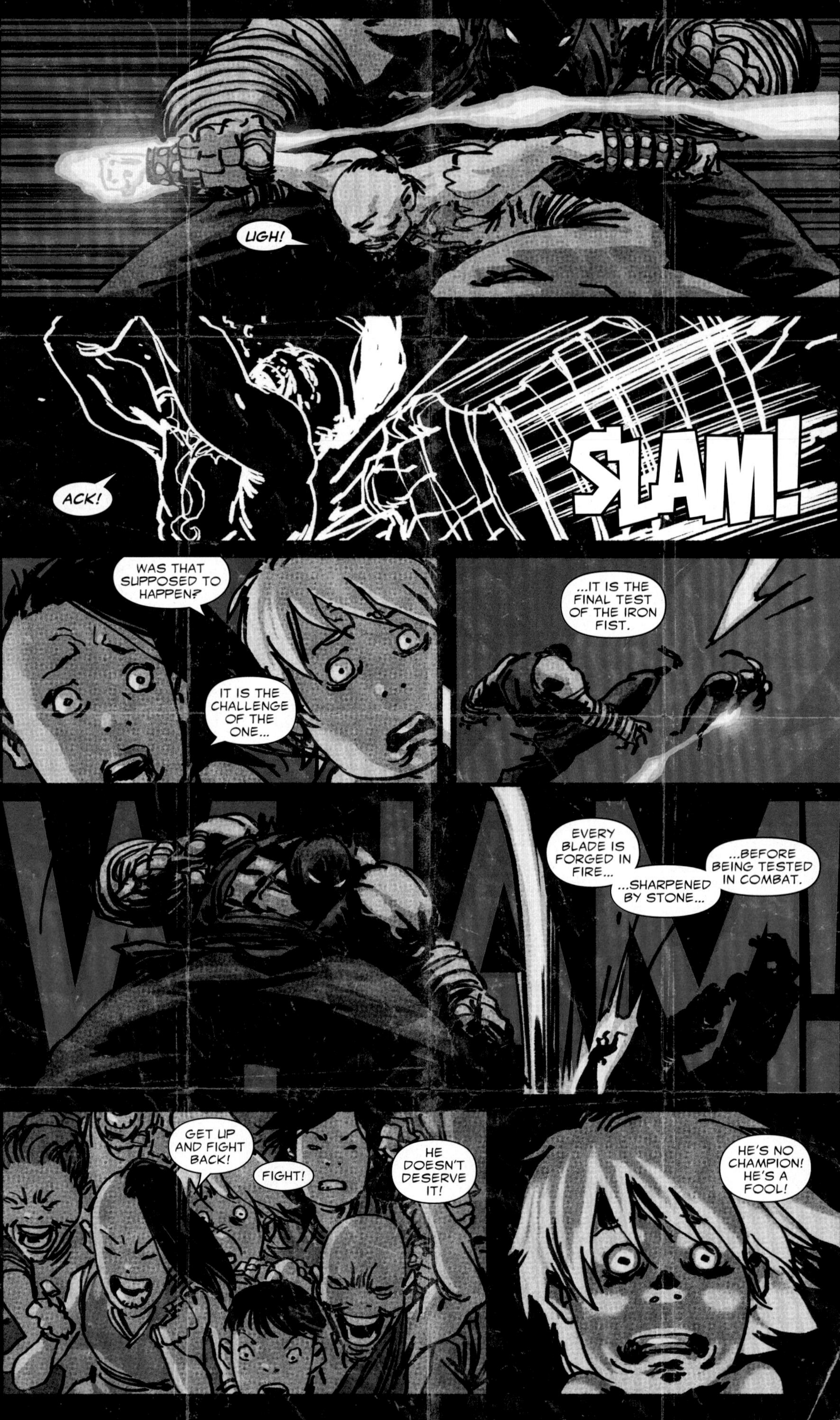
UGH!
ACK!
SLAM!
WAS THAT SUPPOSED TO HAPPEN?
IT IS THE CHALLENGE OF THE ONE...
...IT IS THE FINAL TEST OF THE IRON FIST.
EVERY BLADE IS FORGED IN FIRE...
...SHARPENED BY STONE...
...BEFORE BEING TESTED IN COMBAT.
GET UP AND FIGHT BACK!
FIGHT!
HE DOESN'T DESERVE IT!
HE'S NO CHAMPION! HE'S A FOOL!

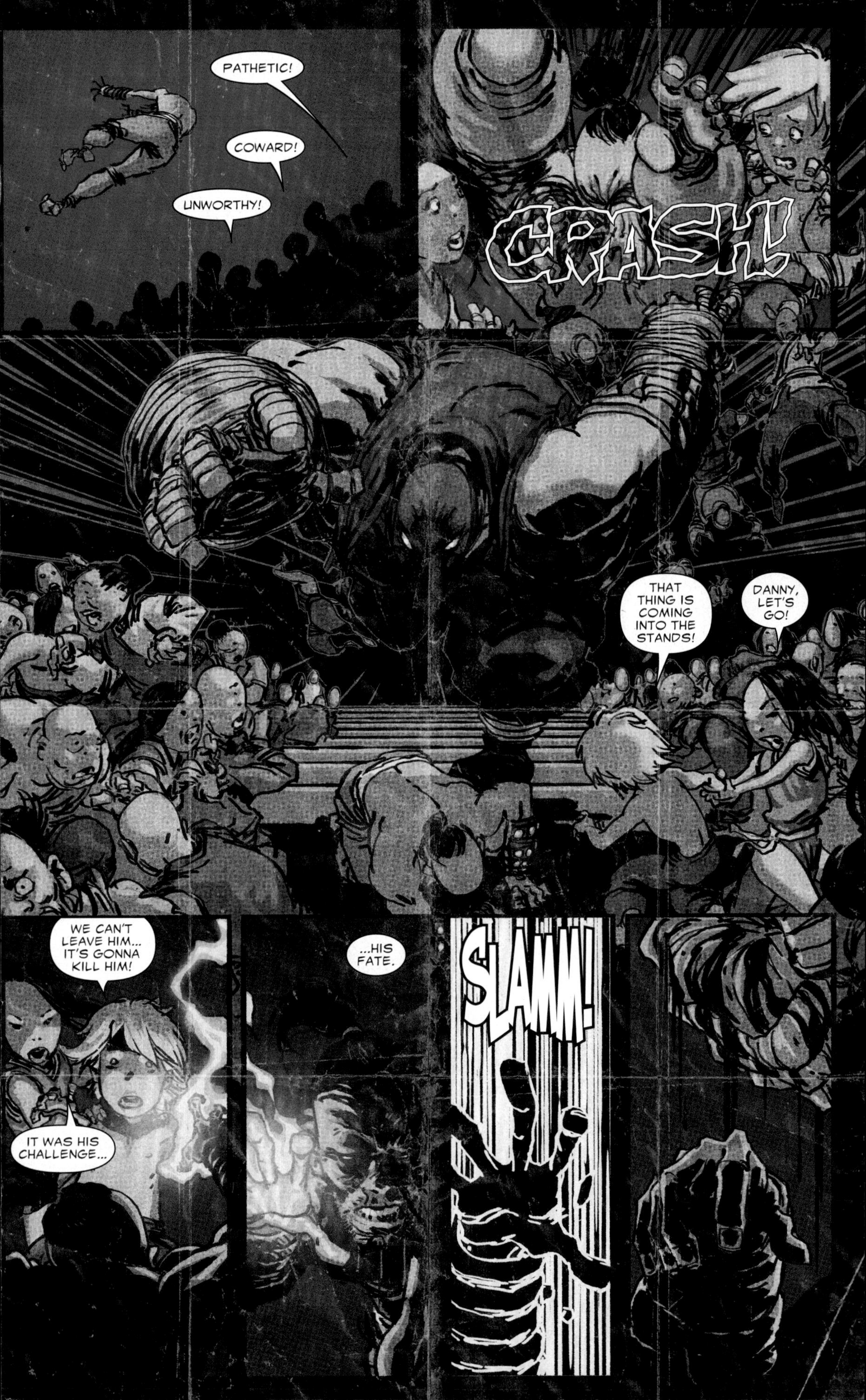
PATHETIC!
COWARD!
UNWORTHY!
CRASH!
THAT THING IS COMING INTO THE STANDS!
DANNY, LET'S GO!
WE CAN'T LEAVE HIM... IT'S GONNA KILL HIM!
IT WAS HIS CHALLENGE...
...HIS FATE.
SLAMM!

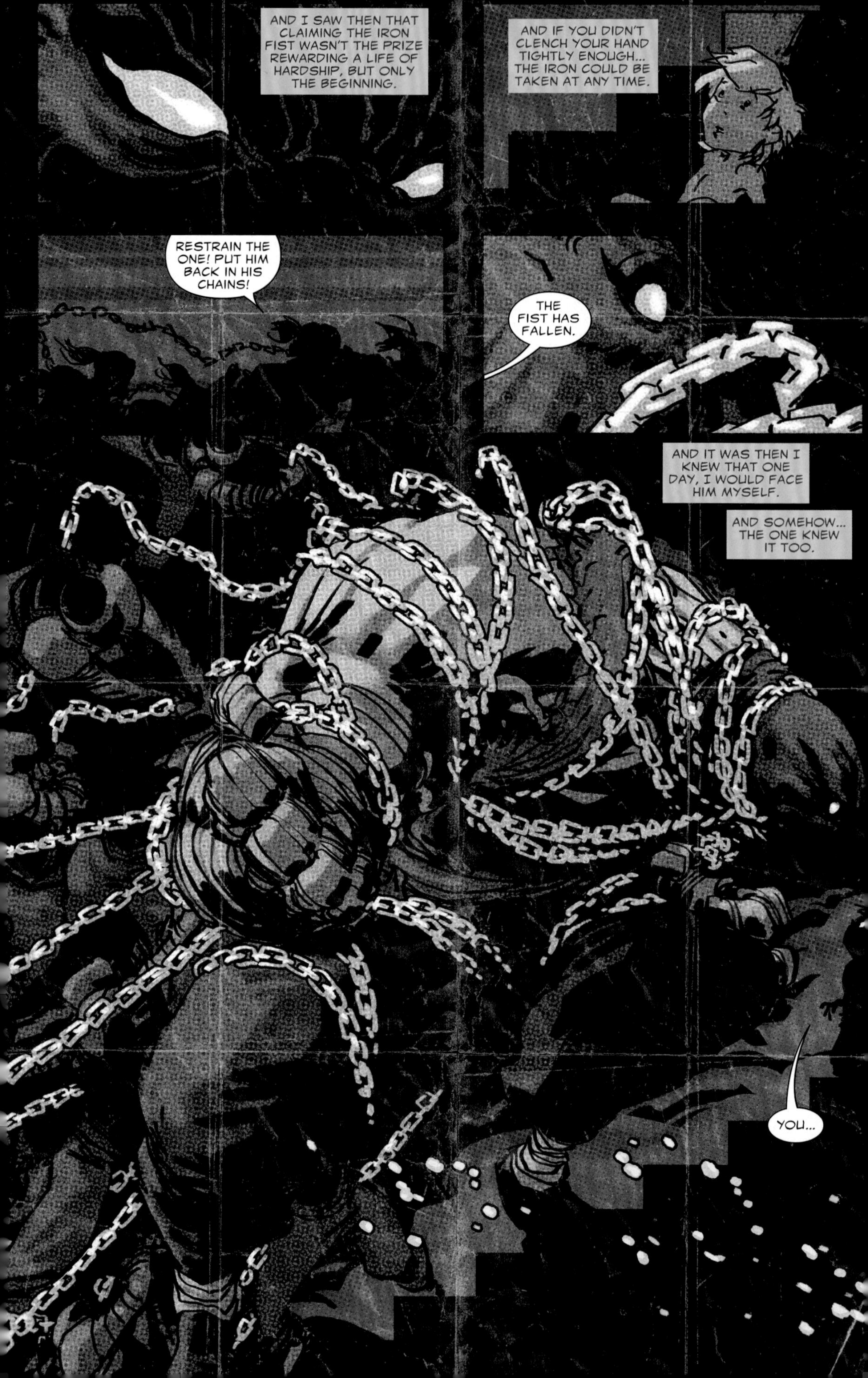
AND I SAW THEN THAT CLAIMING THE IRON FIST WASN'T THE PRIZE REWARDING A LIFE OF HARDSHIP, BUT ONLY THE BEGINNING.
AND IF YOU DIDN'T CLENCH YOUR HAND TIGHTLY ENOUGH... THE IRON COULD BE TAKEN AT ANY TIME.
RESTRAIN THE ONE! PUT HIM BACK IN HIS CHAINS!
THE FIST HAS FALLEN.
AND IT WAS THEN I KNEW THAT ONE DAY, I WOULD FACE HIM MYSELF.
AND SOMEHOW... THE ONE KNEW IT TOO.
YOU...

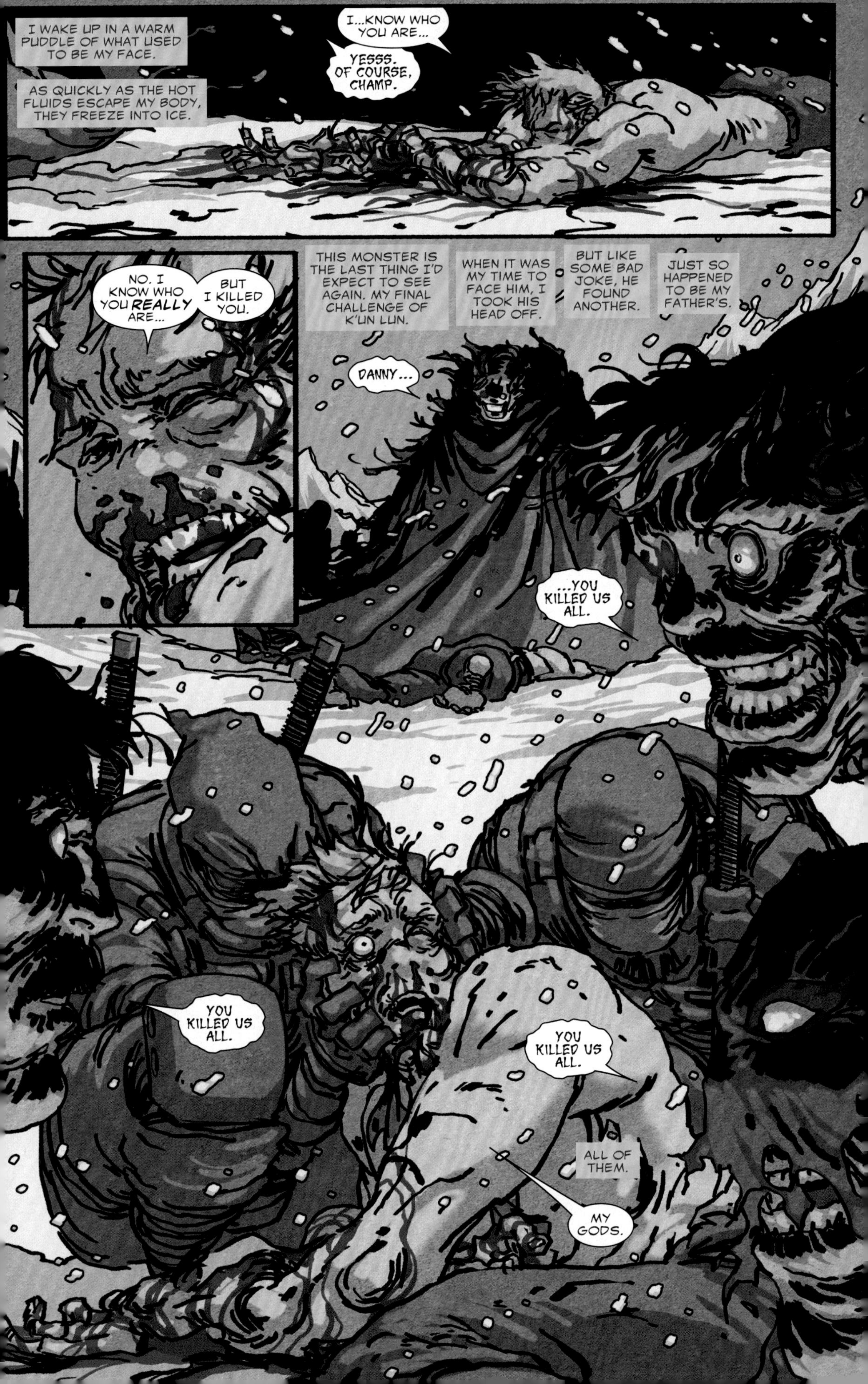
I WAKE UP IN A WARM PUDDLE OF WHAT USED TO BE MY FACE.
AS QUICKLY AS THE HOT FLUIDS ESCAPE MY BODY, THEY FREEZE INTO ICE.
I...KNOW WHO YOU ARE...
YESSS. OF COURSE, CHAMP.
NO. I KNOW WHO YOU REALLY ARE...
BUT I KILLED YOU.
THIS MONSTER IS THE LAST THING I'D EXPECT TO SEE AGAIN. MY FINAL CHALLENGE OF K'UN LUN.
WHEN IT WAS MY TIME TO FACE HIM, I TOOK HIS HEAD OFF.
BUT LIKE SOME BAD JOKE, HE FOUND ANOTHER.
JUST SO HAPPENED TO BE MY FATHER'S.
DANNY...
...YOU KILLED US ALL.
YOU KILLED US ALL.
YOU KILLED US ALL.
ALL OF THEM.
MY GODS.

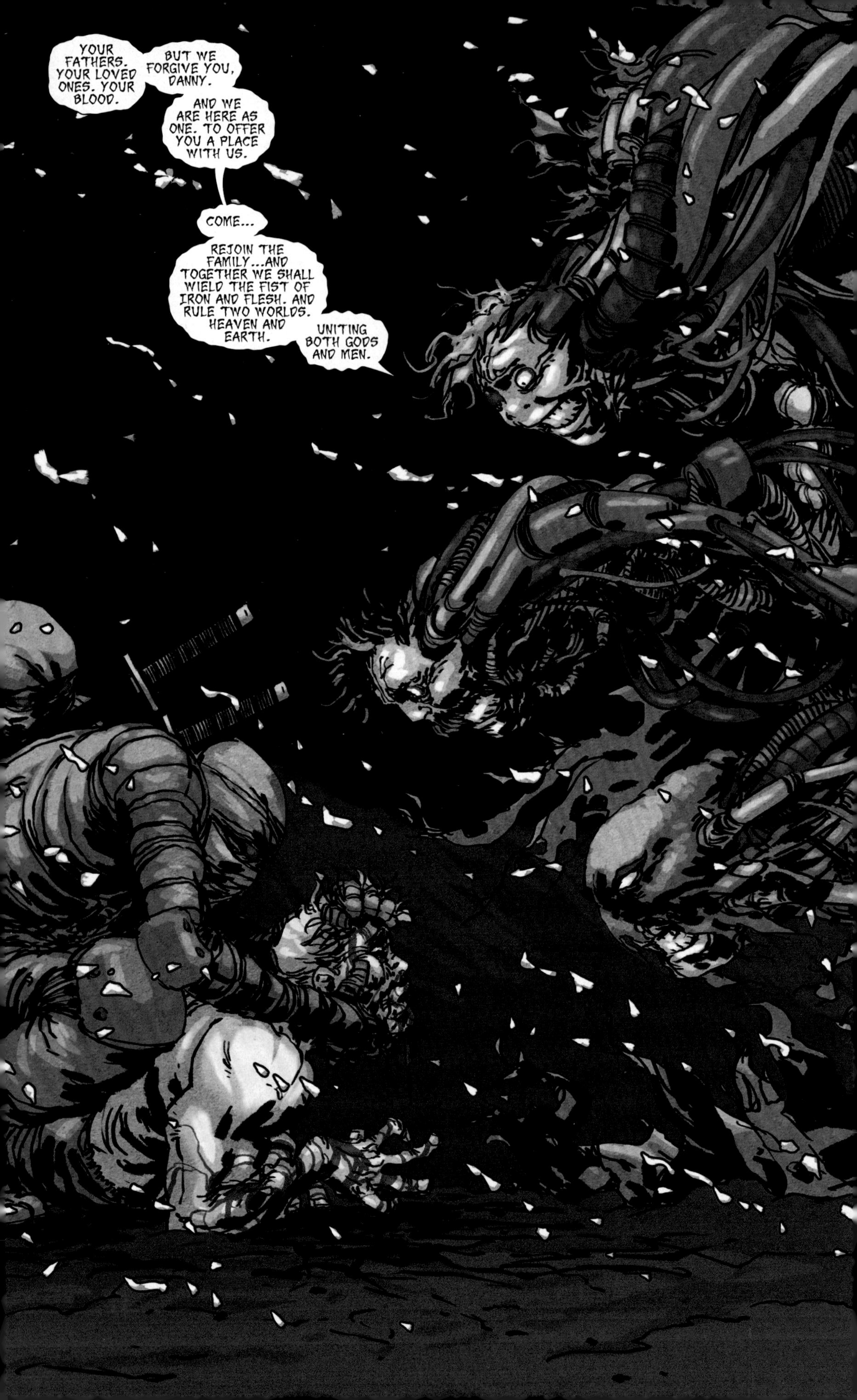
YOUR FATHERS. YOUR LOVED ONES. YOUR BLOOD.
BUT WE FORGIVE YOU, DANNY.
AND WE ARE HERE AS ONE. TO OFFER YOU A PLACE WITH US.
COME...
REJOIN THE FAMILY...AND TOGETHER WE SHALL WIELD THE FIST OF IRON AND FLESH. AND RULE TWO WORLDS. HEAVEN AND EARTH.
UNITING BOTH GODS AND MEN.

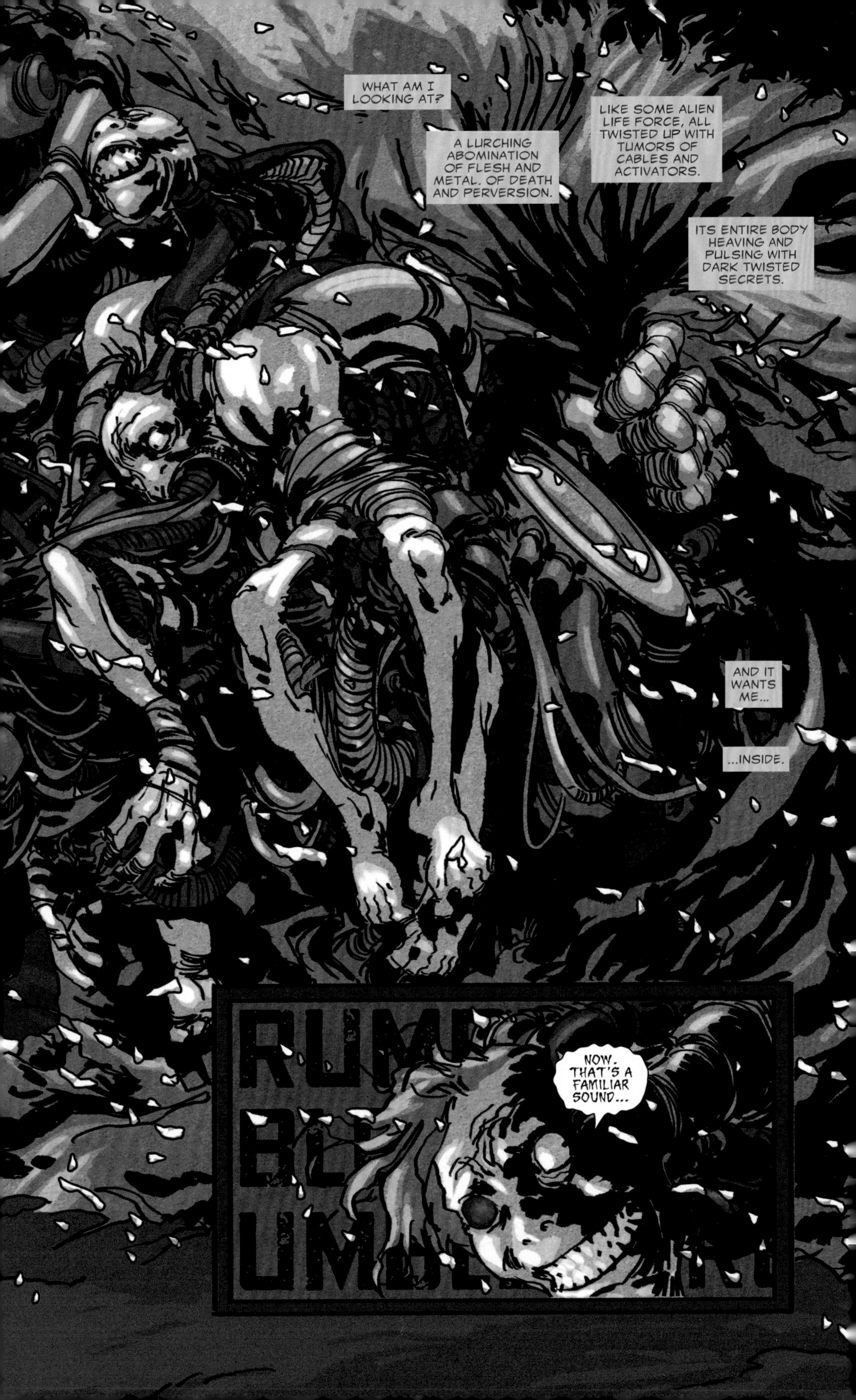
WHAT AM I LOOKING AT?
A LURCHING ABOMINATION OF FLESH AND METAL. OF DEATH AND PERVERSION.
LIKE SOME ALIEN LIFE FORCE, ALL TWISTED UP WITH TUMORS OF CABLES AND ACTIVATORS.
ITS ENTIRE BODY HEAVING AND PULSING WITH DARK TWISTED SECRETS.
AND IT WANTS ME...
...INSIDE.
NOW. THAT'S A FAMILIAR SOUND...

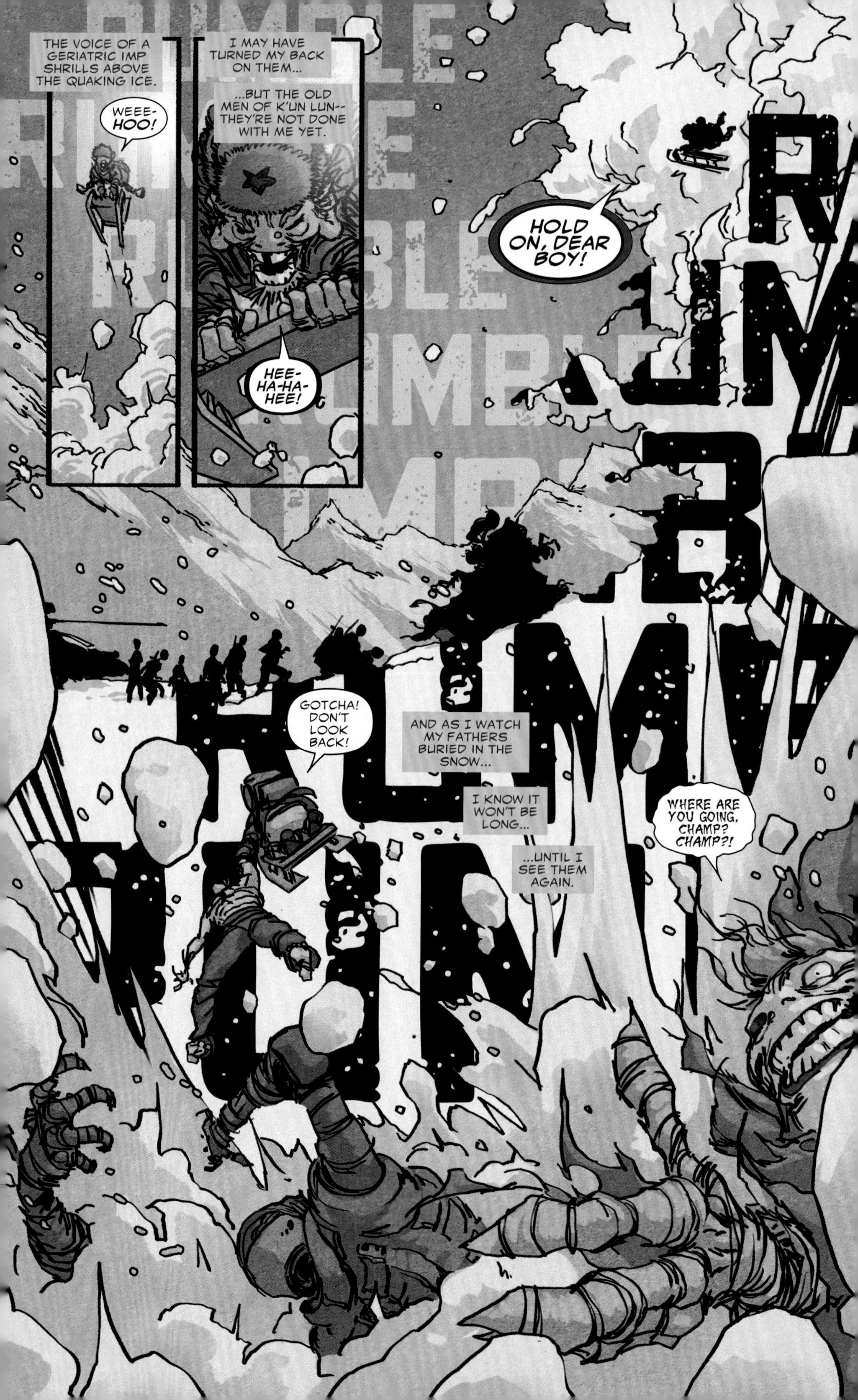

THE VOICE OF A GERIATRIC IMP SHRILLS ABOVE THE QUAKING ICE.
WEEE-HOO!
I MAY HAVE TURNED MY BACK ON THEM...
...BUT THE OLD MEN OF K'UN LUN--THEY'RE NOT DONE WITH ME YET.
HEE-HA-HA-HEE!
HOLD ON, DEAR BOY!
GOTCHA! DON'T LOOK BACK!
AND AS I WATCH MY FATHERS BURIED IN THE SNOW...
I KNOW IT WON'T BE LONG...
...UNTIL I SEE THEM AGAIN.
WHERE ARE YOU GOING, CHAMP? CHAMP?!

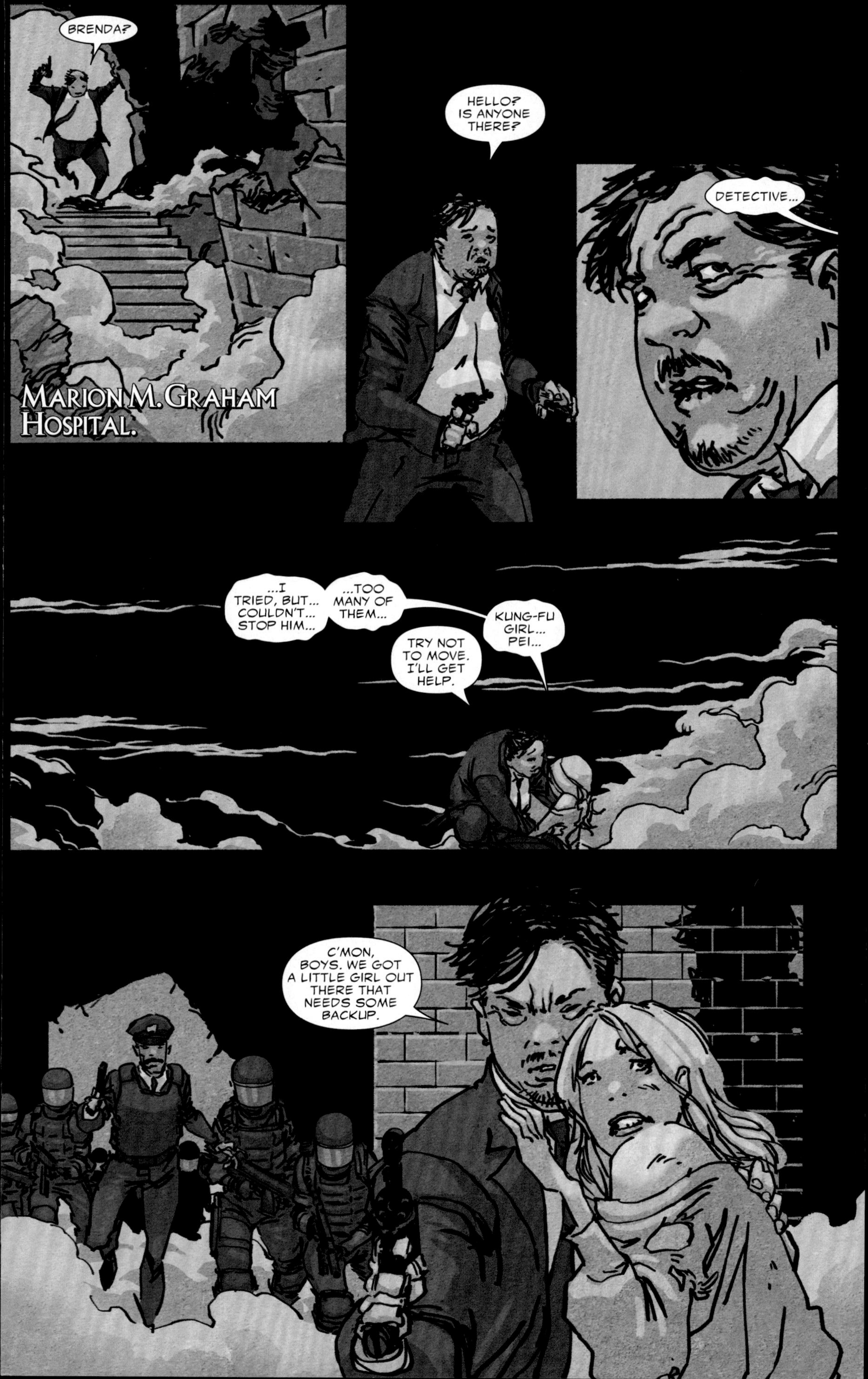
BRENDA?
MARION M. GRAHAM HOSPITAL.
HELLO? IS ANYONE THERE?
DETECTIVE...
...I TRIED, BUT... COULDN'T... STOP HIM...
...TOO MANY OF THEM...
KUNG-FU GIRL... PEI...
TRY NOT TO MOVE. I'LL GET HELP.
C'MON, BOYS. WE GOT A LITTLE GIRL OUT THERE THAT NEEDS SOME BACKUP.

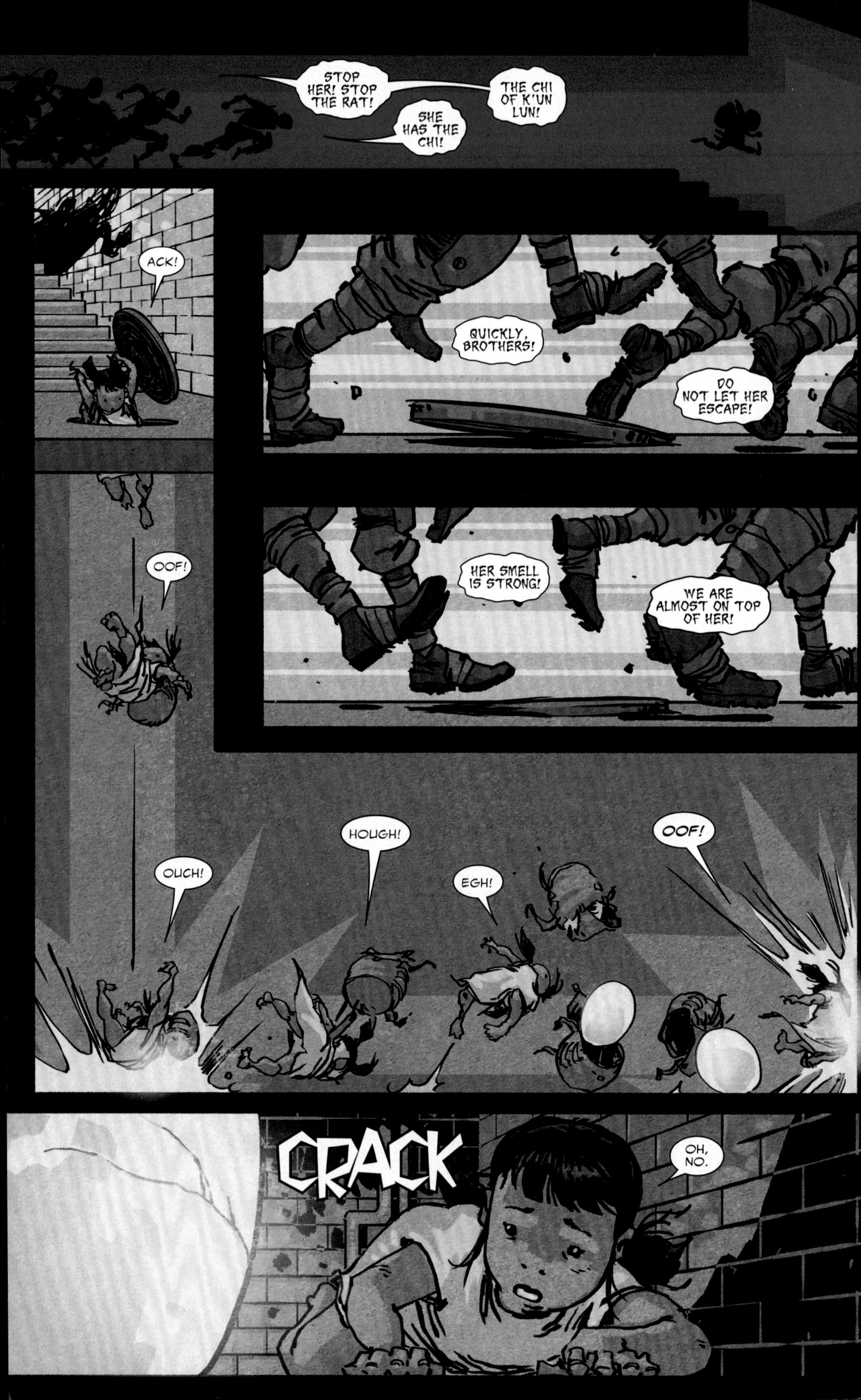
STOP HER! STOP THE RAT!
SHE HAS THE CHI!
THE CHI OF K'UN LUN!
ACK!
QUICKLY, BROTHERS!
DO NOT LET HER ESCAPE!
OOF!
HER SMELL IS STRONG!
WE ARE ALMOST ON TOP OF HER!
OUCH!
HOUGH!
EGH!
OOF!
CRACK
OH, NO.

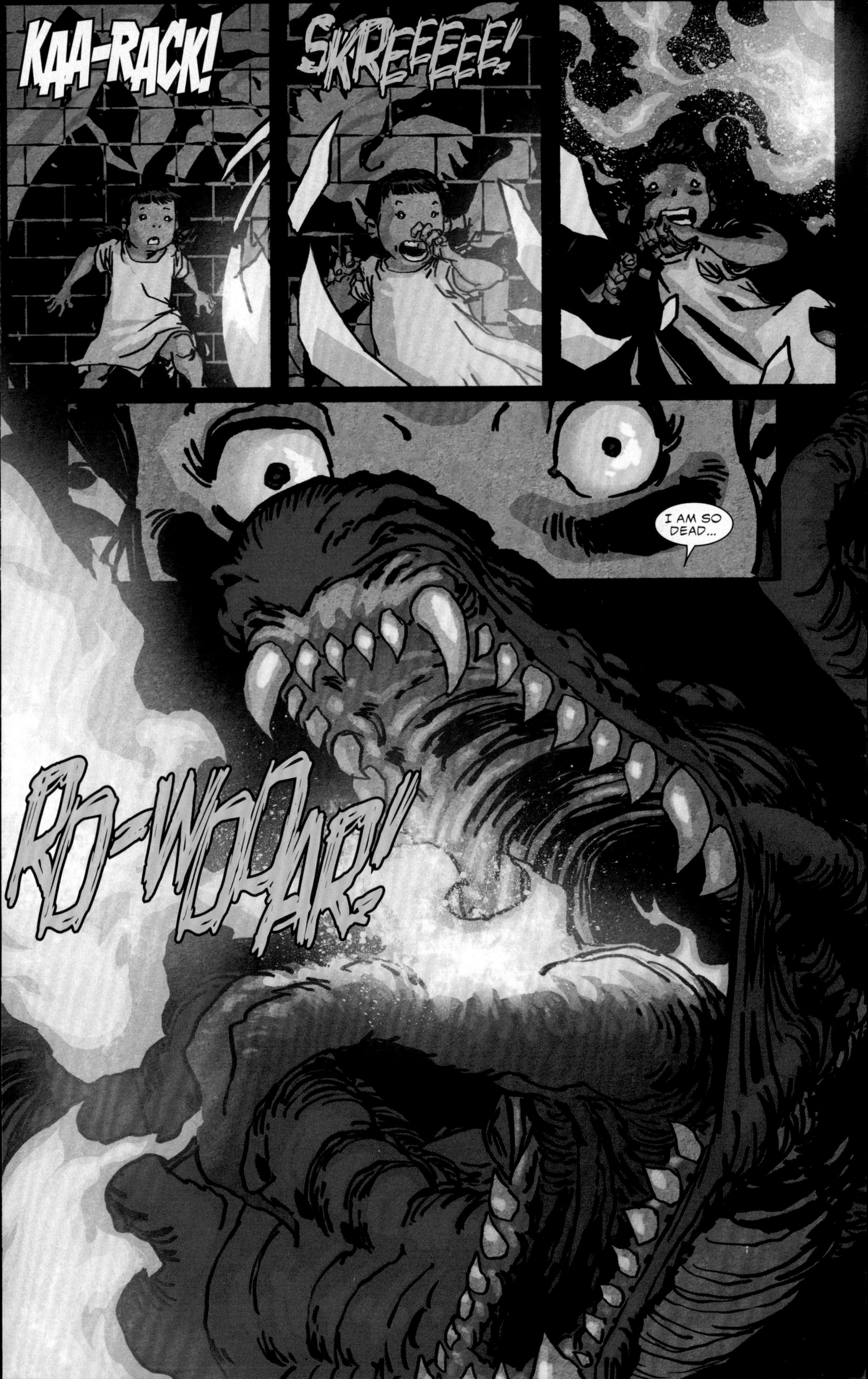
KAA-RACK!
SKREEEEEE!
I AM SO DEAD...
RO-WOOAR!

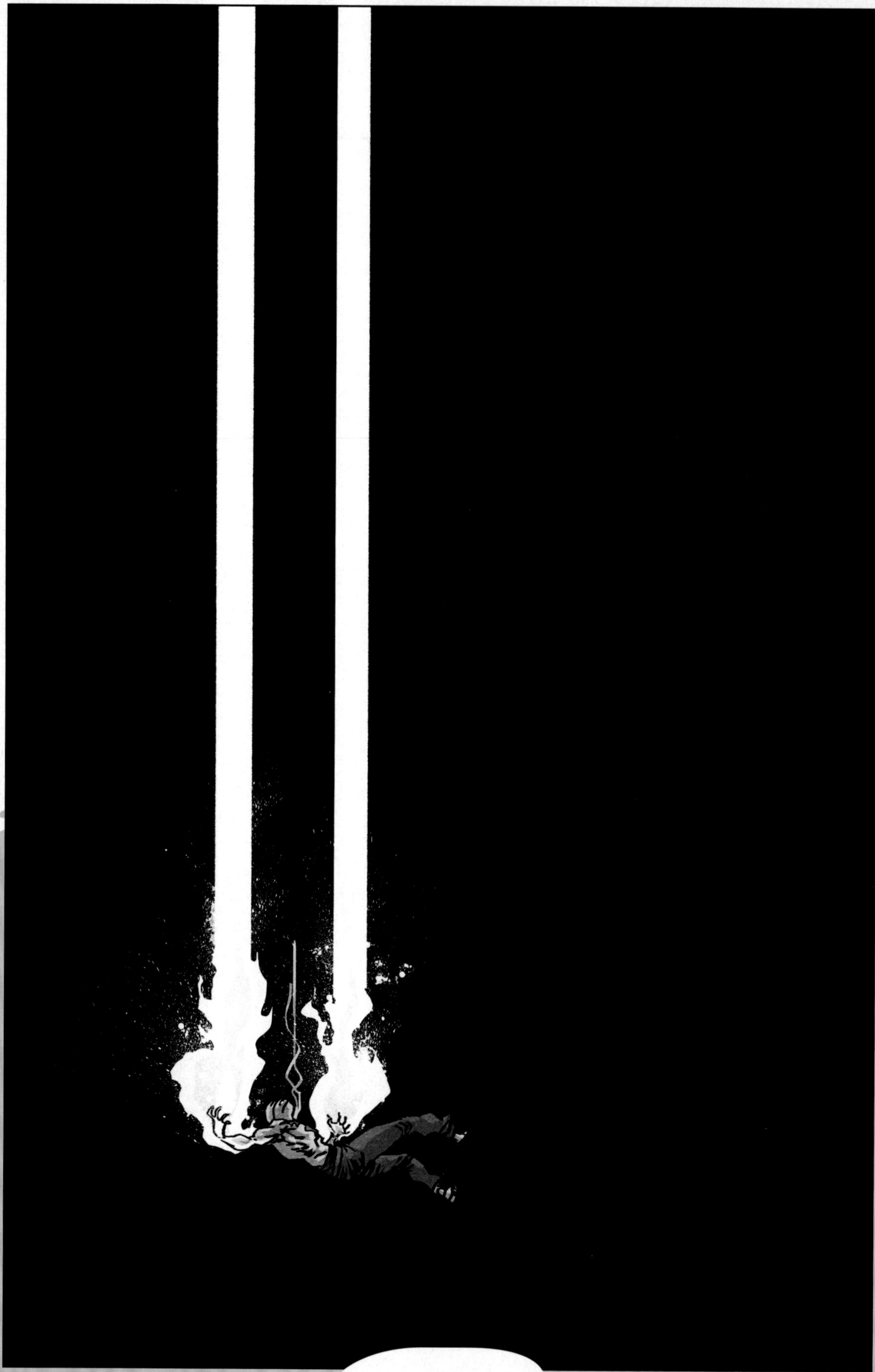

6

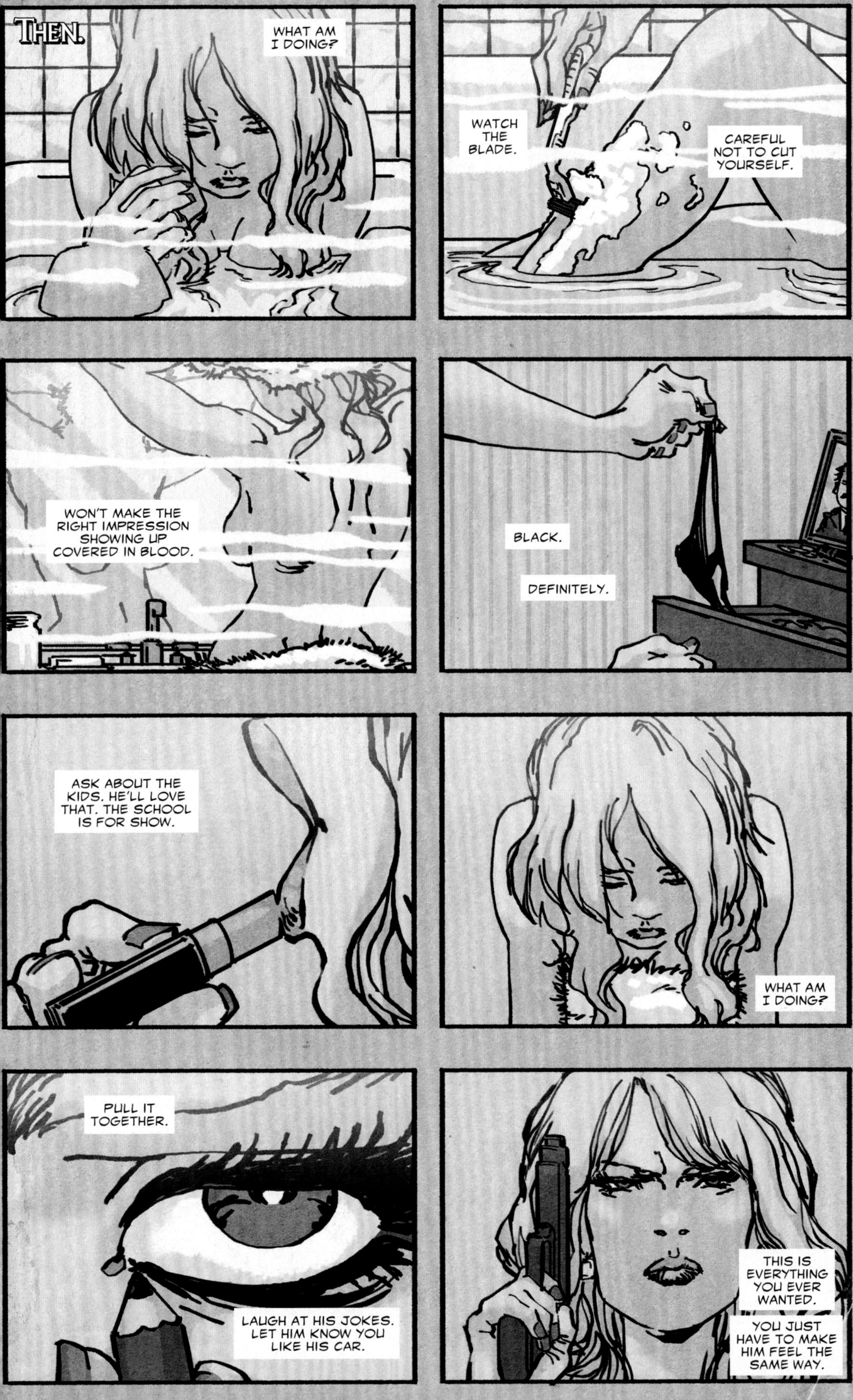
THEN.
WHAT AM I DOING?
WATCH THE BLADE.
CAREFUL NOT TO CUT YOURSELF.
WON'T MAKE THE RIGHT IMPRESSION SHOWING UP COVERED IN BLOOD.
BLACK.
DEFINITELY.
ASK ABOUT THE KIDS. HE'LL LOVE THAT. THE SCHOOL IS FOR SHOW.
WHAT AM I DOING?
PULL IT TOGETHER.
LAUGH AT HIS JOKES. LET HIM KNOW YOU LIKE HIS CAR.
THIS IS EVERYTHING YOU EVER WANTED.
YOU JUST HAVE TO MAKE HIM FEEL THE SAME WAY.

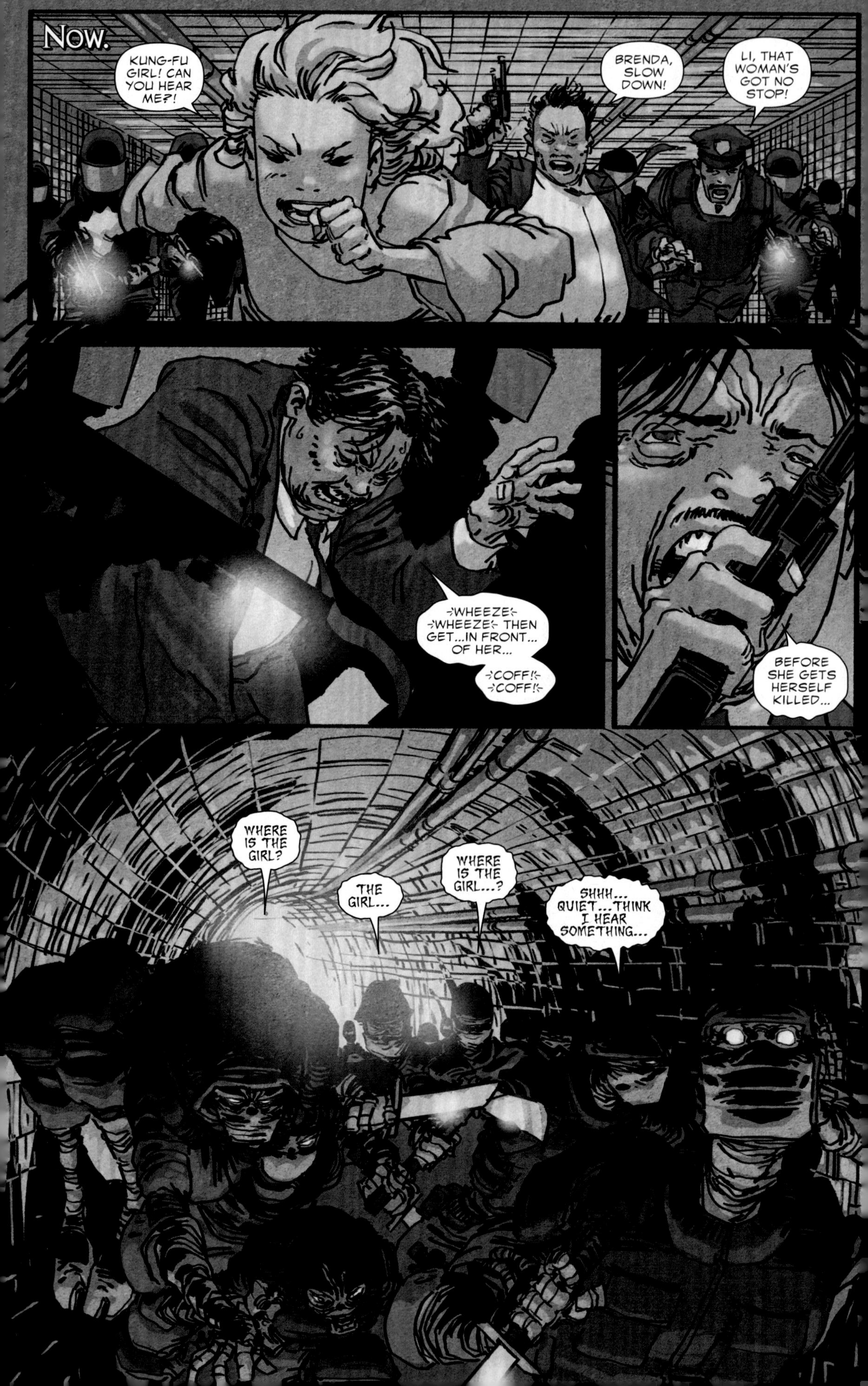
Now.
KUNG-FU GIRL! CAN YOU HEAR ME?!
BRENDA, SLOW DOWN!
LI, THAT WOMAN'S GOT NO STOP!
WHEEZE WHEEZE THEN GET...IN FRONT... OF HER...
COFF! COFF!
BEFORE SHE GETS HERSELF KILLED...
WHERE IS THE GIRL?
THE GIRL...
WHERE IS THE GIRL...?
SHHH... QUIET...THINK I HEAR SOMETHING...

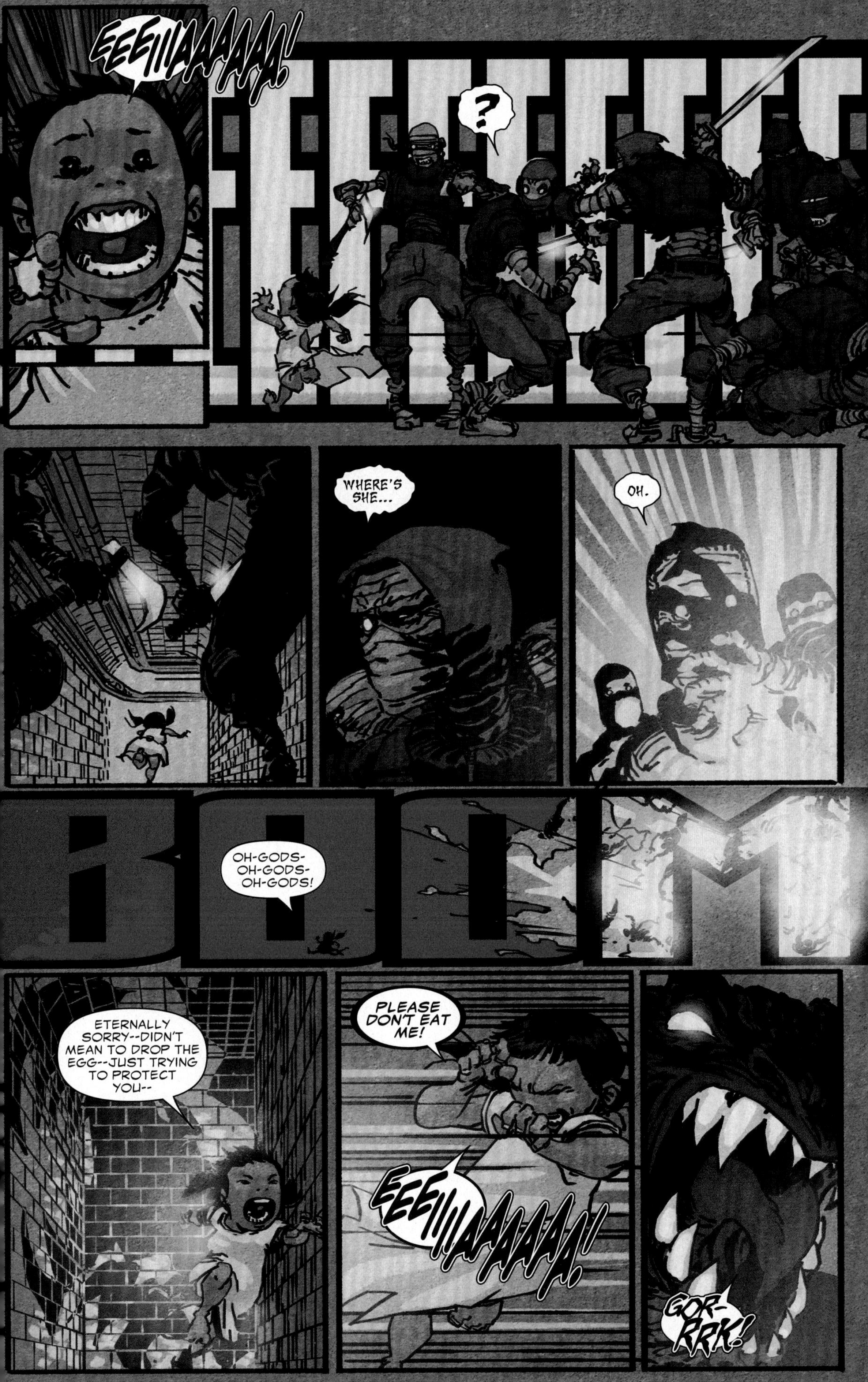

EEEIIIAAAAAAA!
?
WHERE'S SHE...
OH.
BOOM
OH-GODS-OH-GODS-OH-GODS!
ETERNALLY SORRY--DIDN'T MEAN TO DROP THE EGG--JUST TRYING TO PROTECT YOU--
PLEASE DON'T EAT ME!
EEEIIIAAAAAAA!
GOR-RRK!

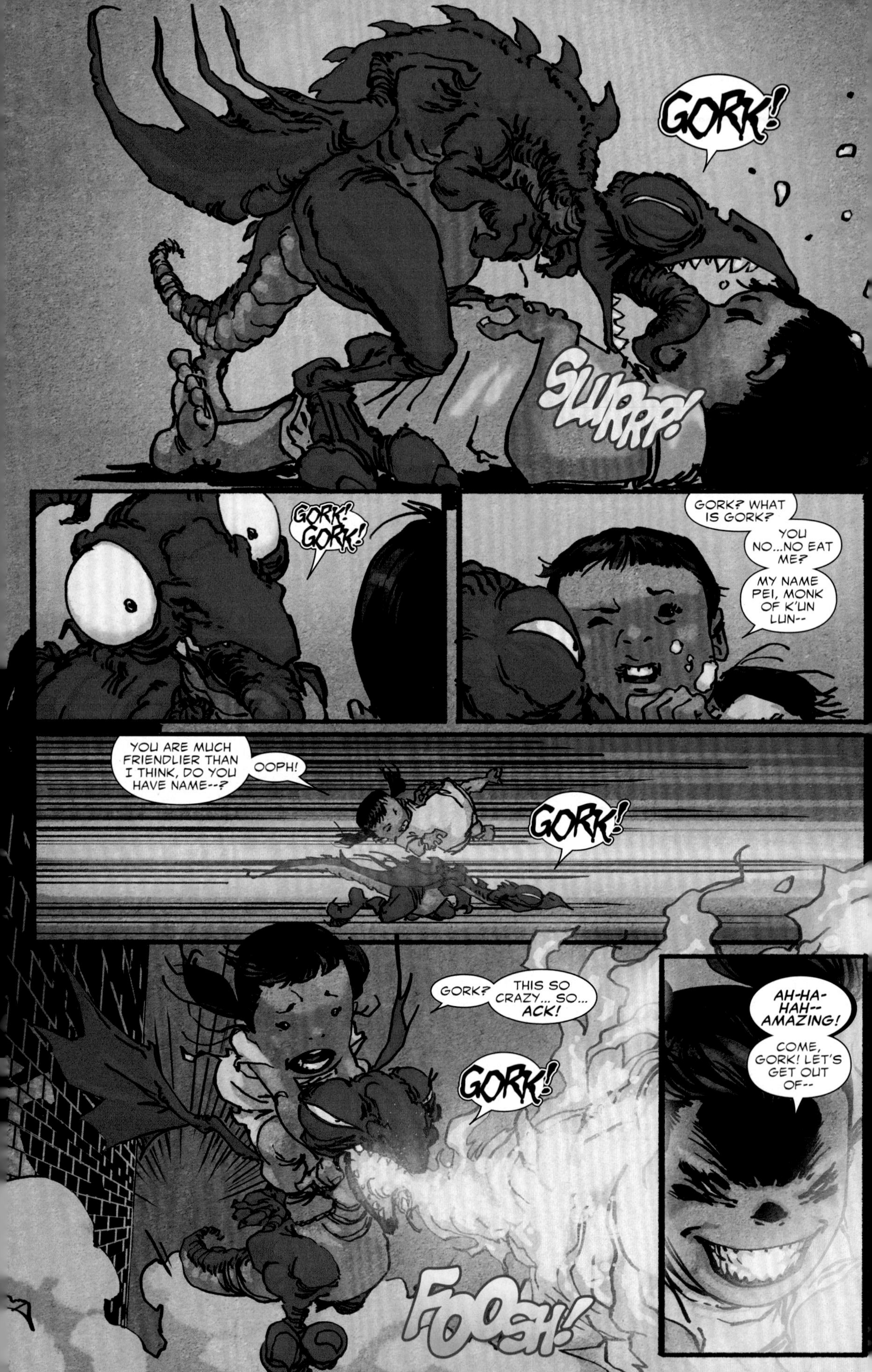
GORK!
SLURRP!
GORK! GORK!
GORK? WHAT IS GORK?
YOU NO...NO EAT ME?
MY NAME PEI, MONK OF K'UN LUN--
YOU ARE MUCH FRIENDLIER THAN I THINK, DO YOU HAVE NAME--?
OOPH!
GORK!
GORK?
THIS SO CRAZY... SO... ACK!
GORK!
FOOSH!
AH-HA-HAH--AMAZING!
COME, GORK! LET'S GET OUT OF--

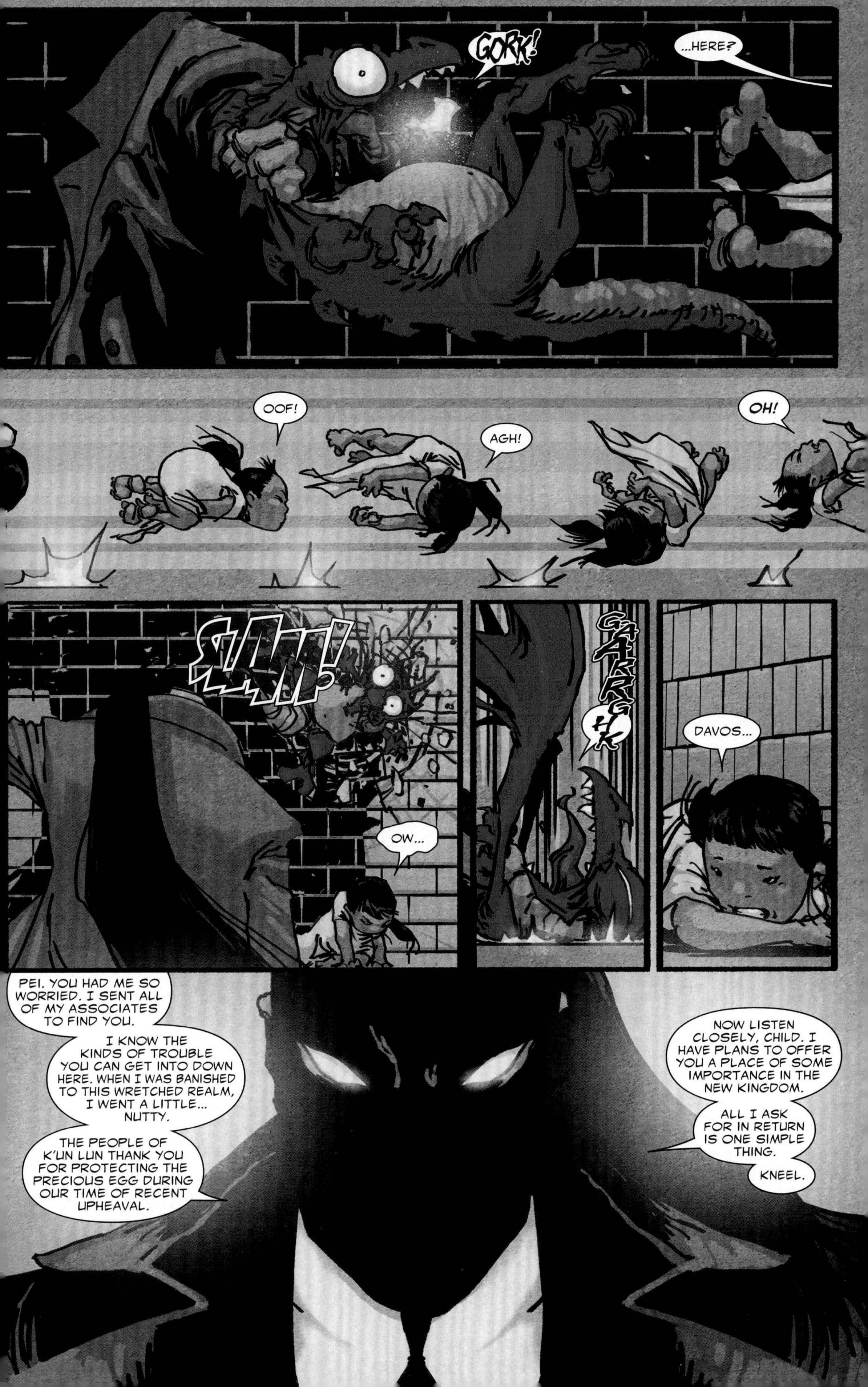
GORK!
...HERE?
OOF!
AGH!
OH!
SLAM!
GAKRGHK
DAVOS...
OW...
PEI. YOU HAD ME SO WORRIED. I SENT ALL OF MY ASSOCIATES TO FIND YOU.
I KNOW THE KINDS OF TROUBLE YOU CAN GET INTO DOWN HERE. WHEN I WAS BANISHED TO THIS WRETCHED REALM, I WENT A LITTLE... NUTTY.
THE PEOPLE OF K'UN LUN THANK YOU FOR PROTECTING THE PRECIOUS EGG DURING OUR TIME OF RECENT UPHEAVAL.
NOW LISTEN CLOSELY, CHILD. I HAVE PLANS TO OFFER YOU A PLACE OF SOME IMPORTANCE IN THE NEW KINGDOM.
ALL I ASK FOR IN RETURN IS ONE SIMPLE THING.
KNEEL.

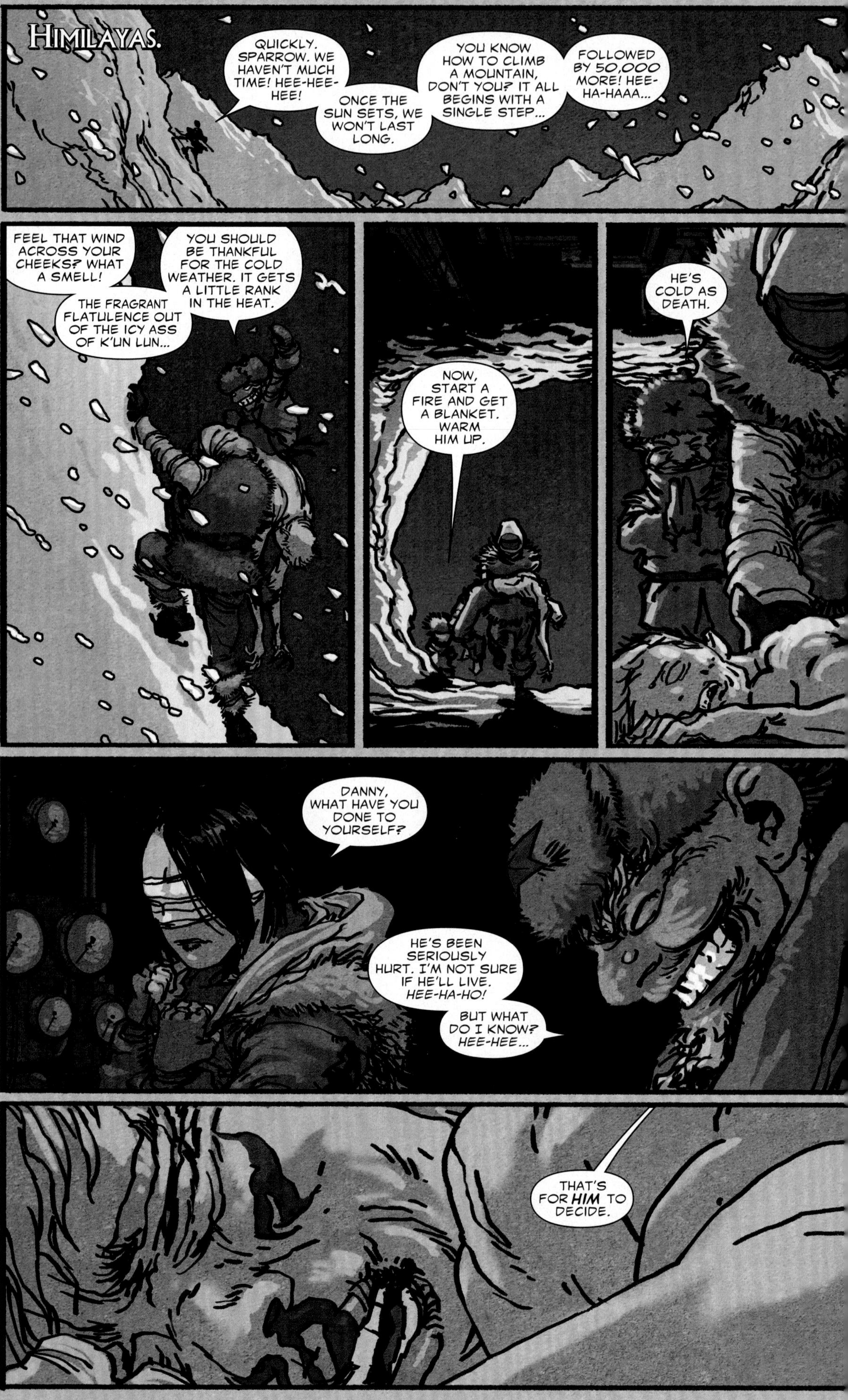
HIMILAYAS.
QUICKLY. SPARROW. WE HAVEN'T MUCH TIME! HEE-HEE-HEE!
ONCE THE SUN SETS, WE WON'T LAST LONG.
YOU KNOW HOW TO CLIMB A MOUNTAIN, DON'T YOU? IT ALL BEGINS WITH A SINGLE STEP...
FOLLOWED BY 50,000 MORE! HEE-HA-HAAA...
FEEL THAT WIND ACROSS YOUR CHEEKS? WHAT A SMELL!
THE FRAGRANT FLATULENCE OUT OF THE ICY ASS OF K'UN LUN...
YOU SHOULD BE THANKFUL FOR THE COLD WEATHER. IT GETS A LITTLE RANK IN THE HEAT.
NOW, START A FIRE AND GET A BLANKET. WARM HIM UP.
HE'S COLD AS DEATH.
DANNY, WHAT HAVE YOU DONE TO YOURSELF?
HE'S BEEN SERIOUSLY HURT. I'M NOT SURE IF HE'LL LIVE. *HEE-HA-HO!*
BUT WHAT DO I KNOW? *HEE-HEE...*
THAT'S FOR ***HIM*** TO DECIDE.

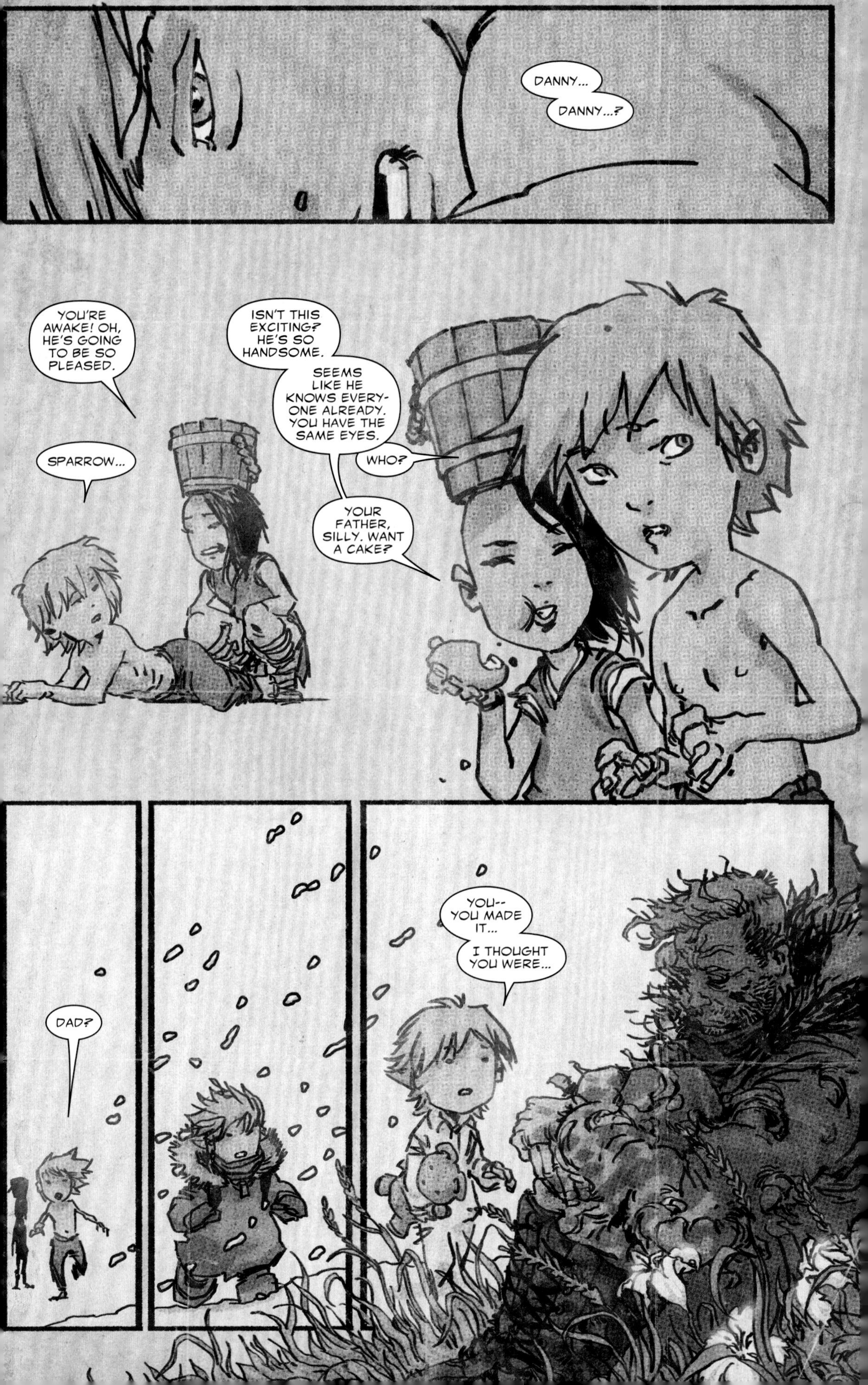
DANNY...
DANNY...?
YOU'RE AWAKE! OH, HE'S GOING TO BE SO PLEASED.
SPARROW...
ISN'T THIS EXCITING? HE'S SO HANDSOME.
SEEMS LIKE HE KNOWS EVERY-ONE ALREADY. YOU HAVE THE SAME EYES.
WHO?
YOUR FATHER, SILLY. WANT A CAKE?
DAD?
YOU-- YOU MADE IT...
I THOUGHT YOU WERE...

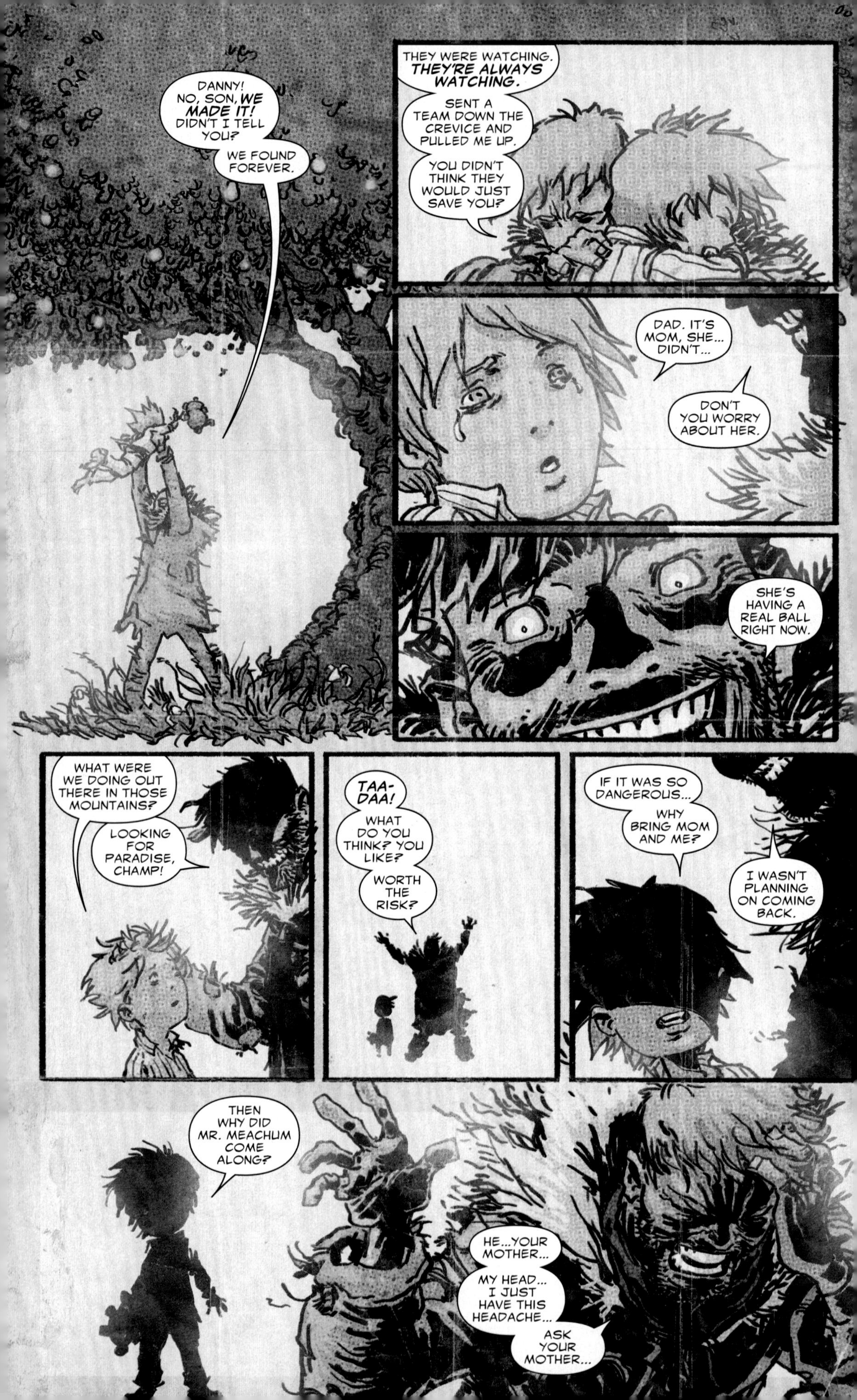
DANNY! NO, SON, WE MADE IT! DIDN'T I TELL YOU?
WE FOUND FOREVER.
THEY WERE WATCHING. THEY'RE ALWAYS WATCHING.
SENT A TEAM DOWN THE CREVICE AND PULLED ME UP.
YOU DIDN'T THINK THEY WOULD JUST SAVE YOU?
DAD. IT'S MOM, SHE... DIDN'T...
DON'T YOU WORRY ABOUT HER.
SHE'S HAVING A REAL BALL RIGHT NOW.
WHAT WERE WE DOING OUT THERE IN THOSE MOUNTAINS?
LOOKING FOR PARADISE, CHAMP!
TAA-DAA!
WHAT DO YOU THINK? YOU LIKE?
WORTH THE RISK?
IF IT WAS SO DANGEROUS...
WHY BRING MOM AND ME?
I WASN'T PLANNING ON COMING BACK.
THEN WHY DID MR. MEACHUM COME ALONG?
HE...YOUR MOTHER...
MY HEAD... I JUST HAVE THIS HEADACHE...
ASK YOUR MOTHER...

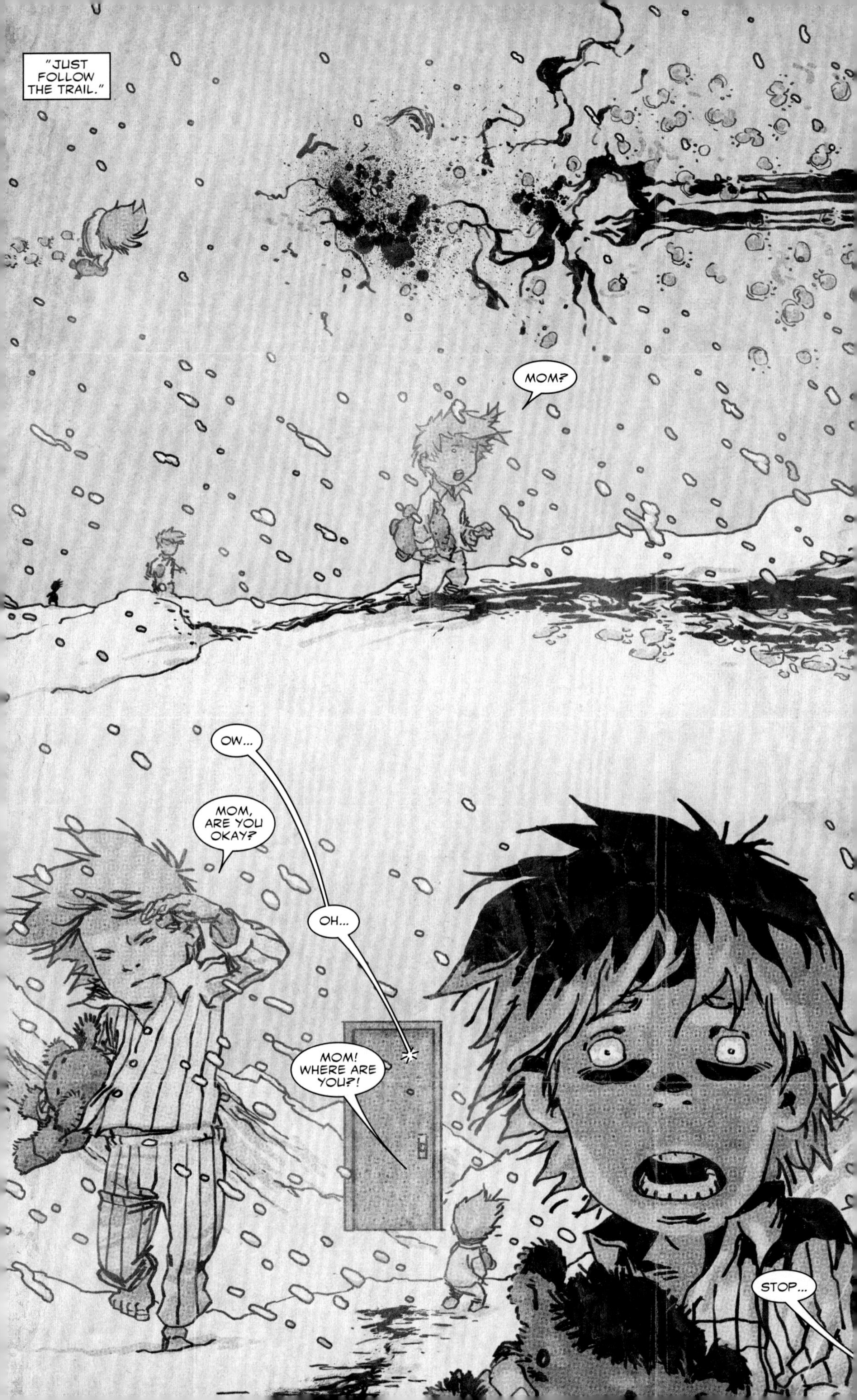

"JUST FOLLOW THE TRAIL."
MOM?
OW...
MOM, ARE YOU OKAY?
OH...
MOM! WHERE ARE YOU?!
STOP...

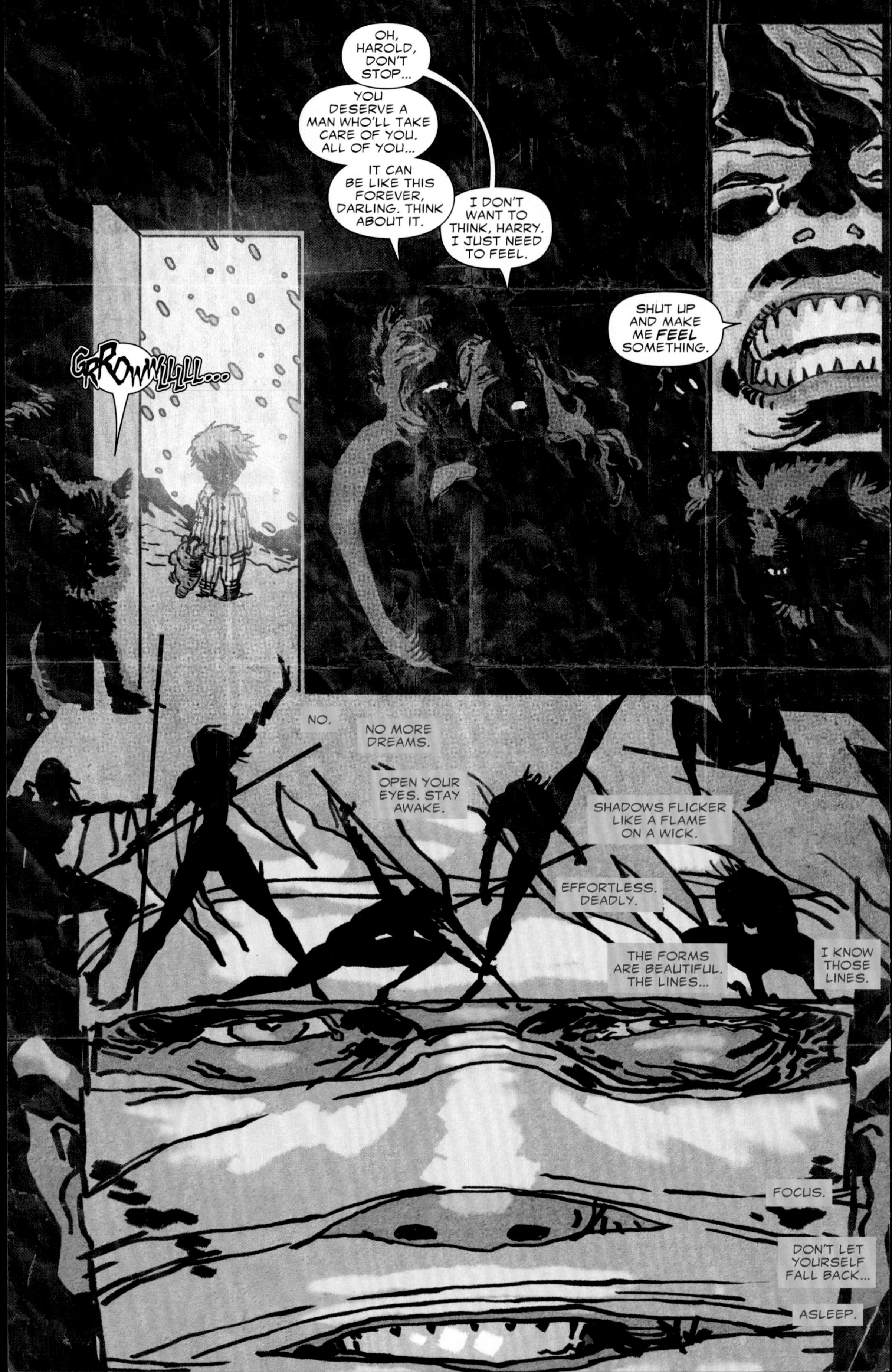

OH, HAROLD, DON'T STOP...
YOU DESERVE A MAN WHO'LL TAKE CARE OF YOU. ALL OF YOU...
IT CAN BE LIKE THIS FOREVER, DARLING. THINK ABOUT IT.
I DON'T WANT TO THINK, HARRY. I JUST NEED TO FEEL.
SHUT UP AND MAKE ME FEEL SOMETHING.
GRROWWLLLL...
NO.
NO MORE DREAMS.
OPEN YOUR EYES. STAY AWAKE.
SHADOWS FLICKER LIKE A FLAME ON A WICK.
EFFORTLESS. DEADLY.
THE FORMS ARE BEAUTIFUL. THE LINES...
I KNOW THOSE LINES.
FOCUS.
DON'T LET YOURSELF FALL BACK...
ASLEEP.

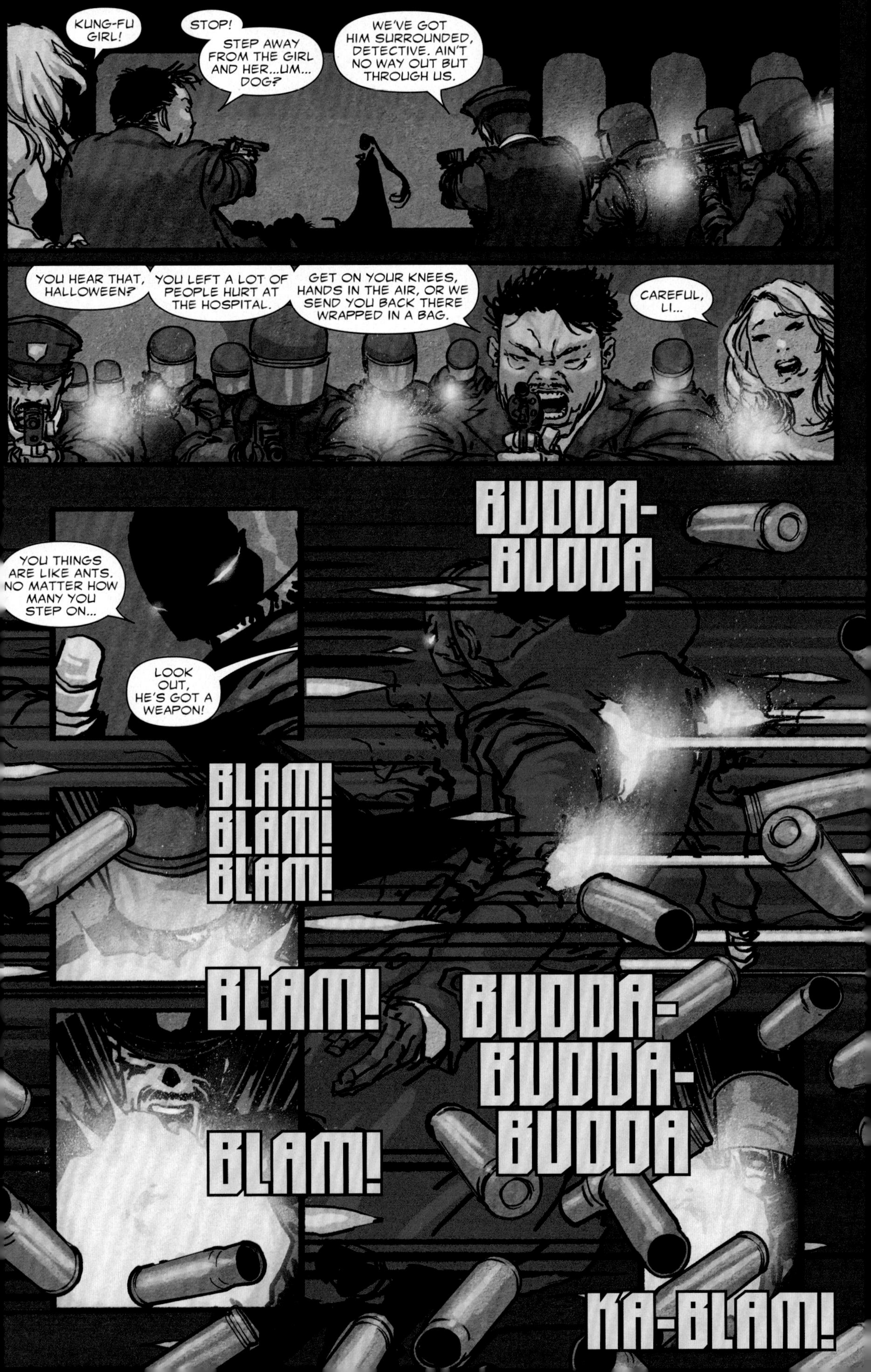
KUNG-FU GIRL!
STOP! STEP AWAY FROM THE GIRL AND HER...UM... DOG?
WE'VE GOT HIM SURROUNDED, DETECTIVE. AIN'T NO WAY OUT BUT THROUGH US.
YOU HEAR THAT, HALLOWEEN?
YOU LEFT A LOT OF PEOPLE HURT AT THE HOSPITAL.
GET ON YOUR KNEES, HANDS IN THE AIR, OR WE SEND YOU BACK THERE WRAPPED IN A BAG.
CAREFUL, LI...
BUDDA-BUDDA
YOU THINGS ARE LIKE ANTS. NO MATTER HOW MANY YOU STEP ON...
LOOK OUT, HE'S GOT A WEAPON!
BLAM! BLAM! BLAM!
BLAM!
BUDDA-BUDDA-BUDDA
BLAM!
KA-BLAM!

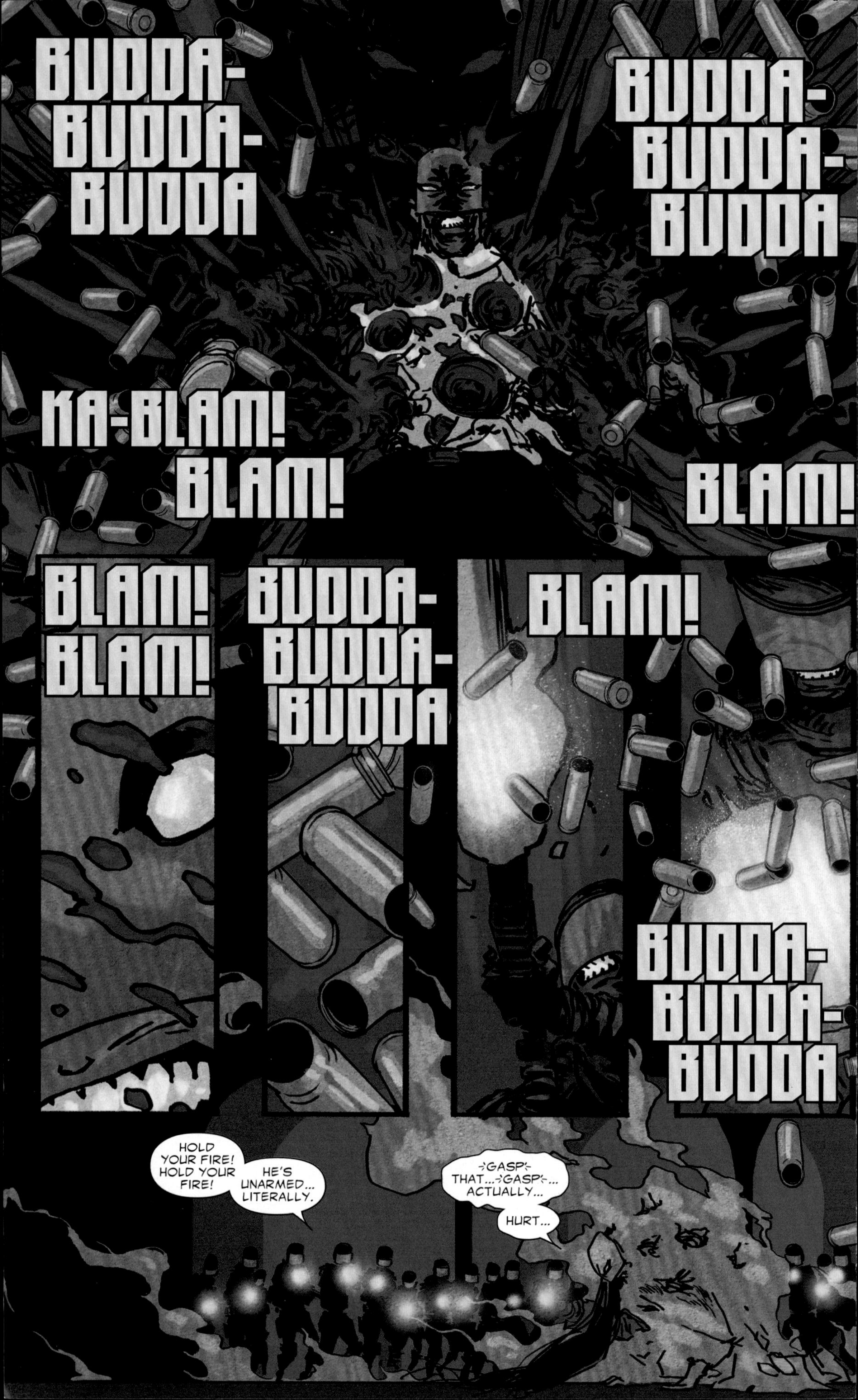
BUDDA-BUDDA-BUDDA
BUDDA-BUDDA-BUDDA
KA-BLAM! BLAM!
BLAM!
BLAM! BLAM!
BUDDA-BUDDA-BUDDA
BLAM!
BUDDA-BUDDA-BUDDA
HOLD YOUR FIRE! HOLD YOUR FIRE!
HE'S UNARMED... LITERALLY.
GASP THAT... GASP... ACTUALLY...
HURT...

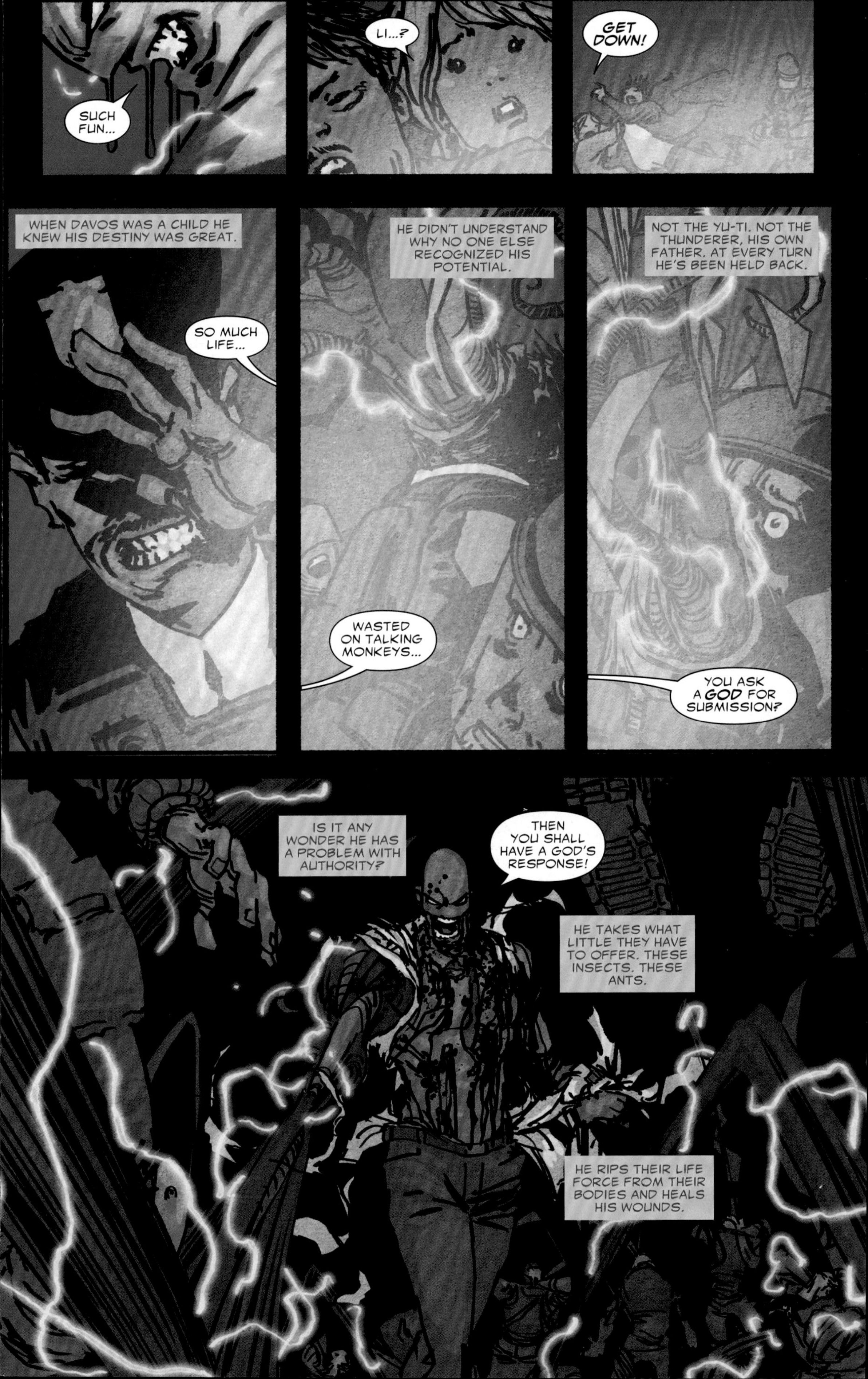
SUCH FUN...
LI...?
GET DOWN!
WHEN DAVOS WAS A CHILD HE KNEW HIS DESTINY WAS GREAT.
SO MUCH LIFE...
HE DIDN'T UNDERSTAND WHY NO ONE ELSE RECOGNIZED HIS POTENTIAL.
WASTED ON TALKING MONKEYS...
NOT THE YU-TI. NOT THE THUNDERER, HIS OWN FATHER. AT EVERY TURN HE'S BEEN HELD BACK.
YOU ASK A **GOD** FOR SUBMISSION?
IS IT ANY WONDER HE HAS A PROBLEM WITH AUTHORITY?
THEN YOU SHALL HAVE A GOD'S RESPONSE!
HE TAKES WHAT LITTLE THEY HAVE TO OFFER. THESE INSECTS. THESE ANTS.
HE RIPS THEIR LIFE FORCE FROM THEIR BODIES AND HEALS HIS WOUNDS.

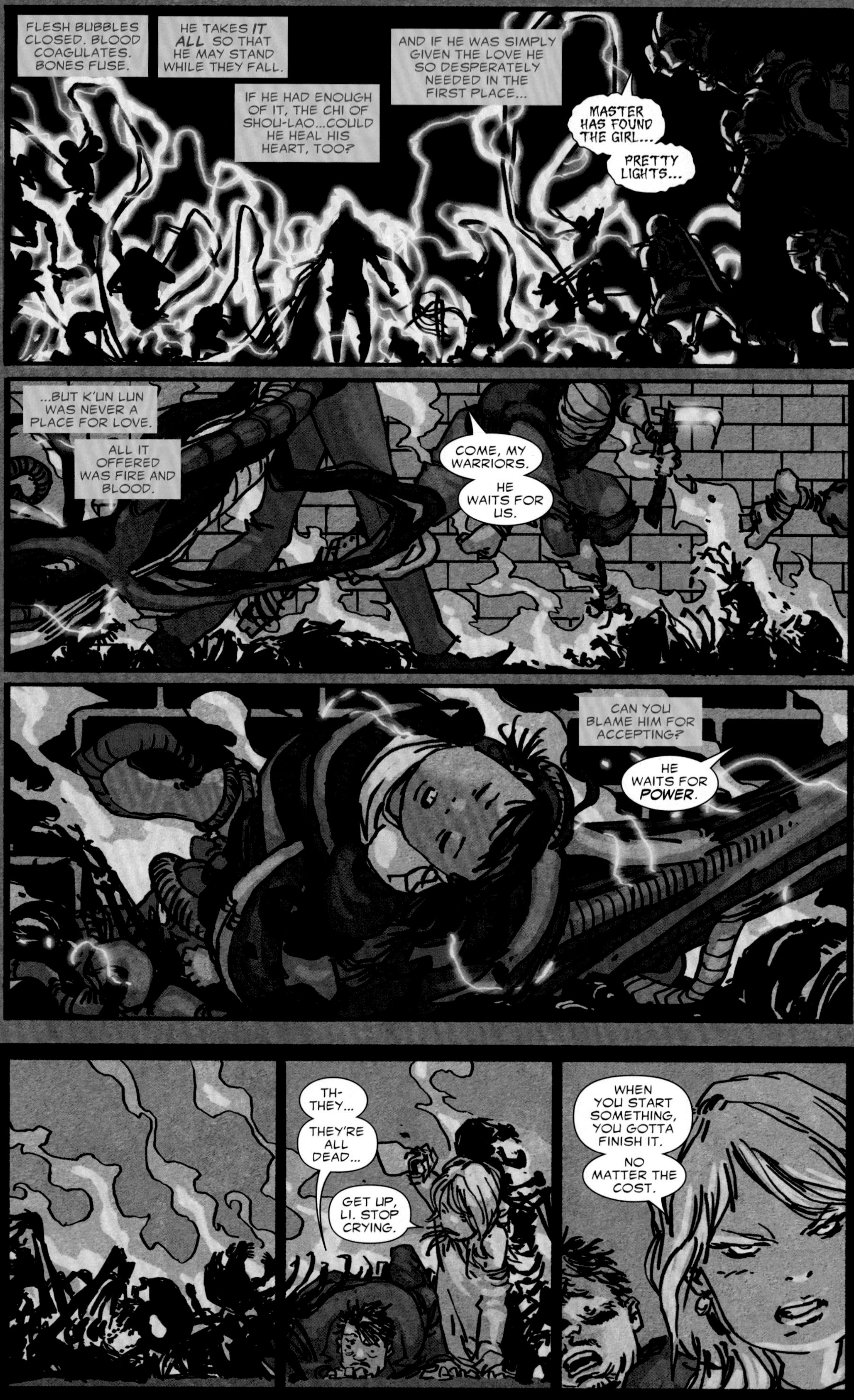

FLESH BUBBLES CLOSED. BLOOD COAGULATES. BONES FUSE.
HE TAKES IT ALL SO THAT HE MAY STAND WHILE THEY FALL.
IF HE HAD ENOUGH OF IT, THE CHI OF SHOU-LAO...COULD HE HEAL HIS HEART, TOO?
AND IF HE WAS SIMPLY GIVEN THE LOVE HE SO DESPERATELY NEEDED IN THE FIRST PLACE...
MASTER HAS FOUND THE GIRL...
PRETTY LIGHTS...
...BUT K'UN LUN WAS NEVER A PLACE FOR LOVE.
ALL IT OFFERED WAS FIRE AND BLOOD.
COME, MY WARRIORS.
HE WAITS FOR US.
CAN YOU BLAME HIM FOR ACCEPTING?
HE WAITS FOR POWER.
TH-THEY...
THEY'RE ALL DEAD...
GET UP, LI. STOP CRYING.
WHEN YOU START SOMETHING, YOU GOTTA FINISH IT.
NO MATTER THE COST.

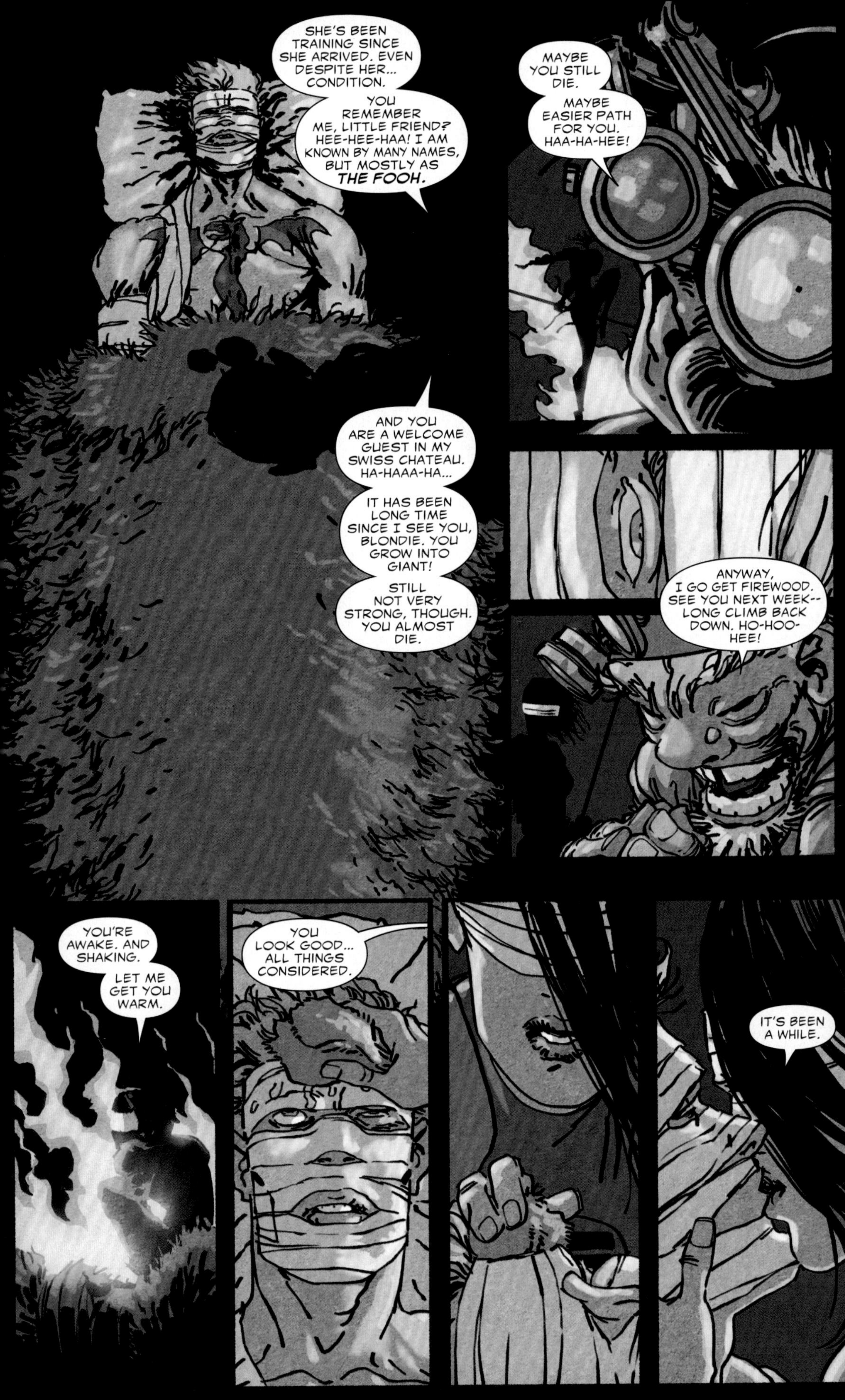
SHE'S BEEN TRAINING SINCE SHE ARRIVED. EVEN DESPITE HER... CONDITION.
YOU REMEMBER ME, LITTLE FRIEND? HEE-HEE-HAA! I AM KNOWN BY MANY NAMES, BUT MOSTLY AS THE FOOH.
MAYBE YOU STILL DIE.
MAYBE EASIER PATH FOR YOU. HAA-HA-HEE!
AND YOU ARE A WELCOME GUEST IN MY SWISS CHATEAU. HA-HAAA-HA...
IT HAS BEEN LONG TIME SINCE I SEE YOU, BLONDIE. YOU GROW INTO GIANT!
STILL NOT VERY STRONG, THOUGH. YOU ALMOST DIE.
ANYWAY, I GO GET FIREWOOD. SEE YOU NEXT WEEK--LONG CLIMB BACK DOWN. HO-HOO-HEE!
YOU'RE AWAKE. AND SHAKING.
LET ME GET YOU WARM.
YOU LOOK GOOD... ALL THINGS CONSIDERED.
IT'S BEEN A WHILE.

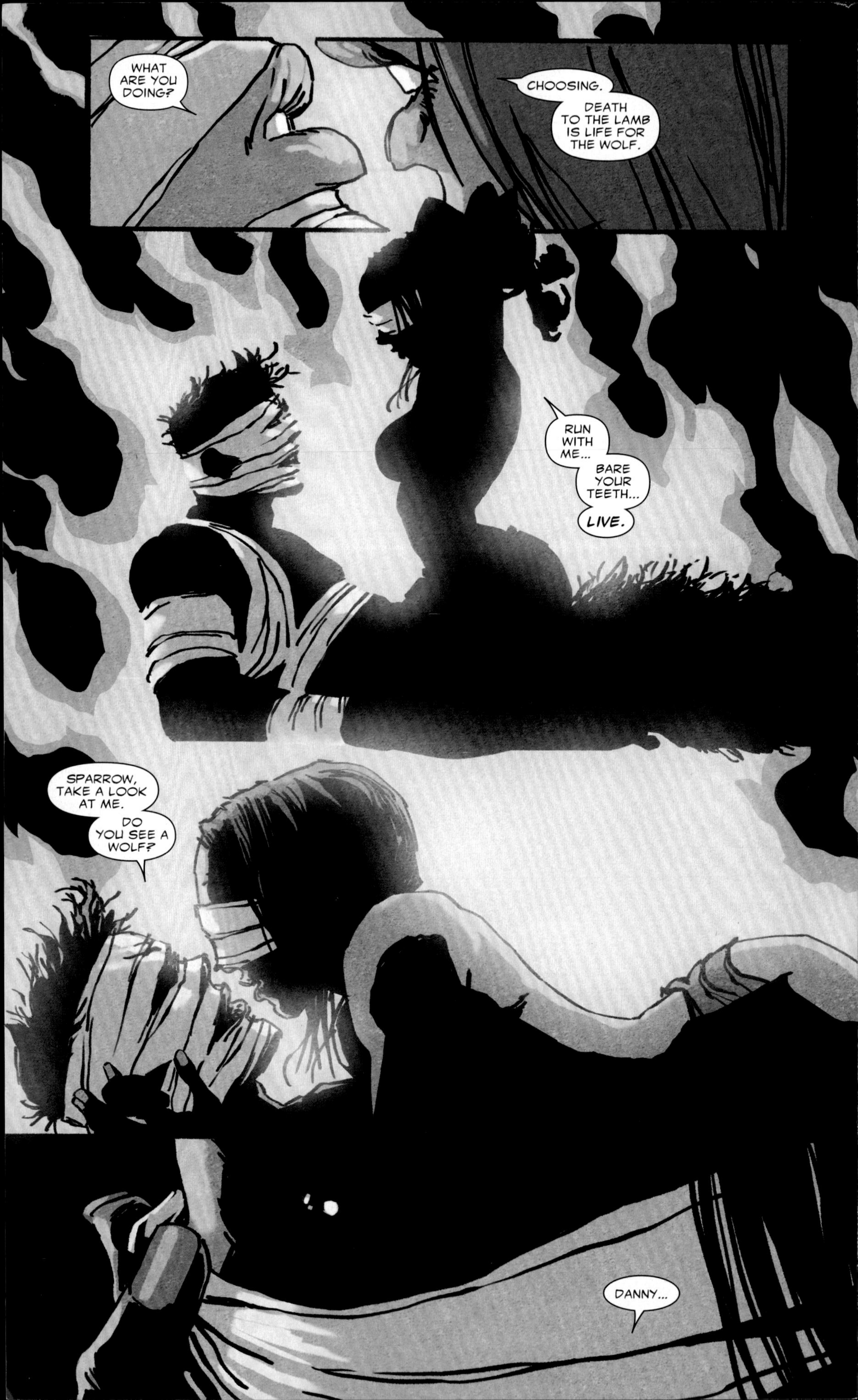
WHAT ARE YOU DOING?
CHOOSING.
DEATH TO THE LAMB IS LIFE FOR THE WOLF.
RUN WITH ME...
BARE YOUR TEETH...
LIVE.
SPARROW, TAKE A LOOK AT ME.
DO YOU SEE A WOLF?
DANNY...

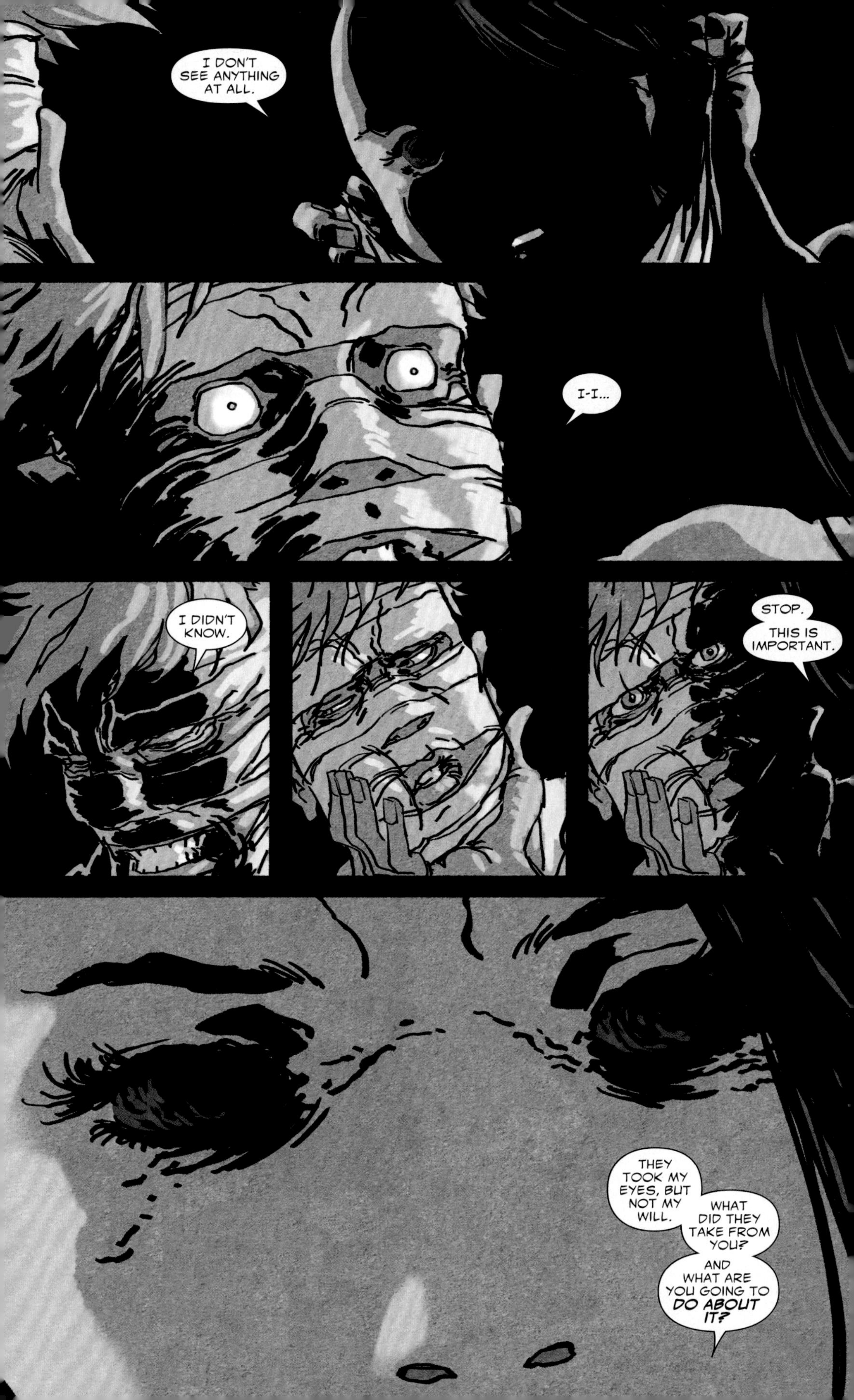
I DON'T SEE ANYTHING AT ALL.
I-I...
I DIDN'T KNOW.
STOP.
THIS IS IMPORTANT.
THEY TOOK MY EYES, BUT NOT MY WILL.
WHAT DID THEY TAKE FROM YOU?
AND WHAT ARE YOU GOING TO DO ABOUT IT?

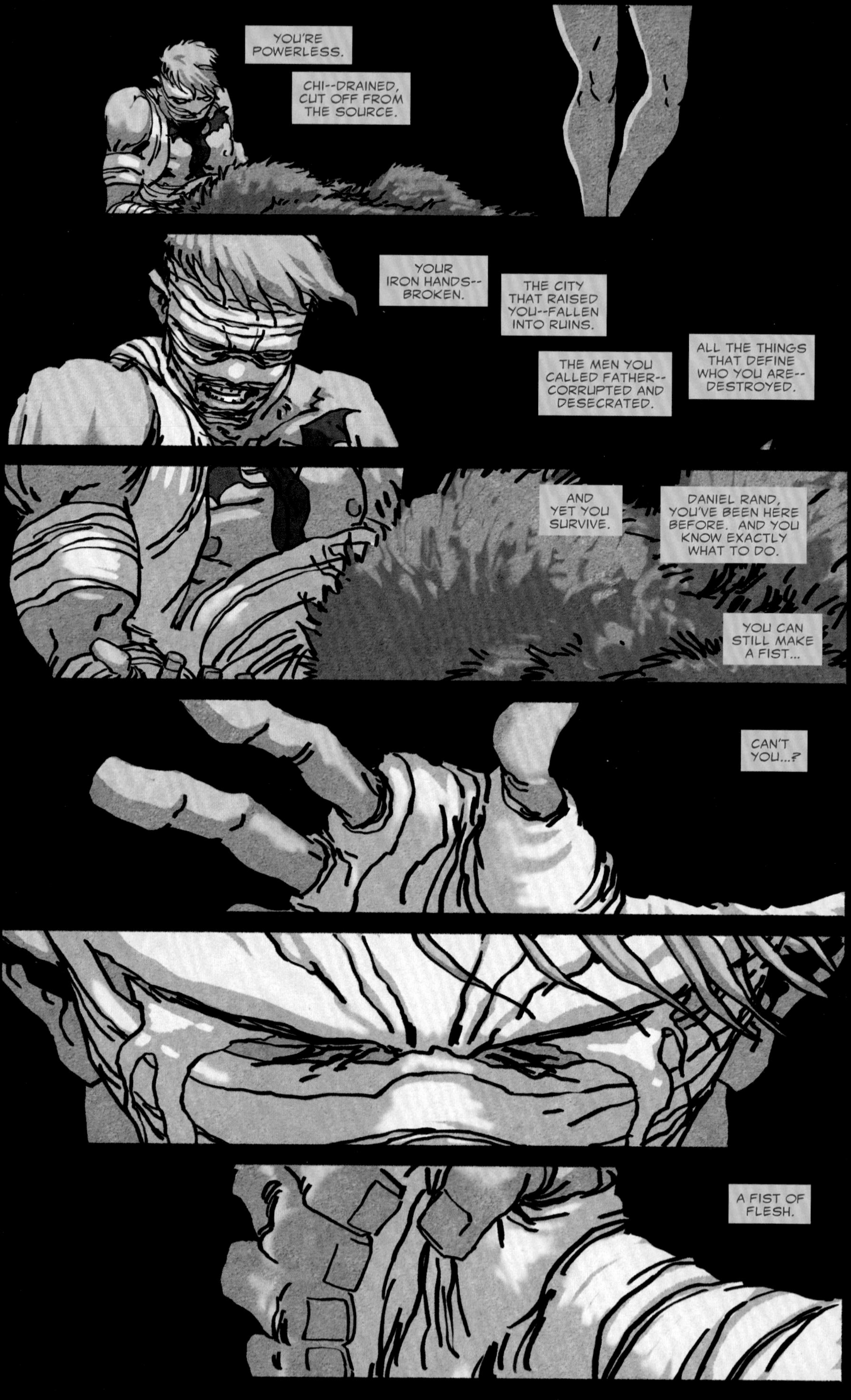

YOU'RE POWERLESS.
CHI--DRAINED, CUT OFF FROM THE SOURCE.
YOUR IRON HANDS-- BROKEN.
THE CITY THAT RAISED YOU--FALLEN INTO RUINS.
THE MEN YOU CALLED FATHER-- CORRUPTED AND DESECRATED.
ALL THE THINGS THAT DEFINE WHO YOU ARE-- DESTROYED.
AND YET YOU SURVIVE.
DANIEL RAND, YOU'VE BEEN HERE BEFORE. AND YOU KNOW EXACTLY WHAT TO DO.
YOU CAN STILL MAKE A FIST...
CAN'T YOU...?
A FIST OF FLESH.

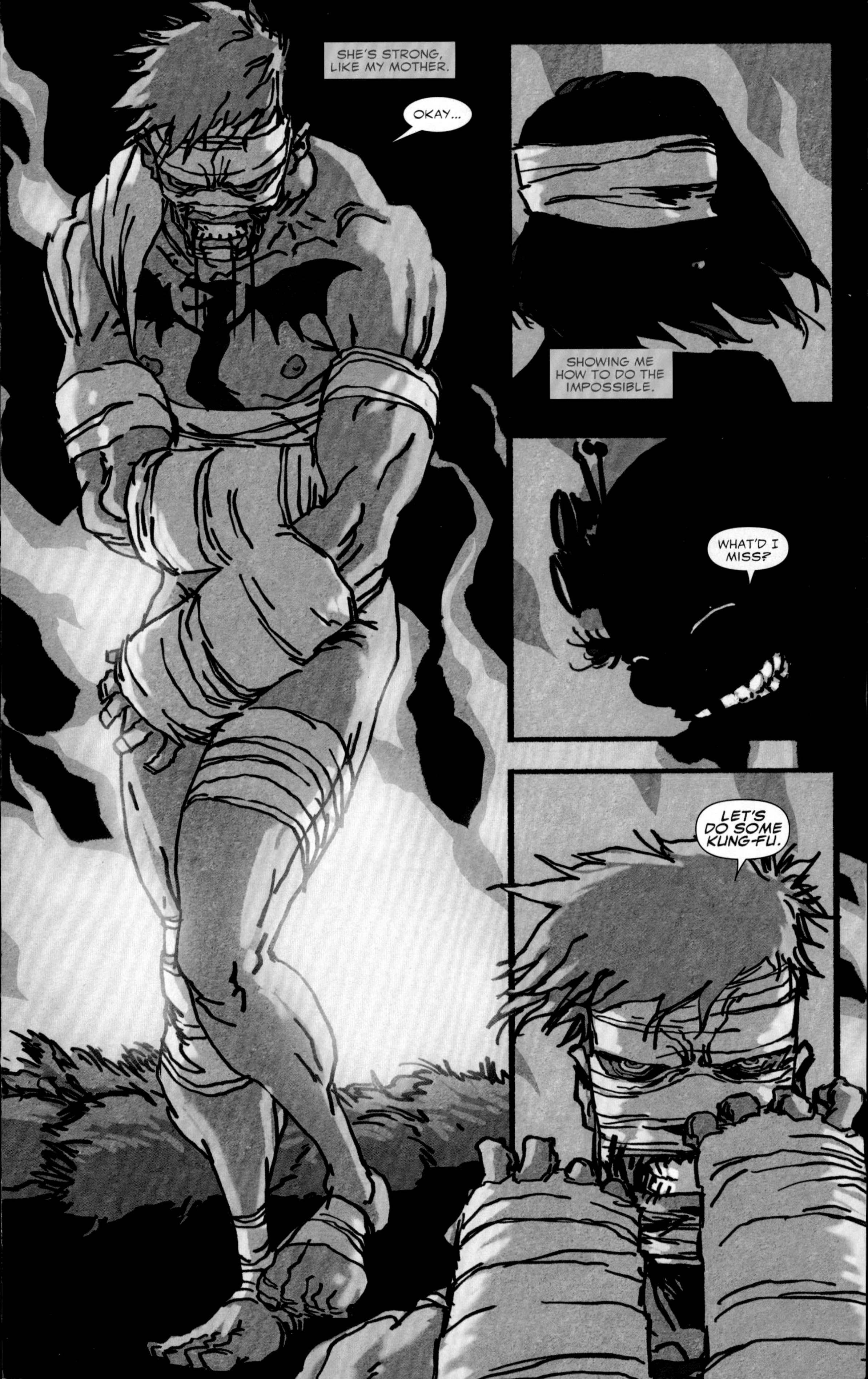
SHE'S STRONG, LIKE MY MOTHER.
OKAY...
SHOWING ME HOW TO DO THE IMPOSSIBLE.
WHAT'D I MISS?
LET'S DO SOME KUNG-FU.

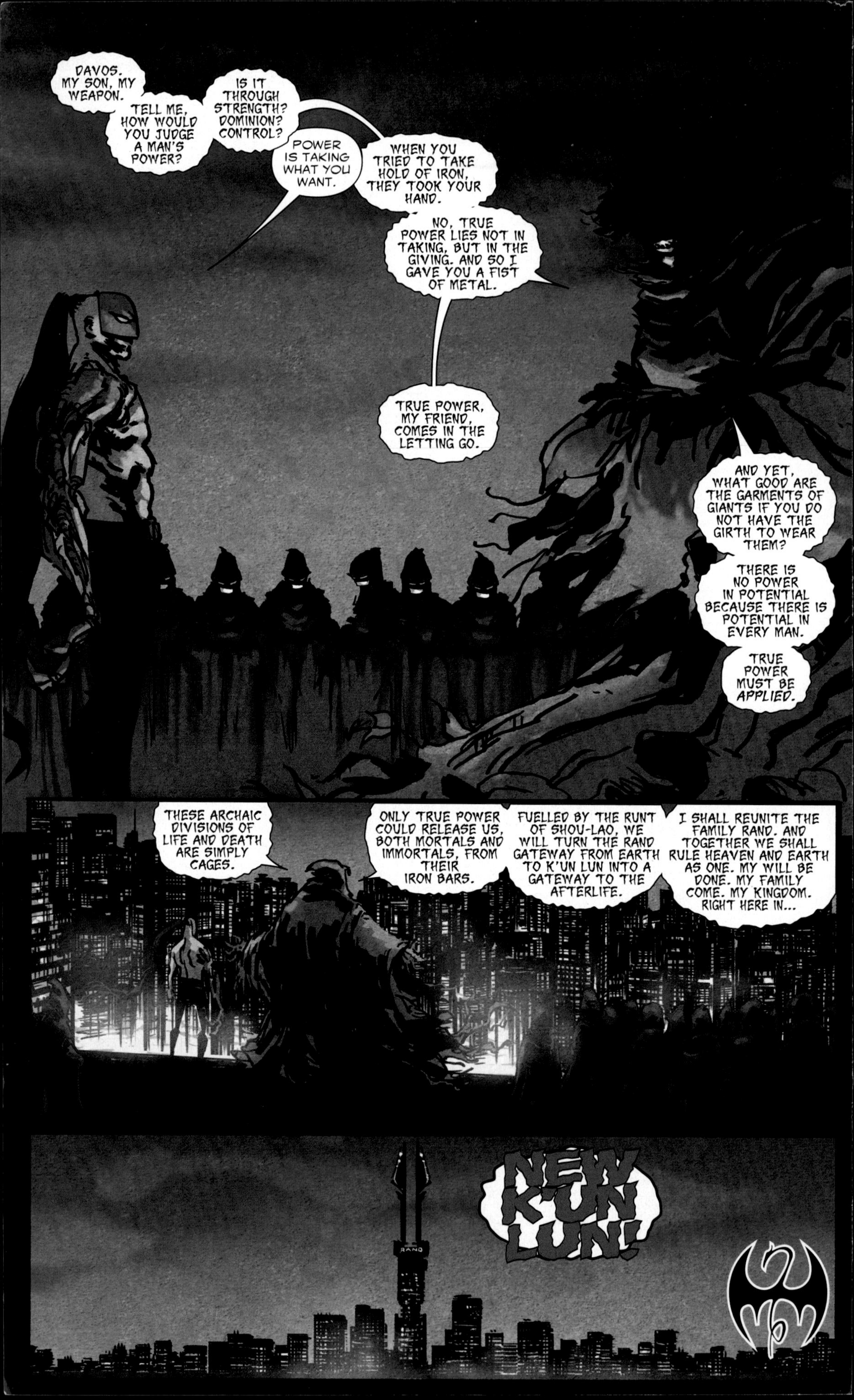
DAVOS. MY SON, MY WEAPON.
TELL ME, HOW WOULD YOU JUDGE A MAN'S POWER?
IS IT THROUGH STRENGTH? DOMINION? CONTROL?
POWER IS TAKING WHAT YOU WANT.
WHEN YOU TRIED TO TAKE HOLD OF IRON, THEY TOOK YOUR HAND.
NO, TRUE POWER LIES NOT IN TAKING, BUT IN THE GIVING. AND SO I GAVE YOU A FIST OF METAL.
TRUE POWER, MY FRIEND, COMES IN THE LETTING GO.
AND YET, WHAT GOOD ARE THE GARMENTS OF GIANTS IF YOU DO NOT HAVE THE GIRTH TO WEAR THEM?
THERE IS NO POWER IN POTENTIAL BECAUSE THERE IS POTENTIAL IN EVERY MAN.
TRUE POWER MUST BE *APPLIED.*
THESE ARCHAIC DIVISIONS OF LIFE AND DEATH ARE SIMPLY CAGES.
ONLY TRUE POWER COULD RELEASE US, BOTH MORTALS AND IMMORTALS, FROM THEIR IRON BARS.
FUELLED BY THE RUNT OF SHOU-LAO, WE WILL TURN THE RAND GATEWAY FROM EARTH TO K'UN LUN INTO A GATEWAY TO THE AFTERLIFE.
I SHALL REUNITE THE FAMILY RAND. AND TOGETHER WE SHALL RULE HEAVEN AND EARTH AS ONE. MY WILL BE DONE. MY FAMILY COME. MY KINGDOM. RIGHT HERE IN...
RAND
NEW K'UN LUN!

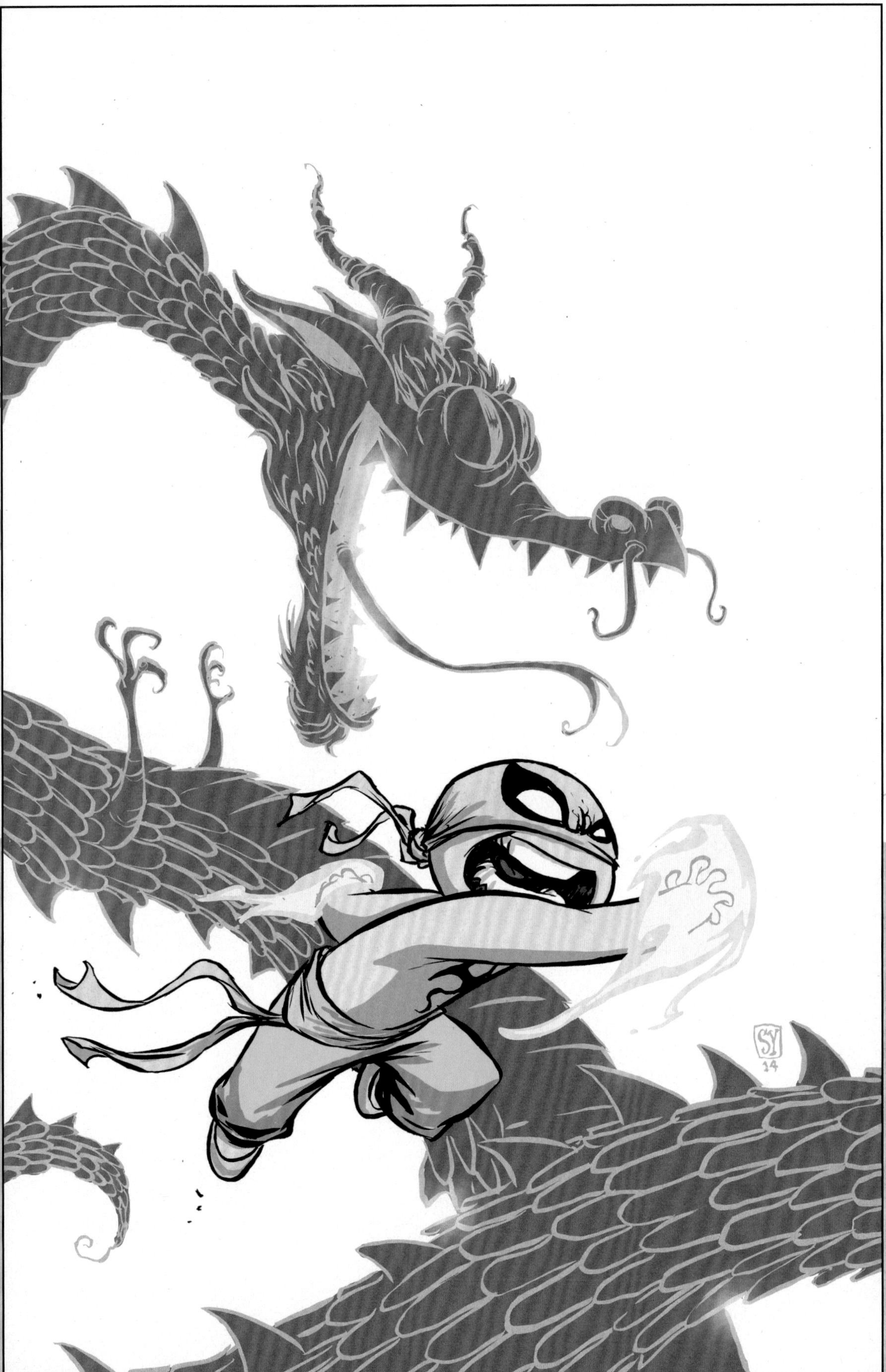

IRON FIST: THE LIVING WEAPON #1 VARIANT
BY SKOTTIE YOUNG

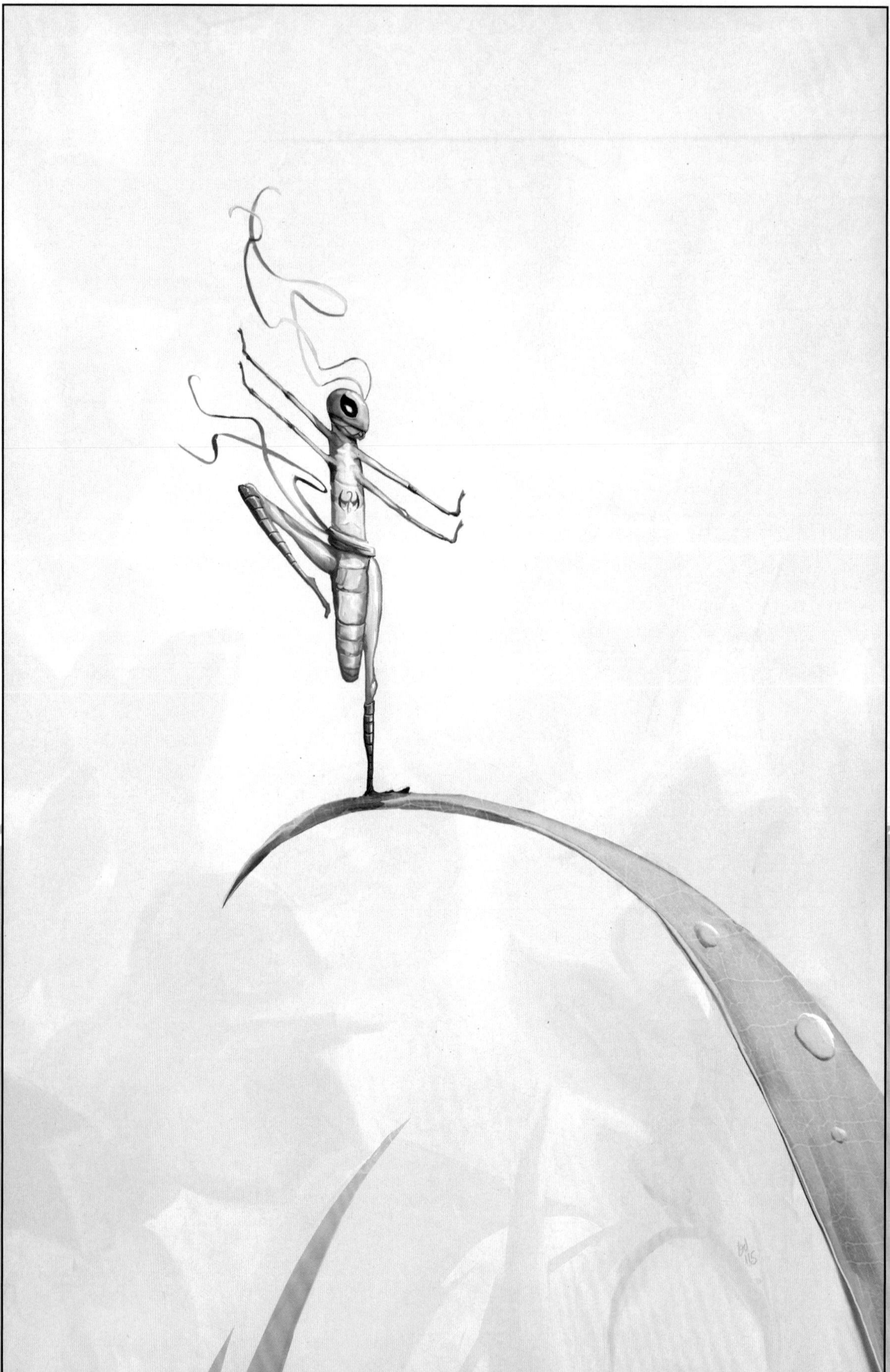

IRON FIST: THE LIVING WEAPON #1 ANIMAL VARIANT
BY MIKE DEL MUNDO

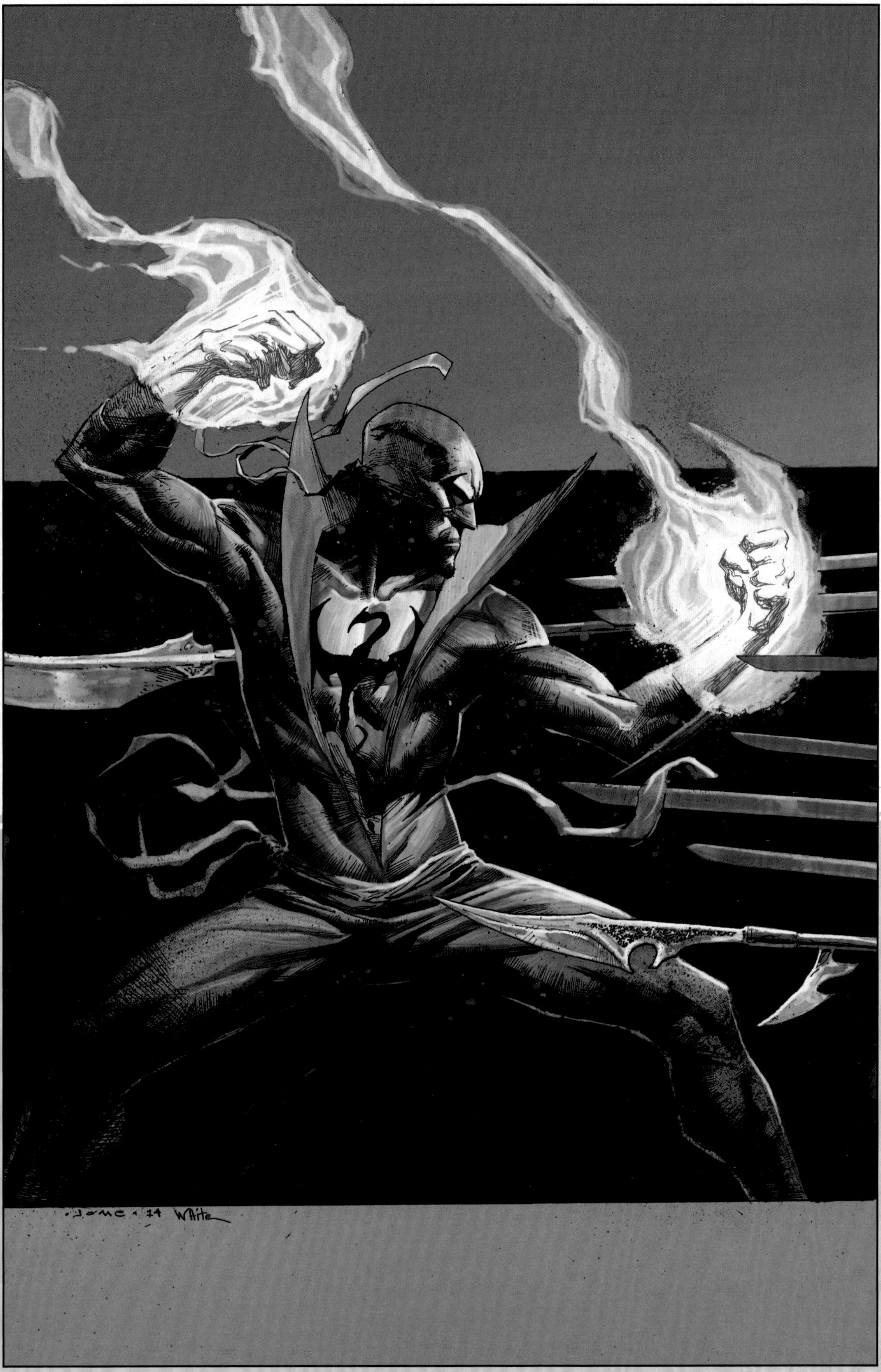

IRON FIST: THE LIVING WEAPON #1 VARIANT
BY JEROME OPEÑA & DEAN WHITE

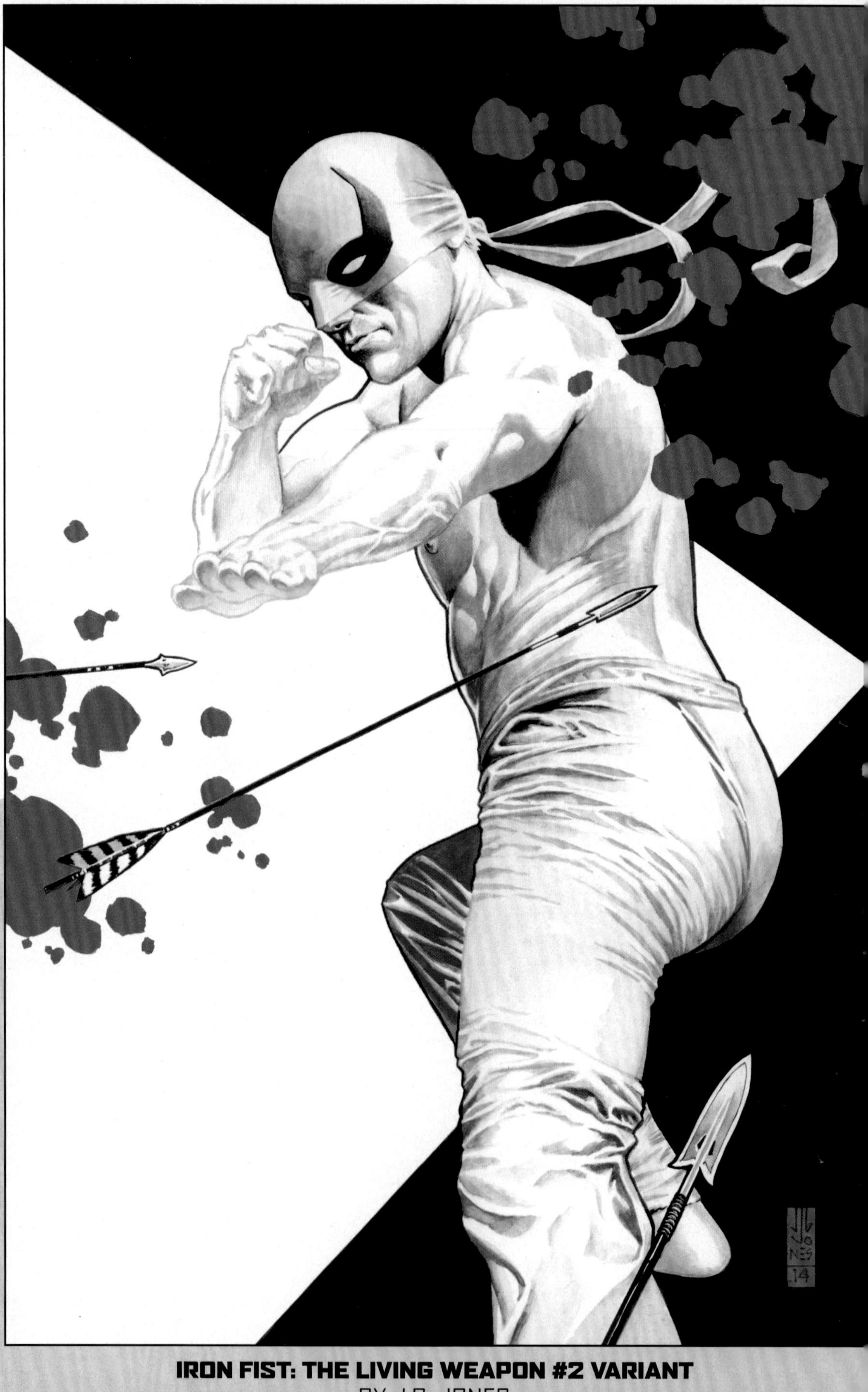
JG
JONES
14

IRON FIST: THE LIVING WEAPON #2 VARIANT
BY J.G. JONES

IN THE DOJO

WITH KAARE ANDREWS

I remember picking that back issue at a comic store. I was maybe 12 or 13? I saw this older comic, high up on the wall. It was a Marvel book from the '60s and it seemed a little different. A few figures with guns standing on blocks, all sort of posing and looking for one another. I immediately bought it. I don't really know why. I just remember the excited feeling that I had to have it, even if it did blow a hole through my allowance.

This strange little comicbook...

Quick side note: Stan Lee taught me--well not me directly--that you should always write comicbook as one word, so it becomes a unique thing and not simply a genre of books filled with comic drawings.

So anyways, this strange little unique comicbook came home with me and I pulled it out of its crisp bag. Now let me just describe the experience as it felt to my young mind, which is more important than how it may actually have happened.

Inside that book, everything seemed a little different. It started out with a title page where the title itself became part of the background that the main character scaled over. There were what seemed to be pages and pages of silent storytelling, followed by some of the most amazing action I had ever seen. There was romance. Style. Intrigue. The story seemed to be written for adults, not kids. There were photographs cut and pasted into the panels as art itself. Everything seemed a little "off," yet there was a unique cohesion to it all that I hadn't quite experienced before. This was not just "words" juxtaposed with "art." Every part of that comicbook was contributing to a singular storytelling experience. The name of that creator was Jim Steranko, and the name of the book was NICK FURY: AGENT OF S.H.I.E.L.D.

Steranko wrote, drew and even colored that book. And it changed my life.

I don't know why we've rigidly divided up the task of creating a comicbook into four or five different components. For some reason, in today's climate, it seems strange to "allow" a penciler to write, that an inker might want to color, or to "permit" a writer to draw. There is a machine where each person is a separate component. Now, I've worked with amazing writers like Mark Millar, Warren Ellis, and Zeb Wells, heroes of mine. And the work we did was a great deal of fun for me, and well received. But there is just no way Steranko could have done what he did as part of a machine. Because if you approach a project like everyone else approaches a project, the results will be like everyone else.

Steranko taught me to do things the wrong way. Don't just write it. Don't just draw it. DO EVERYTHING. Plot. Script. Pencil. Ink. Color. Logo. Get your hands on the whole of it. Make every part of the process uniquely yours. Draw with words. Write with your pencil. Ink with color. Don't be a cog in a machine...

BECOME THE MACHINE.

I hope you stay with me on this experience. I have a lot of things planned for Danny Rand. Some of it will feel "off" and may be flat-out "wrong." But I wouldn't want it any other way.

Let's do some Kung Fu.

-Kaare Andrews

MARVEL AR AUGMENTED REALITY

MARVEL AUGMENTED REALITY (AR) ENHANCES AND CHANGES THE WAY YOU EXPERIENCE COMICS!

TO ACCESS THE FREE MARVEL AR CONTENT IN THIS BOOK*:

1. **Locate the AR logo within the comic.**
2. **Go to Marvel.com/AR in your web browser.**
3. **Search by series title to find the corresponding AR.**
4. **Enjoy Marvel AR!**

*All AR content that appears in this book has been archived and will be available only at Marvel.com/AR – no longer in the Marvel AR App. Content subject to change and availability.

AR INDEX

Issue #1

IRON FIST

THE LIVING WEAPON

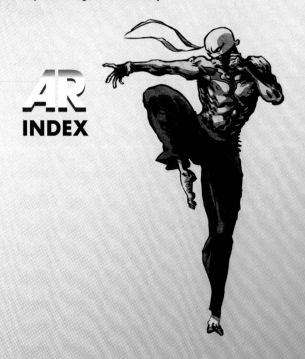

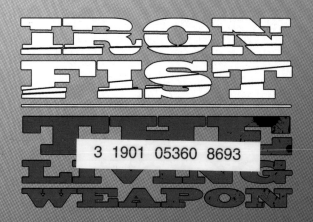